Leadership with Synercube

Anatoly Zankovsky ·
Christiane von der Heiden

Leadership with Synercube

A dynamic leadership culture
for excellence

Springer Vieweg

Anatoly Zankovsky
Psychologisches Institut
Moskau, The Moscow Area
Russia

Christiane von der Heiden
Synercube GmbH
Leverkusen, Germany

Translation from the German language edition: Leadership mit Synercube. Eine dynamische Führungskultur für Spitzenleistungen. © Springer-Verlag Berlin Heidelberg 2015

ISBN 978-3-662-49051-8   ISBN 978-3-662-49052-5   (eBook)
DOI 10.1007/978-3-662-49052-5

Library of Congress Control Number: 2016940849

Printed on acid-free paper

This Springer Vieweg imprint is published by Springer Nature
The registered company is Springer-Verlag GmbH Berlin Heidelberg

Foreword

When, in July 2013, a Boeing of an Asian airline crashed while approaching for landing in San Francisco, experts quickly reached a mutual conclusion: the main cause of the disaster was the communication and leadership culture inside the cockpit. Analysis of the recordings from the cockpit made clear that while the team of pilots was acutely aware of the danger in hand, the situation was not resolved using any team management methods that involved the full and optimum use of the available human resources. Instead, the chief pilot opted to apply a unilateral style of leadership based on the principle of order and obey—in other words, "top-down" communication, a leadership behaviour which is common practice in many Asian countries.

The crash in San Francisco confirms the findings of a study conducted by aircraft manufacturer Boeing that, as far as airplane crash statistics are concerned, countries where a more authoritarian leadership style prevails are overly represented.

These findings indicate that even in the highly technified world of aviation, cultural factors play a conspicuous role. Notable studies (GLOBE, HOFSTEDE, THOMAS, TROMPENAARS) have revealed how diversely the culture factor affects human behaviour. This explains why cultural studies are becoming increasingly more significant in behavioural science.

Zankovsky can be credited with having made the culture phenomenon a fertile subject field for leadership theory.

In his capacity as professor of social psychology at the renowned Russian Academy of Sciences in Moscow and through various research visits to Germany and Japan, Zankovsky has devoted decades of his time to the theory and practice of leadership behaviour. He also has long-term experience in leadership training in an international context.

The leadership theory developed by Zankovsky is based on the group-dynamic approach conceived by Blake/Mouton, who developed a two-dimensional managerial grid model in the middle of the last century. This model involves "concern for results" and "concern for people" as the core leadership dimensions, with their respective characteristics represented in a behavioural grid.

His extensive empirical research led Zankovsky to extend this two-dimensional behavioural grid to include a "concern for culture" dimension, thereby turning the managerial grid into to a Synercube.

Leadership is three-dimensional. This is the quintessence of the new leadership model that enables diverse leadership processes to become more tangible than ever before.

Moreover, extending the leadership dimensions to include the culture factor has paved the way for new approaches when analysing and describing leadership behaviour in an intercultural context. Thus, the leadership theory developed by Zankovsky also represents a far-reaching approach for Intercultural Management, a field that is gaining in significance given the increasing interconnectedness of today's international economies.

The Synercube is at the core of a comprehensive training system, where orientation towards results, people, as well as values and culture are imparted as central leadership features.

Not without good reason, leadership psychology is considered to be one of the most complex areas of modern social psychology. With his three-dimensional approach, Zankovsky has contributed greatly to the development of leadership theory and therefore deserves our gratitude and appreciation.

Osnabrueck, Germany   Hans-Wolf Sievert
16 October 2014

Contents

Leadership in a Changing World

1.1 Leadership: Past, Present, and Future

Today the problem of leadership is a popular issue not only in modern organizational life but also in society in general. The leadership disease has overtaken all continents, penetrating in all life spheres: education, sport, science, art, and even family relations. Companies and enterprises are striving to be a leader in the market, political parties pin hopes on new charismatic leaders, heads of democratic states and strong-hand dictators are equally well-disposed to be called "leaders", as hasty journalists usually tag them. Whole countries and nations would be glad to acclaim themselves the leaders of the world.

Leadership is studied by many social sciences, either of which seeks its own way of understanding it. Traditionally, the leader is supposed to be a member of the group, who is the first to face a collective task by taking on the arrangement and organization of the group activity. In addition, leaders show higher levels of commitment, involvement, and impact on the decision-making. Other members recognize the leader, i.e. they build up the relations that presuppose their role as the leader's followers.

The problem of leadership in organizations came up for the very first time in the 1920–1930s. A more professional attitude among managers was preconditioned by the business demand. Without underestimating the contribution of other sciences, we must point out the decisive role of psychology in meeting the demands of business circles and launching the first leadership studies. Starting with works of Lewin and Lippitt (1938), psychological leadership researches gained the status of the recognized scientific area of investigation. At that time, the first laboratory and field studies were carried out, the first theories created, the first monographies published, and the first training programs worked out (Winkler 2010; Zankovsky 2000; Kouzes and Posner 2010).

From the viewpoint of management and administration practice, it was the behaviourist approach towards leadership that proved to be the most successful. Within this approach, the basic factors responsible for efficient leadership

© Springer-Verlag Berlin Heidelberg 2016

A. Zankovsky, C. von der Heiden, *Leadership with Synercube*,

DOI 10.1007/978-3-662-49052-5_1

behaviour were accentuated (Misumi 1984; Blake and Mouton 1985; Hersey and Blanchard 1982). All this allowed for the creation of practical behaviour technologies of forming and developing efficient leadership skills, which during the 1950–1990s helped boost the professional efficiency and the level of expertise among managers in organizations of different types.

While recognizing evident scientific and practical achievements, we must point out that today many organizations face a serious shortage of leaders at all management levels.

Google search query "lack of leaders" puts forward no less than 200 million links! The statistics says that today the work time of corporations' senior managers is 2.5–4 years at average, which is twice as short as a few decades ago. Over recent years the number of CEOs having been fired has grown four times. Besides, the major reason for sending off today is poor leadership skills and not low financial performance, as it used to be. In the presence of unemployment many organizations have near 25 % of their top and mid-level management posts vacant, because there are no worthy candidates! Lots of companies are worrying about the personnel shortage that they associate with a leadership crisis.

No wonder the famous management guru Warren Bennis (1989) had to say perplexedly:

> Where have all the leaders gone? Why don't we have real leaders today? All the great leaders that are coming to mind were living in the past; all of them have left the scene. So where have they all gone? They lost themselves among the production lines of their factories, joining with the production background. They disappeared on a distant orbit in pursuit of immediate gain. Instead of inspiring people, they are only able to intimidate them with serious problems and the need to reckon with today's realities.
>
> We urgently need leaders now. We need them because the quality of the managers themselves became worse. We need them because the challenges we face are acute, as never before. And as a man cannot live and act without a mind, no society can function without leaders, its thinking centres.

But why is the shortage of leaders so palpable now in the twenty-first century?

The main reason is likely to be associated with those radical changes that took place within the last two decades. Indeed, these changes in various life spheres are so manifold and dynamic that the passed times seem tranquil and snail-paced.

Bill Gates (2008) once noted that previous stages of economic development were marked by long periods of stability with brief sparks of revolutionary changes. Evolutionists call it punctuated equilibrium. Today's digital information shapes a specific ever-changing business environment that evolutionists might have termed punctuated chaos—the state of permanent maelstrom with sporadic breaks. The pace of change is disturbingly fast.

Some of these changes directly affect the basic principles of organizational activity and the system of requirements, traditionally specified for leaders. We shall name the central ones:

1. Change of the environment wherein the organization is operating. Globalization transformed the world anew, altering international, public, and social institutions and business philosophy.
2. Change of organizations themselves. High levels of indeterminacy and instability force organizations to be fast-paced and flexible. Organizations become more virtual, changing both content and form of administrative and management functions (for instance, control and supervision function).
3. Changes in the nature of work. The work has become more complex and knowledge-based, while the members of the working process become more and more interdependent.
4. Multicultural personnel. Cultural and confessional diversity requires additional communication skills, as well as tolerance and civility.
5. Opinion pluralism and individualized consciousness. Organization staff members tend to discard unquestioning obedience and blind loyalty; the diversity of viewpoints requires novel approaches in dealing with the personnel.
6. New idea of leadership in modern social sciences. There is an evident shift from behavioural models (how should a leader behave himself?) to personality paradigms (why does a leader behave himself in this particularly way?). New theories of leadership have emerged: transformational leadership, charismatic leadership, authentic leadership, symbolic leadership, leader-member exchange theory. The idea of the destructive ("toxic") leader has been developed (Schumacher 2014).
7. Shift in the leader's role within the organization. Leadership is no longer perceived as a group process, but as a defining factor in the organization's functioning in general, i.e. leadership has become organizational. The responsibility and risk taken by the leader redoubled considerably.

As is known, dramatic changes make people feel vulnerable and unworthy, stupefied, perplexed, and frustrated. It is not easy to stay calm in a situation like that, and many leaders fail to pass the test.

How can one become and remain a leader in an ever-changing world? How can a model of efficient leadership be altered? Where can new leaders find resources for being able to meet new demands? What styles of leadership and what skills will be highly sought after?

It is of vital importance to find comprehensive answers for all these questions, as the models of leadership that were highly efficient during the "punctuated equilibrium" period no longer work. New times imperatively require new approaches.

1.2   How Is the World Changing, and What About Me?

The subject of rapid changes is so popular and widespread today that one can think we are dealing with something new and poorly explored, especially in the context of organizations and leadership. Yet a closer look clearly reveals the fact that changes are inseparable from our lives. The seed brings forth the first green shoots, and then come the stems, leaves, and flowers to finally bear a ripe fruit. We see the ever-changing nature of vegetative life.

A child's body and the psyche system are forming; education and experience are constantly changing his knowledge, skills, behaviour, and personality in general (sometimes beyond recognition). The same is relevant to a social group or organization: their functioning is a constant change of structures, processes, goals, etc. Even the rocks, which may seem dead, inevitably change their form. In other words, life in all its forms is a series of unceasing changes that start from its germ.

The amazing pace of today's progress does not mean that the tendencies and laws, described by the thinkers and scholars of long ago, are no longer relevant.

Nearly 2500 years ago, Heraclitus of Ephesus (520–460 B.C.) famously noted that "everything flows". Socrates (470–399 B.C.), one of the greatest sages of Antiquity, was the first to call the opposites and conflicts the source of all changes. Focusing on contradictions both in thinking and in talking, he introduced the term dialectics, perceiving it as an art of dispute and argument that can lead to the truth (by revealing and analysing contradictions).

Great German thinker Georg Hegel (1770–1831) also contributed to the theoretical apprehension of changes' fundamental ground. In his famous dialectics, the concept of contradiction is regarded as the "engine", an immanent impulse of each and every change and development process. Contradiction serves as a unity of mutually exclusive and all at once mutually implying opposites.

The objective world and consciousness are developing through bifurcation into mutually exclusive opposite aspects or tendencies. Their interrelations, i.e. the struggle and the resolution, outline every system as something whole, qualitatively defined. On the other hand, this tension is an immanent impulse that triggers changes, development, and transformation, acquiring a new quality. The progress of science has proved out the heuristic value of Hegel's ideas: the modern scientific worldview is entirely dialectical. Indeed each and every system is regarded both as a concrete unity and as an immanently split entity. The evolution of science has made contradiction a basic principle of scientific investigation, while the divergence within natural and social processes is considered their intrinsic and essential quality.

Accordingly, we can say that today's acceleration of changes and development in all spheres of human activity is a result of unprecedented diversity and sharpening of contradictions that humankind actually faces. Only dialectical thinking, the dialectical approach to natural phenomena, social life, and work of consciousness can reveal the real tendencies and driving motives of their development.

1.3   Leadership and Organizational Changes

Organizational changes turned into a subject of scientific research more than 50 years ago, attracting the attention of experts. The separate domain of management—the organizational development (OD)—has been distinguished.

As pointed out, all kinds of changes come from opposite tendencies that are present in every process, phenomena, event, human, or any other being. Every system consists of subsystems or components that are developing non-uniformly, i.e. the interaction between subsystems can vary considerably. The unity and struggle of these opposites provide for the immanent development of any organizational system. We can highlight three efficiency-determining subsystems within the activity of organizations:

1. Senior leadership/owners
2. Personnel/staff members
3. Environment (economical, social, political), wherein the organization functions

The interaction of the subsystems mentioned above determines the main management tasks that can ensure organization's survival, integration, and development. These tasks are:

1. The optimization of inner processes and structures
2. The organization's adaptation to the environment

The first task can be reduced to the optimal solution of all organization's inner problems, while the second one deals with extra-organizational challenges. The first task is primary, as the adaptation to the environment is only possible when all intra-organizational conflicts are resolved and the organization is functioning as a whole and stable entity. The possibility to meet environmental challenges depends on how leaders managed to cope with the first task.

The interaction of these subsystems creates conflicts and contradictions, which eventually specify the direction of further change and development. Each element is expecting to gain a certain profit from organizational management, not to mention that none of them believes meeting organizational goals can be harmful. The goals of these elements can be fully, partially, or not congruent at all.

Is it possible for organizational leaders to define and choose the goals that will satisfy everyone more or less associated to the organization?

Take, for instance, the expectations of the owner, the staff members, the ecologists, and the public authorities. The owner is interested in the top profit, inter alia by cutting down non-production spending (ecology, personnel) and optimizing taxation. Staff members hold an interest in higher wages, social protection, favourable working conditions, and opportunities for education and going up the ladder. Reducing expenses on these issues will seem unacceptable for most of them. The ecologists' agenda includes the protection of the environment, so they will never accept the cuts on ecological issues, whereas the public authorities regard organizations as major taxpayers.

Given that the organization's efficacy in the context of globalization becomes dependent on a variety of non-business factors or overseas resources, we can say that the modern organization is turning into the scene of interactions and clashes of the numerous organizational and extra-organizational factors that are vital for the organization's survival and development.

Therefore, a modern leader's key competence is going to be the dialectical way of thinking and acting, i.e. the ability to identify the basic inner contradictions and, by properly resolving them, to ensure the necessary organizational changes. If a leader fails to do that, changes will come unexpectedly in the form of crises and destructive conflicts.

Thus, the first principle of efficient leadership and change management is the uncovering of basic contradictions and the understanding of the dialectics of organizational life.

1.4   The Organization as a Continuous Contradiction

In general, contradictions within organizational life are neglected by the management until they turn into a destructive conflict that reflects the intensification of contradictions. Only then do managers start to seek the cause of the conflicts, realizing that it was preceded by a complex and long history of implicit and explicit contradictions that had been neglected. If it has not come to open conflict, everything is considered to be fine, while minor tensions are regarded as an accepted degree of necessary and inevitable evil. That is why it comes as no surprise that the majority of managers believe there are no serious contradictions in conflicts in their organizations.

However, if one wants to avoid tacit destructive contradictions and uncontrolled changes, one must remember that each and every organization is a system of continuous contradictions and conflicts between. Among others, there are contradictions:

- The common goal of the organization and individual goals of staff members
- Praising individual progress and collective work
- Delegation and duties
- Organizational culture and organizational changes
- Formal and informal organizations
- Result- and personnel-oriented approach
- Maximum profit and ethical imperatives

As already mentioned, the main task for an organization is the optimization of its inner processes and structures. In this respect, each and every organization is a system of inner contradictions and conflicts that are to be resolved in order to ensure its survival and development. At the basis of the system of organizational conflicts lies the interaction of two main subsystems: the owner/senior leadership and the personnel/staff members. Thus, the organization turns out to be a contradictory process of theses subsystems' interaction, both of them having different and sometimes opposite goals, interests, and demands.

In psychological terms this contradiction manifests itself in two opposite tendencies: centripetal and centrifugal. The former pushes a staff member (an individual) towards the organization (i.e. the subsystem of senior leadership/ owners), towards the cooperation and the search for common goals and interests. Within this tendency the organization becomes a tool for meeting the individual demands: being part of the organization he gains not only means of existence but also the opportunity for well-being and development. The second tendency forces an individual to escape organizational pressure, while the necessity to subject individual interests to the demands of the organization inevitably leads to the feeling of resistance and the unwillingness to cooperate with others on behalf of alien organizational goals.

This contradiction is dialectically inherent to any organization, constantly subverting its wholeness. The organization can endure as an organism only if centripetal forces consistently dominate over the centrifugal ones, if the drive towards wholeness is stronger than the drive towards disintegration.

1.5   Power as the Basic Organizational Process for Resolving Conflicts and Contradictions

What, then, can provide for the organization's survival and development, placing integration above disintegration and cooperation above competition?

One of the attributes of each and every organization is the presence of a common goal, which underlies all structural and functional characteristics. However, as we already mentioned, the goals of the two basic subsystems—the owner/senior leadership and the personnel/staff members—may be fully, partially, or not congruent at all.

How, then, can a common goal which will guide all staff members be articulated? Usually it is one of the senior managers' or owners' objectives—an individual goal of a certain group of organization's policy makers. But how can an individual goal become a common one? How can it ensure steady orientation of staff members in a certain direction, even if it is only partially or not congruent to their own goals and interests?

There are famous zoo psychological experiments that make a hungry monkey reach a banana, fixed on a ceiling. To get the forbidden fruit a monkey has to use boxes that researchers had put into a cage in advance. By placing the boxes against each other, the monkey can reach its goal. Each monkey separately can quickly manage to do that. However, when there is a group of animals facing the task, they are focused only on individual efforts, not regarding other species as partners. A "cooperation" like that always leads to clashes and fights for boxes. Sometimes, when the necessary construction is finally made, one of the monkeys decides to use the box at the very bottom and takes it. All this results in a failure to achieve the goal, while all the monkeys remain hungry, become tired, and frustrated.

This is a good example of a certain type of "organization", wherein individual goals of all members agree with the common goal, but still the goal cannot be reached. And what organizational activity would we expect when individual goals and interests are only partially or not congruent to the common one at all!

The common organizational goal must be one, relying on some force or process that can ensure its supremacy over all individual endeavours and thus giving way to centripetal tendencies. If a process like that is not present, even the most clever and prolific goal has no chances to rise above the whole bunch of mediocre plans. And the opposite is true: the most awkward scheme can beat a brilliant plan if the former is based on some process that ensures its priority. It is also noteworthy that an individual goal can become common only if its priority over the other ones is relatively stable.

Thus, the first sine qua non of an organization's existence and development is not just a presence of an abstract common goal, but a certain force that can overcome centrifugal tendencies and grant the individual goal the status of a common one.

The best example of a force like that is the organizational power—a process that ensures stable priority of the common goal over individual interests of staff members, using a wide range of organizational and personal instruments (Zankovsky 2000).

The evolution of organizational forms—from most primitive to modern models—can be regarded as the development of power and the sophistication of means that ensure the priority of the common goal over individual ones. It is also noteworthy that dozens of thousands of years ago mankind lived in tribal communities, so the setting-up of the first organizational form, the state, was an extremely difficult and decisive move. String evidence suggests that it had happened much later than historians used to believe. Even today the phenomenon of "Arab Spring" makes us realize how thin the line is between organization (the state) and intergroup chaos.

Over the long history of mankind the main means that ensured the priority of a certain goal was violence.

Today in the age of democracy, personal freedom, and tolerance, one may think that power itself is an unnecessary anachronism and the organization can function according to new principles, which offer everyone an opportunity to take part in articulating the common organizational goal and choosing the area of its activity.

Organizational power is an *organizatiogenic* (organization-creating) process, as we can postulate the fact of the organization's existence as stable and goal-oriented only if there is a process like that, which confirms the priority of a certain goal over the plans and interests of this or that staff member. If there is no such process, or if it is very feeble, then the existence of the organization as a whole, purposeful community becomes inevitably challenged.

Today organizational power seems to look more attractive: it gives more individual freedom and has a variety of means to impact on a person without using direct violence. Still its essence is the same—to ensure stable priority of one's goal over the others' by all means available (violence included).

The process of organizational power is an attribute of any kind of organization, regardless of its common goal or its agent's personal characteristics. Being an instrument for changing goals and behaviours of the organization's members, i.e. being an instrument of psychological impact, organizational power is embodied in a system of means that can exercise power impersonally in the shape of formal functional interconnections, professional duties and instructions, norms and rules. In fact this system can function without an agent of organizational power, if the subordination of individual goals to one common goal is clear and unambiguous.

The process of organizational power is an integral part of the organization of any level: whether it be a state, a big industrial group, a Marine division, a social fund or a small enterprise. The notion that exact and positive-acting power can be only authoritarian seems the product of ideology or ignorance. The process of organizational power is equally necessary to authoritarian and democratic organizations, if certain results are to be obtained and certain goals reached.

To resolve the conflict of common and individual goals the modern organization uses six types (French and Raven 1959; Raven 1965, 1992) of power:

1. *The power of reward.* People are ready to change their behaviour if they know it will help them to satisfy their demands, earn more, promote, enjoy recognition, and win prizes and presents. That is why the one who controls the distribution of benefits and privileges has the real power and can have an impact on the behaviour of those who value such stimulations.
2. *The power of punishment.* This type of power is based on fear. An individual conforms with it for fear of negative consequences that can follow disobedience. This power is maintained by threats of physical violence, pain, deprivation of liberty and satisfaction of basic needs, and even death. On the organizational level a manager can use the power of violence by dropping a remark, giving a reprimand, imposing a fine, transferring a staff member to a low-paid small-scale job, or even firing him.
3. *The power of position.* The formal position of a manager gives him an opportunity to have an impact on the behaviour of his subordinates, presupposing their duty to obey and be led. This type of power is secured by the whole system of legal regulations, traditional norms, and organizational instructions. That is why it is usually called legitimate.
4. *The power of information.* Everyone constantly needs important organizational information. A manager controls the communication channels to a large extent. Thus, by regulating information flows in his department, he can influence his subordinates. Human needs, motivations, values and attitudes, as well as decision-making largely depend on intra-organizational communication and informational support. So, those who control access to information and are able to use it properly have the real power.
5. *The expert power.* A staff member with good professional knowledge and skills also gains power: he runs the machines, software and hardware, he is aware of all legal rules, he controls the condition of other workers. Besides, the more specialized the organization's activity is, the more it becomes dependent on experts.

6. *The referent power*. The desire to be like another individual, to imitate his behaviour, to think like him, to share his goals and values—all that gives a referent individual (the one who enjoys being a role model) a real opportunity to change attitudes, beliefs, and behavioural patterns of other people. If a manager has this kind of referent power, his subordinates will perceive his goals as their own.

At the same time, the fact that the power has been formed is not a guarantee of the organization's being efficient, socially oriented, democratic, and humanistic. At the turn of the twentieth century a European politician said that even a cook can rule the country. Unfortunately, we have to agree: anyone can manage an organization (or a state) if we do not take into consideration the efficacy or morality of the management. Be it a cook, a sergeant-major, Barack Obama, or Vladimir Putin—one can do that only in the presence of organizational power.

Being a tool to ensure the priority of one goal over the other ones, power can be used to achieve any goal that is possible with certain resources available. That is why the subsequent chapters of the book will dwell in the direction and the substance of the goals that underlie the functioning of the organization.

1.6 Leadership as an Optimal Way of Overcoming Basic Organizational Contradictions with the Help of Personal Power Sources

Leadership as part of the organizational power system can help us to understand this phenomenon from novel perspectives. Both power and leadership focus on the same: to align the goals and the behaviour of the members of the organization. Though leadership is not explicitly repressive, it also has a certain faculty for social pressure.

When facing a problem or a need to use power, a manager confronts a dilemma: how one can force or inspire a subordinate to obey, what type of power to use. The above-considered types of power can be qualified as organizational (the power of punishment, reward, and hierarchy), personal (competence and charisma power), or organizational-personal (informational power).

A grouping like that is a new way to look at the differences between the chief-manager and the leader. The structural position within the organization gives the chief-manager an access to all six types of power. The position of the chief-member automatically allows him to use the powers of punishment, reward, and hierarchy itself. Ideally the chief-manager can have three other powers—informational, charismatic, and competence. However, the organization cannot automatically grant the manager with personal powers. The individual himself can only develop charismatic characteristics and professional skills. The organizational-personal quality of informational power is preconditioned by the fact that information without the necessary expertise cannot be used efficiently. Or vice versa, communicative and professional skills without the full access to information do not grant a manager this type of power. Of course, having a quick eye, good memory, and powerful analytic thinking, a manager can predict the necessity of important organizational decisions by himself, but this exception only proves the general rule. In any case, only by having the three latter types of power can the chief-manager also be a leader.

The renowned psychologist Douglas McGregor considered leadership the best possible form of power (McGregor 2005). Identifying with his manager-leader, who is doing his best to achieve the goal, a staff member shifts this identification onto this goal, perceiving it as personally significant. In this context, the manager is coming to be regarded not as an individual but as a goal-bearer, its embodiment. As long as the manager is pursuing his goal, his effort will inspire his subordinate. But if the manager becomes less goal-oriented, the subordinate's identification will fade away, i.e. the manager will cease to be a leader. That is why, McGregor asserts, as the gravitation cannot be attributed to the object, that leadership cannot be considered exclusively as a manager's personal characteristic.

Ideally the leader is supposed to have knowledge, experience, and abilities that will help him, regardless of his position, to influence thoughts and deeds of staff members, leading them to the common goal.

1.7   From the Dialectics of Conflict Towards the Dialectics of Cooperation and Competition

On the behavioural level, the dialectical approach manifests itself in an ability to reveal and overcome contradictions present in a conflict.

Managers one-sidedly tend to believe that each and every conflict can have only negative implications. Indeed, it is the negative (destructive) aspect that initially reveals the conflict, making us focus on tensions and contradictions. Then we begin to realize that there is nothing new about these contradictions.

This aspect of the conflict is usually called destructive, as it can lead to disagreement and inconsistency. Moreover, the destructive conflict is said to be independent of its reasons. Instead it is specified by emotional attitude and ad hominem arguments, multilateralization, and intensification of negative attitudes (expansion of the conflict).

However, in order to realize the importance of changes and development, all members of the organization must receive inner and outer impulses, stimuli, and messages. If everything is functioning not the best way it can, but steadily and evenly, the majority of staff members will reasonably prefer not to change anything. The so-called destructive aspect of the conflict in this context can be a kind of spotlight, displaying the implicitly present contradictions, and—on the other hand—it can pinpoint the area of potential growth and development most affected by the conflict. The dialectical approach allows us to regard the destructive aspect of conflict also as an alarming one, which can trigger a process of functional resolution of contradictions and bring forth a deeper apprehension of the problem.

The very fact of recognizing the problem and all existing differences contributes to the development of cooperative interaction within the conflict, thus making optimal resolution possible.

As R. Dahrendorf (1992) pointed out, the proper regulating of conflict's creative force promotes the evolution of social structures. Conflicts can finally result in more thorough management decision-making, help to realize neglected problems, motivate to examine the whole range of viewpoints more closely, and encourage accepting constructive criticism.

Taking into account all the advantages of the constructive conflict, we should keep in mind the fact that its destructive (alarming) aspect initially attracted our attention and gave momentum to the search of new solutions. Thus, both sides of the conflict are to be considered in their reference to each other, i.e. dialectically.

The point will look more vital and vivid if we see these two aspects of the conflict as the pattern of each and every interactional contradiction, which is always associated with cooperation and competition. In other words, the constructive aspect of conflict implies cooperation and the destructive (alarming) one implies competition.

However, at this point we face a paradox: when trying to resolve the conflict, we rely on the constructive aspect, that is to say, on the ability to cooperate (therewith denying the destructive aspect). And at the same time modern theory and practice of management proclaim competition as the main source of development.

We even have a special branch of economic theory called competition studies that explores how competition is organized. One of the founding fathers of this branch, Michael Porter of Harvard University (1990, 1998), said the success on the market depends on acquiring competitive advantage. Modern economic theory, in spite of the diversity of perspectives, is still largely based on the notion of competition, regarding it as the only noteworthy form of economic interaction.

The dominating idea of competition being a basic mechanism of changes is genetically connected to Darwin's theory of evolution that set competition as a natural effect of the struggle for limited resources. Yet the application of evolutionism to social life aroused reasonable criticism back in Darwin's days (Darwin 1975; Denton 1986; Erwin 2000; Lewin 1980).

Cooperation, or cooperative interaction, implies coordinated efforts (their arrangement, combining, summing up) of a group of individuals. Psychologists have different ways to describe cooperation and competition, using such terms as partnership and rivalry, concord and conflict, association and dissociation.

Deutsch (1994) sees the main difference between competition and cooperation in the objective. In the social context of cooperation, an individual can achieve the goal only when other members of the group have managed to do the same (win/win approach). Thus, cooperation leads to the following:

- All individual efforts depend on the activity of others.
- Each individual gains reinforcement by his particular role within the cooperation structure.
- A collective confidence in achieving the goal is strengthened.

In the context of competition, the goal achieved by one excludes this possibility for the others (win/lose approach).

Taking into consideration all the above-described, one can think we deem competition studies useless and claim that only cooperation can be considered a source of potential change. However, both opposite tendencies have their pros and cons. If competition is dominant, constant rivalry can lead to disagreement and disengagement; if cooperation is dominant, the strive to agree by all means can result in unreasonable compromises and stagnation. Only shifts from one to another and mutual denial can boost the cooperative aspect of competition and the competitive aspect of cooperation, thus enabling changes and development.

When we analyse mutual shifts from destructive conflicts to constructive ones, from competition to cooperation in the context of organizational interactions, we should pay attention to the problem of directedness of organizational activity. We all witness efficient conflict resolution, dynamic development, and high productivity of certain departments and organizations which have selfish, anti-social and even criminal goals (the fact can become clear only afterwards). It is not surprising that for decades already, the business community has been worried about the ethical norms in the trade.

Constructive and destructive conflicts, cooperation and competition, and the dialectical approach in general are the only way to describe behavioural and psychological patterns, while the directedness in both cases is designated by the wider frame of activity, by the global business environment and corporative culture, which includes cooperation and competition. That is why, when analysing conflicts and interactions, one needs to regard them not only in the context of behavioural technology, but also in light of a certain ideal model. A model like that presupposes the goal that, if achieved, can harmonize and improve all the subsystems of organizational interactions.

1.8 Education by Overcoming a Conflict (Diagogics)

The key role of contradictions as changes' driving force attests the fact that in the modern, constantly evolving world contradictions and the process of their resolution will become a major issue in educating the new types of leaders. By revealing and resolving organizational contradictions, a manager can control organizational changes, as well as efficiently perform his main functions. A manager's job can be reduced to the decision-making process: the one who does not make any decisions, cannot be called a manager. As a rule, the necessity to make decisions arouses not in normal, routine work, but in the situations when complex and ambivalent tasks are present. And the decision made is always a process of choosing the optimal one out of several alternatives, which implies the resolution of inner conflict.

Thus, in the modern context a key backbone skill is the ability to reveal and resolve intra and extra organizational contradictions. Besides, this skill becomes both an instructional issue and a method. By the term diagogics we mean the instructional method of resolving conflicts.

The task of revealing and resolving contradictions is a difficult one. Many types of intellectual activity and behaviour models in an organization are determined by its rules, technologies, norms, and traditions that do not necessarily stipulate any forms of dealing with the conflict, but can be regarded as formal ways of resolving contradictions. Staff members should not and do not have to reflect about when they are to come to work or how to present the accounts (e.g. Annual Financial Report).

Things go in a similar way in education. If a coach gives a task and describes the right way to fulfil it, their work cannot be considered a diagogic solution. Trainees can take part in scientific researches by gathering the material, but if they do not solve proper scientific problems, revealing the interconnections and contradictions of the phenomenon under study, this kind of education is in no way different from traditional. True diagogic is associated with an opportunity for an independent individual (or group) to search for the solution and resolution of contradictions. Education can be called diagogic only if it is aimed to teach a trainee to resolve contradictions within a certain theoretical or technical (practical) problem, generating and highlighting the conflict.

Attempts to use new knowledge and individual changes inevitably are scarcely notable within a comfortable, customary environment. You cannot change a child's behaviour without changing the relationship models within the family; equally, in the organization one can change the behavioural patterns of staff members only if the whole system of relations is changed. The organization itself acts as the unit of change and development. The principles of diagogic education are based on R. Blake's and J. Mouton's (1962) synergogics and at the same time expand it. This means the educational environment, wherein cooperation and constructive resolving of conflicts induce mutual changes and learning.

The traditional model of instructional education (familiar to everyone since early childhood) implies the authoritative and powerful figure of the teacher, passing his knowledge onto his pupils from above downwards. Besides, the traditional model inevitably causes the trainee's dependence on the trainer, and all the responsibility rests with the teacher. How then can a fresh and solid motivational attitude towards individual change and development be created? What can encourage staff members to strive for changes and development?

The energy that is necessary for changes to come is cellared in the group interaction and in the group in general. As far back as in the late 1940s, group therapy among military men proved to be much more efficient than individual therapy (Bion 1946). It was discovered that a group contains powerful therapeutic resources. Positive changes were also boosted by a higher degree of personal involvement.

Research of group processes also shows that, when a teacher or a coach uses the traditional educational model, trainees (consciously or instinctively) develop one of four basic attitude models towards him:

Dependence—they feel dependent, trying to insinuate themselves into his confidence
Confrontation—they reject the powerful figure, regarding the teacher as their rival

Avoidance—they try to isolate themselves, regarding the powerful figure as dangerous or useless

Unionization—they try to unite in groups to deal cooperatively with all difficulties and challenges

In fact one is not just trying (consciously or not) to choose a behavioural model, but to decide on a strategy of overcoming a conflict. In other words, group interaction in general and group education in particular are inevitably implemented through continuous resolving explicit and inner conflicts. Generally, among these strategies you will not find cooperation, which is the only one that allows to set efficient group activity and to overcome the "win/lose" mechanism.

Research showed that when the teacher or a coach purposely limits his impact on the group, he causes "unconscious group tension" (Bion 1961), as it becomes impossible to use traditional models and solutions. All this triggers the process of searching for new perspectives and new strategies, and the group starts to explore novel behavioural patterns. This very moment is marked by the first real change of both individual and group activity.

When the responsibility is being shifted onto the group itself, a new model of group activity is forming. At this very instance each group starts to open up, revealing a previously hidden progressive potential that can be experienced by every member of the group. This potential implies the ability of each and every member of the group to change over the long run.

It also ought to be noted that people in general are blind and indulgent as far as their behaviour is concerned, even if it interferes in their work and career. Resolving inner conflicts between oneself and others, oneself and external conditions, the individual again uses the above-listed strategies: dependence, confrontation, avoidance, and unionization. Each of them assumes the form of a certain psychological defence that prevents an individual from regarding oneself and one's behaviour impartially. Those barriers constitute severe impediments for education and development by assuming a self-deceiving form—from denying the facts and information filtering to rationalization and self-indulgence.

Further, if some fact-based information comes from a coach or a certain staff member or manager, an individual tends to reject or, at least, flatten it. But if the feedback comes from the group, the individual takes it seriously, feeling strong support and potential for changes and improvement. What we see now are great opportunities for using the group and the organization in general as a key unit for the profound and permanent change of each and every staff member.

But how can a training process really be created without its main structural element—a trainer-trainee dyad? How can we override the phenomenon of motivation fade, which manifests mainly in the failure to carry over-acquired knowledge and skills into the real organizational environment?

The key point is to remove a powerful figure from the process of group education. No matter how prescriptive or not the teacher may be, he is always perceived as the powerful figure, even more powerful than the tough top-manager, whose influence is always implicit. It is necessary to create educational conditions that will allow groups themselves to manage the process of learning. Besides, the group needs special conditions that will help them to realize all tacit and hidden models of behaviour (also making them a topic for discussion).

Group behaviour is actualized in stable, consistent models, but as a rule people do not have a common understanding of them, so it has to be articulated within a certain frame. We should have a general theory, so that the group discussion is focused on particular behaviour patterns. A theory like that can speed up the process of education, emphasizing only relevant issues and giving a neutral interpretation. It can also help group dynamics to acquire the necessary structure without the involvement of the powerful figure of the trainer. Hence a theory can be used, among other matters, as a structure-forming tool in the educational environment.

Thus, the theory is seamlessly included in the process of organizational development, with efficient exclusion of the trainer's figure and formation of the necessary conditions for group education (such conditions comprise dialectical thinking and constructive conflict resolution, i.e. diagogics). The most important instructional elements of diagogics are:

1. Preparatory studies of theory (preliminary training) in order to develop a common understanding of initially formless views on behaviour and to get ready for peer coaching.
2. Regular reflection on the group activity's quality, based on preliminary set criteria for common progress assessment.
3. An atmosphere of constructive intergroup competition within the framework of common organizational goals.
4. Conditions for articulating and clarifying individual values and attitudes.

Thus, diagogics is aimed at working out a common theory, with exclusion of the trainer's influence, and creating (by means of mutual cooperation and constructive conflict resolution) an educational environment that allows individuals and groups to master a comprehensive set of personal attitudes and orientations, integrated into the company's corporative culture. A unique competition-cooperation educational atmosphere allows improving the manager's intellectual activity and behaviour, to acquire an appropriate leadership style and to elaborate a specific way of thinking, usually referred to as scientific, critical, or dialectical.

References

Online-first Published Book Chapter

Winkler I (2010) Contemporary leadership theories. Contributions to management sciences. Springer, Berlin. doi:10.1007/978-3-2158-1

Literature

Bennis W (1989) Why leaders can't lead. Jossey-Bass, San Francisco, CA

Bion W (1961) Experiences in groups – and other papers. Tavistock, London

Blake R, Mouton J (1962) The intergroup dynamics of win/lose conflict and problem-solving collaboration in union-management relations. In: Sherif M (ed) Intergroup relations and leadership. Wiley, New York, pp 94–140

Blake R, Mouton J (1985) The managerial grid III: the key to leadership excellence, 3. Aufl. Gulf Publishing, Houston, TX

Dahrendorf R (1992) Der moderne soziale Konflikt. Essay zur Politik der Freiheit. DVA, Stuttgart, p 392, 394

Darwin C (1975) On the origin of species: a facsimile of the first edition. Harvard University Press, Cambridge, MA

Denton M (1986) Evolution: a theory in crisis. Adler and Adler, Bethesda, MD

French J, Raven B (1959) The bases of social power. In: Cartwright D (ed) Studies in social power. Institute for Social Research, University of Michigan, Ann Arbor, MI, pp 150–167

Gates B (2008) Business at the speed of thought, 2nd edn. Penguin, London

Kouzes J, Posner B (2010) The truth about leadership. Jossey-Bass, San Francisco, CA

McGregor D (2005) The human side of enterprise. McGraw-Hill, New York

Misumi J (1984) The behavioral science of leadership (aus dem Japanischen). Yuchikaku, Tokyo

Porter M (1990) The competitive advantage of nations. Free Press, New York

Porter M (1998) On competition. Harvard Business School, Boston, MA

Raven B (1965) Social influence and power. In: Steiner I, Fishbein M (eds) Current studies in social psychology. Holt, Rinehait, Winston, New York

Zankovsky A (2000) Organizational psychology. Flinta, Moscow

Journals

Bion W (1946) Leaderless group project. Bull Menninger Clin 10:77–81

Deutsch M (1994) Constructive conflict resolution: principles, training and research. J Soc Iss 50 (1):13–32

Erwin D (2000) Macroevolution is more than repeated rounds of microevolution. Evol Dev 2:78–84

Hersey P, Blanchard K (1982) Leadership style: attitudes and behaviors. Train Dev J 36:50–52

Lewin R (1980) Evolutionary theory under fire. Science 210:883

Lewin K, Lippitt R (1938) An experimental approach to the study of autocracy and democracy: a preliminary note. Sociometry 1:292–380

Raven B (1992) Power/interaction model of interpersonal influence. In: French J and Raven B thirty years later. J Soc Behav Pers 7(2):217–244

Master Thesis

Schumacher S (2014) Leadership dimensions: an empirical integration. Master Thesis, University of Osnabrueck, Osnabrueck

Synercube: A Scientific Theory for Shaping Efficient Organizational Relationship

2

2.1 The Organization as an Open System

In terms of system approach, any organization is a set of elements and their interconnections, which function as an integral whole (Katz and Kahn 1966). In order to maintain this wholeness, organizations need *resources* (information, energy, funds, personnel, materials, equipment, etc.) that can be gotten from outside and are necessary for the organization's activity. While functioning, an organization transforms resources into *results* (product, goods, services, information, etc.) that are brought back to the outside environment, returning a profit. In turn, the profit allows getting new resources and resuming the transformational cycle. Thus, each and every organization is an open system that is constantly interacting with the outside environment (s. Fig. 2.1).

As biological organisms, organizations grow and survive due to a favourable correlation between resources used and results achieved. To sustain itself in the long run, an organization should have an output at least equivalent to the input expenses on resources, transformational process, and normal functioning. If the output results do not allow reproducing expensed resources and efforts, the organization loses its resilience. Thus, the efficiency of the transformational process acts as a decisive condition of the organization's survival.

The history of business shows how even huge organizations that possess a great deal of resources ceased to exist because of the inefficient transformational process and inevitable lack of significant results. And vice versa, successful companies can achieve good results even in the presence of resource shortage, when their transformation works efficiently.

Rationale for paradoxes like that is the complexity of the transformational process that encompasses a variety of organizational, technical, and human factors. For a long while, problems were thought to stem from the insufficient technological level (consequently, a solution was associated exclusively with technological progress). However, it turned out that the problems with the transformational process result mainly from difficulties in staff members' organizational interaction.

© Springer-Verlag Berlin Heidelberg 2016
A. Zankovsky, C. von der Heiden, *Leadership with Synercube*,
DOI 10.1007/978-3-662-49052-5_2

Fig. 2.1 The organization as an open system

At first glance the management of joint efforts and fruitful interaction seems an easy task: one has to provide each staff member with information on what to do and how to do it, to create favourable and reasonable working conditions, to supply everyone with equipment and tools, to envisage the necessary educational projects. This way, you should have all necessary preconditions for efficient teamwork. That had been a popular view, and managers were focusing on resources, results, and technological aspects of the transformational process. However, the neglect of joint working and cooperation combined with poor awareness of organizational interactions' inner mechanisms used to lead to serious failures, regardless of the organization's size, type, or specialization.

2.2   Paradoxes and Mysteries of Teamwork

The majority of tasks that people face can only be accomplished through joint efforts. Working together a group of people can achieve results that can never, even by making inhuman efforts, be achieved by an individual alone. Be he the most talented, hard-working, smart, and strong, his potential capabilities to achieve prominent results are limited.

It is impressing, how in the absence of technologies and machines huge structures like the Egyptian pyramids or the Great Wall of China were made only by organizing and joining the efforts of many people. A thousand-fold physical increase of a single human effort results in a colossal might capable of creating manmade mounts.

Neither social nor technological progresses have changed these rules. And now, when trying to fulfil his purposes, a manager is thinking about how to unite and coordinate the efforts of his working group members, be it a department or an organization. In the organizational environment there is (and for long there has been) an established opinion that teamwork (the mere fact of fellow workers' presence) has a beneficiary effect on the productivity of the individual. In order to demonstrate an increment like that, a simple arithmetic metaphor is used: $1 + 1 > 2$ or $2 + 2 > 4$.

The results of scientific research would not give us the evidence of the collective increment like that. As far back as the late nineteenth century, French professor Maximilian Ringelmann showed the dramatic lapse in productivity of an individual starting to work in a group (Ringelmann 1913; Moede 1927).

By comparing the results of individual and group activity within the experiment on lifting the load with the pulley, Ringelmann expected that group effort would be at least equal to the sum of individual efforts. In other words, two men together had to show a result similar to the sum of their separate efforts. However, the study showed almost linear dependence between the number of men in a group (from 2 to 8) and average individual productivity. Thus, in a 2-member group each one was losing 7 % of individual efficiency, in a 3-member group it was 15 %, and in an 8-member group it was 51 %. So in the latter case, each one lost more than half of the individual potential (Steiner 1972; Ingham et al. 1974; Kravitz and Martin 1986).

Current researches show smaller losses, but still confirm the generality of Ringelmann's effect: when working in a group, one loses part of his individual productivity. Thus, we face a mysterious psychological phenomenon that can complicate organizational activity every time the interaction of individuals is necessary.

This fact is usually interpreted in terms of motivational factors: within a group an individual is less motivated to make biggest efforts, as he knows that his contribution will dissolve in collective results. Émile Durkheim once noted that "the group thinks, feels and acts not as a sum of its members' behaviours. Starting out from the individual, one cannot understand the processes arising within a group" (Durkheim 1924, 1950).

The group is forming, developing, and acting according to its own specific laws that cannot be deduced from the psychology of the particular individual.

Psychology now has a body of scientific data on group behaviour. This data, besides being able to explain Ringelmann's effect, can also help us find the means of radical teamwork improvement.

Group activity goals, the ways it is formed and the formal requirements to its structure and functioning are set, as a rule, by a larger organizational system. At the same time, the group phenomena and processes have regularities and particularities of their own. Though most groups are in a state of constant change, a number of consequent stages can be marked out (see Fig. 2.2).

The first stage is group forming, or a formal association of individuals. People, who met each other a while ago, find themselves united in a formal group. At first they behave cautiously, attentively watching their new partners' every step. The stage is characterized by the indeterminacy of group goals, structure, and leadership. Group members are testing the waters, trying to define their role and to choose a behavioural pattern appropriate for the situation. If any work is being done, it is based primarily on individual performance. The stage comes to an end when individuals start to perceive themselves as members of the group.

The storming stage is a certain form of intra-group conflict. Individuals accept the group as a fact, but resist the control exercised on them as its members. Different forms of activity are starting to be clarified and sorted. As a rule, decisions are being taken by the majority (while interests of minor subgroups are ignored). Besides, the necessity to choose a leader provokes another conflict. With this stage finished, the group assumes a relatively stable hierarchy of inner leadership.

The third one is the norming stage, i.e. establishing a close relationship, common norms, and values. On this stage group consolidation is under way. The group

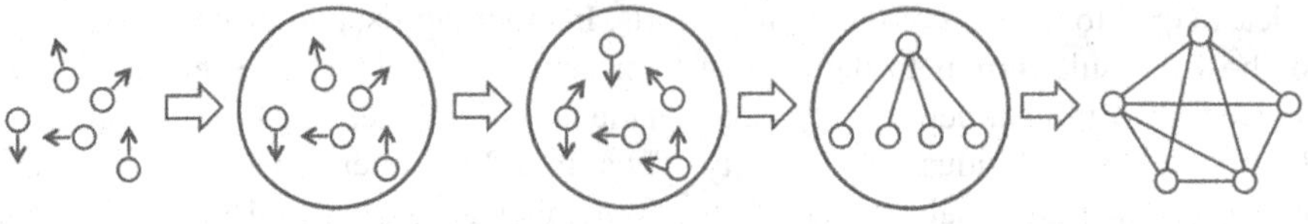

Fig. 2.2 Stages of group formation

begins to function exactly as a group. Each member has the precise impression of others, of their skills and personal characteristics; each member's role and function becomes settled: everyone knows his role and realizes the responsibility associated with it. The group develops strong self-identification (intra-group identification) and team spirit. The stage ends with the formation of a clear-cut structure. Every group member now knows what behaviour others expect from him in this or that situation. Those who are not happy with their roles have to accept it and stick to common rules and requirements. The atmosphere in general becomes positive, the tension of initial stages subsides, and the common goal finally moves to the foreground.

The last one is the performing stage. The group is formed as a psychological entity; the new structure is becoming ultimately functional and accepted by all members. All of them are industrious, energetic, common goal-oriented—they seek self-improvement and are willing to work for the group's benefit. All tasks are being accomplished with common responsibility. The group energy shifts from interaction to performance. The peak of this stage is a state of group synergy,[1] when group members tend to level activity differences and recognize each other's value as a member, in terms of being part of the integral whole.

The atmosphere within the group becomes warm and friendly, all its members feel safe and proud of being part of it. A deeper integration takes place: aside from proper group values, activity values are becoming common for all the members. The teamwork itself becomes so significant that it begins to constitute a basis for the group's existence. Only now can the group be called a team that can both efficiently function and allow each of its members to satisfy a wide range of needs, including self-respect and self-actualization.

Boundaries between the stages are not that clear and distinct. Moreover, when facing new contradictions and problems, the danger of regression to the stage of intra-group conflict arises. And if the group is stuck on the storming stage it can even be split into parts. In this case, the desire to cooperate among staff members dramatically drops, giving space to "subgroups" of individuals, having little to do with common group goals. These subgroups start to compete and fight for leadership, while the efficacy of the group begins to decline. If the group fails to overcome

---

[1]The term is one of the elements of the theory's name, which is *Synercube theory*: *syner*—synergy, implying the group synergy described above; *cube* is a three-dimensional figure, representing three-factor description of organizational leadership.

these disintegration processes, a continuous destructive conflict or even a complete disintegration seems inevitable. If the group and its leaders manage to overcome the crisis, the group resumes constructive progress.

In real life, all the above-described stages can be hardly marked out in their pure form (only in special or critical contexts). Usually two or more parallel or even oppositely directed processes run on. That is why all the stages should be considered a general frame that is aimed to emphasize the dynamics and reveal the problems.

Once again: to become efficient, a group should pass through certain stages, each of them posing specific problems and contradictions. All of them are to be overcome on the group's way towards synergy.

It is important to emphasize that managers have been regarding the organization as a set of individuals, and group interaction as a mechanical sum of individual efforts. It was not until the 1930s–1940s that the idea of different quality of working in groups and individually came around. One of the biggest contributions was the famous Hawthorne experiments, carried out in the 1920s–1930s in Chicago and led by George Elton Mayo (1933) (Roethlisberger and Dickson 1939).

Initially, experiments were aimed to define the impact of physical conditions on the work performance. It emerged that their impact had been pretty much overestimated. Some factors that had been neglected turned out to be crucial.

Within one of the experiments they compared the performance of two groups of female workers. One was working normally, while the other was under the constant supervision of researchers, who were recording the progress, mistakes, working conditions, and everything that was going on. Throughout two years and six months, while the experiment was being conducted, the work performance of the second group constantly increased. Moral climate was also good. The number of absences due to illness was thrice as little as in the organization at average.

Working conditions were identical in the two groups, so the progress could have been explained only by greater attention and management's care. Women also reported that taking part in the experiment was interesting for them, that they began to regard their work in a new light as an important, significant one. The mere fact that their managers decided to undertake a study like that was perceived by the workers with enthusiasm as a demonstration of interest in their labour.

These experiments importantly showed that the efficiency of work performance depended on individual motives, abilities, and skills in a minor way. In some groups a comprehensive plan of financial reward was tested. It was expected that a worker's performance would boost, if directly connected with financial gains. It turned out that workers were boosting productivity as a group, and not individually. Their productivity depended on the group standard that is to say not the standard imposed by the manager, but established independently within a group. Workers were even misreporting to draw real performance figures to planned ones. In other words, the group had its own performance standards.

The Hawthorne experiments made a great contribution to the study of group behaviour: they showed that organizational efficiency can be increased only when managers are aware of group processes. Besides, it was shown that care and attention to people's emotions impact the performance more than any type of financial stimulation. These experiments were the first to reveal the contradictions between formal organizational goals and informal ones, set by the group itself.

From then on management started to study all kinds of group processes and to look for ways and methods for boosting group interaction and team work.

2.3   Organizational Interaction Mechanisms

Organizational interaction, as we have already pointed out, is a vital element of the transformational process. In order to focus exclusively on this interaction, let us simplify the model of organization as an open system by reducing the transformational process to organizational interaction—see Fig. 2.3.

This model of organizational interaction includes three elements: R—resources, I—interactions, and O—output.

Resources constitute the basic point of an interaction. This element embraces finances, information, energy, materials, equipment, and human resources in the form of staff members' personal qualities, their education, skills, knowledge, experience, enthusiasm, and devotion.

Interactions include all types of behaviour, actions, or relations of individuals in the group that can affect the transformational process, i.e. the use and transformation of resources for achieving organizational goals. This also includes the way people interact, their ability to work as a group, and to transform resources into top outcomes. The sphere of interactions is associated with HOW people work, not with WHAT they do.

Output is the result of the activity—products, services, information, knowledge, or creative ideas. It can show whether resources were used properly and whether interactions were effective.

We are going to focus on the interaction zone (I-ZONE). The quality of the I-ZONE determines the efficiency of the $R{\rightarrow}O$ transformation.

When the I-ZONE is arranged improperly, the majority of resources are being wasted or used inefficiently. Unresolved conflicts prevent people from paying attention to their personal drawbacks and from understanding the current problem. If staff members are afraid of their colleagues' or managers' negative attitude, then resources are used inefficiently. For instance, when staff members treat each other with apprehension, they ignore the outcome of their work, focusing, instead, on self-defence. They would rather yield, hide in a shell, or even stop working. The morbid atmosphere suppresses creative work—no one wants to risk, if there is no

Fig. 2.3 Model of
organizational interaction

Resources   Interactions   Output

support and understanding from colleagues. Improper interactions inevitably lead to dramatic consequences in the organization's activity.

When, however, the interaction in the I-ZONE is arranged properly, staff members work in an atmosphere of mutual trust and respect. Thus, resources are being used efficiently. Individual energy (that was previously used to find excuses or hide weaknesses) can now be used to provide cooperation, to find new solutions, and to assume reasonable risks. If current problems are discussed with integrity, staff members will not be afraid of negative consequences and will look for the right decision openly and sincerely. Such support-oriented atmosphere of openness boosts personnel's devotion and zeal. People begin to take up challenging tasks, explore, and create, as they are no longer in danger of being accused or stigmatized.

The synergy effect takes place when resources are reproduced. In such a case, the results of teamwork surpass the sum of individual efforts. The synergy effect is reached when the group defines its goals collectively and tries to do its best to achieve them. Synergy implies a high level of mutual respect and trust, as well as the ability to overcome all conflicts in a constructive way.

It is impossible to gain more with fewer resources only by increasing the number of employees, working hours, or investments. Thus, each and every organization faces the same dilemma: to keep fighting Ringelmann's effect in the I-ZONE or to work for synergetic interaction.

So, why does the I-ZONE, being that important, stay on the fringe of management's attention? There is a scope of organizational, personal, and psychological reasons for that. We will list the most significant of them:

1. In the modern organization a manager's career highly depends on resources and outcome figures. The way of using resources and outcomes is decisive for a manager's further promotion in organizational hierarchy. In such a case the I-ZONE is left neglected.
2. The modern organization imposes a heavy load of responsibilities on a manager, mainly associated with results and outcome. Overload and lack of time would not allow a manager to focus on the I-ZONE, so the emphasis is always shifting from the process to the outcome.
3. Individual psychological characteristics and unique life and professional experience result in very different beliefs and personal values. Thus, each staff member has his own perception of the relationship framework in the I-ZONE, while having a common one seems like quite an unattainable objective. Besides, inevitable fears, defences, and other problematic emotions constitute an additional burden on the way to productive interaction and teamwork.
4. Most staff members of the organization do not have enough knowledge to understand the regularities of group interaction.

2.4   Management Tools in the Search of Group Efficiency

Among group processes, the most important one is leadership, which determines the group's ability to interact with other departments, to organize itself, its area of activity, and its norms. Thus, being aware of leadership principles, one can foresee a group's development, the type of interaction in the I-ZONE, and the outcomes.

The question of leadership was taken for the first time in the 1930s as a part of Kurt Lewin's research (Lewin and Lippitt 1938). Since that moment, psychological approaches to leadership have been recognized as an independent research area. To date numerous experiments have already been carried out, fundamental discoveries made, theories created, monographs and handbooks written (Zhuravlev 2005; Parygin 1973; Bennis and Nanus 1985; Conger 1990; Locke 1991; Vroom 1973; Vroom and Jago 1978; Yammarino and Bass 1990; Yukl, 1994; Blake and Mouton 1964; Fiedler 1967; Hersey and Blanchard 1993; Stogdill, 1974).

K. Lewin's study and the results of Hawthorne's experiments triggered the use of the so-called behaviourist approach to leadership. The approach aims to find the main factors associated with a leader's behaviour.

Many years of research and investigation resulted in bringing the two main factors that ensure a leader's efficiency into light. The 2-factor model of leadership has become popular among psychologists ever since. However, these two factors are recognized by different names: work/staff oriented management (Likert 1961), structured activity and attention to people (Bass 1960; Fleischman and Harris 1962), human/task-oriented approach (Blake and Mouton 1964), task/relation-oriented approach (Hersey and Blanchard 1982; Fiedler 1967; Reddin 1970), directive/participative leadership (Bass 1990), support/progress-oriented leadership (Filley et al. 1976), employer/employee-oriented leadership (Tannenbaum and Schmidt 1973), control and engagement/activity (Lawler 1992), and support-oriented leadership (Misumi and Shirakashi 1966, Misumi 1972, 1985).

The best application of the approach was Robert R. Blake and Jane S. Mouton's Managerial Grid Model (1964), a specific framework of the interaction in the I-ZONE.

The Grid has the two above-mentioned factors as its axes. The first one is concern for production and the second one is concern for people.

Concern for production. Production results can be either short or long term. The horizontal axis numbered from 1 to 9 shows the concern for production. This outcome-oriented quality encompasses all kinds of activities that contribute to the pursuing of organizational goals: planning, control, coordination, and clamp-down. For example, the concern-for-production leader would ask for regular reports, control all work, and do everything possible to make staff members finish their tasks in time.

Concern for people also ranges from 1 to 9. Concern for people is a leader's ability to build relations. High level of this concern means that the manager is able to consider and understand other people's opinions, thoughts, and feelings. He pays attention to their professional and personal problems and is concerned about

Fig. 2.4 Leadership styles in
the two-factor-model
(by R. Blake and J. Mouton)

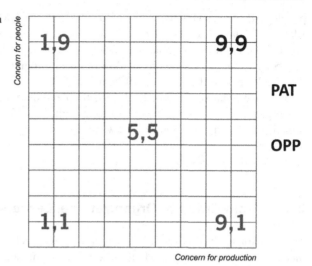

Concern for production

their progress and well-being. Properly expressed, concern for people gives them confidence and allows all group members to build up relationships that will result in fair outcomes.

Each of the Grid's axes has nine ranks. Thus, we have 81 boxes, hence, 81 leadership styles. But the number is unreasonably big, as the differences between this or that style would be very subtle. However, the Managerial Grid model was not aimed to describe leaders' behaviours quantitatively. Rather it showed their main tendencies in the context of tasks at hand.

These two concerns are interdependent, i.e. they cannot be regarded separately, and the understanding of the two factors' interdependence is the key to a leader's personality. For instance, high concern for people can be expressed differently in accordance with the level of concern for production.

R. Blake and J. Mouton distinguished seven leadership styles (Fig. 2.4).

According to this model, seven leadership styles are based on three levels of concern—high, medium, and low. Five main styles—1.1, 9.1, 1.9, 5.5, and 9.9—have numeric names, and two others are called paternalistic (PAT) and opportunistic (OPP). They present a combination of the main styles, which reflect basic attitudes towards the powerful figure: dependence/concession, confrontation, avoidance, alliance, and cooperation. Besides, R. Blake and J. Mouton made an attempt to reveal the motivation of each style on the basis of the common desire to avoid negative consequences and to strain after aimed results.

Researchers designated the 9.9 style as the most effective and sensible. 9.9 unites a high concern for production with a high concern for people. Top results are achieved by candid, honest, and constructive cooperation. 9.9-oriented leaders know that the personal contribution is vital for the performance of the organization. By leading after 9.9, a leader is capable of achieving results through and with other people. All other styles regress behind 9.9 (Blake and Mouton 1982, pp. 20–43; Blake and Adams McCanse 1992, p. 267). The 2-factor model of leadership proved highly efficient in shaping successful leaders. For more than half of the century it has been used in organizational development programmes worldwide (Larson et al. 1976, p. 628 ff.; Nystrom 1978, p. 325 ff.).

Yet, as we stated in Chap. 1, globalization and dramatic changes of labour and the organizational world have led to a radical shift of the leaders' role in organizations. In this context, new up-to-date approaches to leadership are necessary.

2.5   From Group to Organizational Leadership

The 2-factor leadership models considered above, including the Managerial Grid model by R. Blake and J. Mouton, are but the models of group leadership in hierarchic bureaucratic organizations, acting in a stable predictable environment with a number of specified goals.

In the context of constant changes, contradictions, and instability the leader, having no specified goals, finds himself in a difficult situation. What decision is to be made, if the problem is unprecedented? What opportunity is to be used, when conditions are constantly changing? What is to be considered a top-priority: staff, society, organization, group, or my own self? Towards what goal should the leader lead his subordinates? These questions have never been as critical as they are today.

Concerns for people and production are still relevant, but not sufficient. How can one be concerned about the outcome, if the outcome itself is not clear? How can one be concerned about people, when the differences among people across cultures, nationalities, and individual worldviews are unbridgeable?

Furthermore, some studies show that leadership, reduced to two factors, can exercise potent influence onto the group behaviour, even if the leader's goal comes into conflict with individual attitudes and is unsocial. Thus the traditional model of group leadership acts as behavioural technology, which can alter behaviour regardless of the goals imposed by the leader. Today leadership is no longer a group process, it determines the activity of the whole organization, i.e. leadership has become organizational. It changes the whole paradigm of leadership, which is now a form of organizational power (that uses mainly personal and informational resources) and a moral and axiological benchmark (Zankovsky 2011).

A leader's value orientation is a key element of his inner personal structure, as it separates significant from insignificant, essential from unessential. It is a sort of consciousness axis, ensuring personality stability and continuity of certain behavioural patterns expressed in the trends of one's needs and interests. Thereby value orientation acts as a key factor of a person's motivation.

2.6 Organizational Leadership

The moral aspects of goals, set by the leader, his personal value system, and orientation prove to be decisive. Value-orientation enables to distinguish between essence and irrelevance. It is an axis of awareness that defines the stability of a personality and provides continuity in behaviour. This is shown in bias of needs and interest. That is the reason why value-orientation is the most important factor that directs a person's motivation (Fig. 2.5). For a goal set by a leader for his employees, his orientation, personality, and values, the moral tenor is essential. The most tragic is the case when a qualified leader has an adverse mindset and leads his organization to a dead end and self-destruction. Even the most skilful leader, when lacking moral guidelines, will end up like that. Suffice it to recall memorable examples of big American corporations' bankruptcies, fostered by their leaders' egotism.

The leader's value orientations and moral attitudes prove to be vital in the context of informational and technological globalization, when the organization experiences tough competition and indeterminacy, not having solid activity landmarks (Creusen et al. 2013; Schumacher 2014).

As a manager's career evolves, his values orientation becomes more and more decisive.

In this respect, we can state that organizational leadership is a value-oriented leadership, requiring proper moral attitude from the manager. Thus, the model of organizational leadership has to include not only behavioural but also certain axiological dimension, a value dimension. In other words, it has to include three factors.

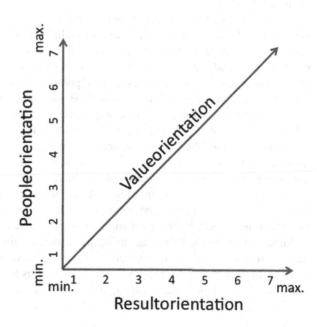

Fig. 2.5 The three-dimension-model of leadership

2.7   Organizational Leadership and Corporate Culture

The values system is formed within different life and educational conditions. That makes them heterogeneous, contradictory, and subject to certain hierarchy: some values can be sacrificed for the sake of others. Values are multiple and diverse. Some opt for spiritual values, trying to assimilate cultural heritage and find answers to perennial questions. Others choose transcendent values—God, salvation, the afterlife. On the personal level, each of us frames his values system by himself, although many aspects are determined and biased by the current historical moment, cultural context, and educational background.

To reconcile numerous individual values systems, those of the organization's staff members, is a big challenge. But first and foremost comes the task of reconciling the leader's values system with a common organizational goal. This is the corporate culture's mission. Each and every culture is based on a certain system of functions. The major one is to preserve and reproduce organizational experience, enriching it and passing it on.

The *communicative function* of corporate culture means the ability to form conditions and means of communication. The culture sets forth certain rules and forms of communication appropriate for the organization's operational climate.

The *normative function* implies maintaining the order and coordinating organization's needs and interests with the work of departments, groups, and individuals. It is culture itself that is responsible for norms, standards, and rules.

The *meaning function* is implemented when corporate culture makes the work meaningful. Besides, corporate culture is responsible for organizational socialization, which is staff members' ability to learn organizational norms, values, social skills, and qualities.

In corporate culture, as in any other professional culture, we can distinguish between two levels: everyday (real) and specialized. Everyday culture is a level of acquired knowledge, customs, norms, and skills that a person must have in everyday organizational life and work. Hiring a man to work in the organization shows that he possesses the everyday level of corporate culture. To master the skills of specialized culture, one needs training and specific organizational socialization. On this level professional socio-cultural experience and basic organizational values, which form the core of corporate culture, are accumulated.

Both levels are closely interrelated and influence each other, with cultural information being constantly exchanged between them. The exchange is carried out through specific communication channels: corporate codes, the mission of the organization, organizational training and development. However, the organizational leadership constitutes the most powerful transmission channel, exercising power and using both information and personal resources.

Important corporate values act as ideals, which are the values regarded in the perfection that is still to be reached. Regarding this or that value as the ideal, reaching beyond the limits of a given reality, allows us to grasp not only the trans-individual but also the transpersonal quality of values. They act as the best criterion for orientation in the world and as the support for personal self-determination of every staff member in the organization (including, above all, leaders).

Thus, corporate culture serves as a value oriented and meaningful space of organizational leadership and is present in two forms: the ideal and the actual. Indeed, everyday corporate culture is mosaic, individualized, and contradictory, while the ideal corporate culture as a system is based on the value orientations elaborated by the world-wide business community and leading corporations. An ideal corporate culture like that is reflected in the corporate codes and organizations' missions. It serves as a reference value system both for the organizational leader and for the actual corporate culture, i.e. values system really existing in the organization at the given moment.

In this context, the corporate culture can be defined as a system of ideals, values, norms, rules, and relationships, elaborated by leading public organizations and advanced corporate community, which acts as a reference value system both for the organizational leader and the actual organizational culture, i.e. the values system prevailing in the organization at the given moment.

We need to point out that:

1. This system of ideals is not a once-and-for-all given standard, but rather it is a constantly changing and improving, dynamic system.
2. Even the most efficient organization cannot essentially utterly and completely achieve these ideals. It can only be more or less close to them.
3. This system is not identical to the sum of the ideas on what a perfect organization is all about, prevailing among staff members. Even the bad accountant can have his ideals about submitting financial statements, but they are usually very far from the ideals and requirements of modern corporation's financial culture.

To identify the basic values and principles of an ideal corporate culture, we summarized the main approaches to leadership styles and corporate culture, as well as corporate codes of major multinational companies and judicial documents that preset the establishment of such codes. We have analysed the following documents, defining fundamental aspects of the corporate culture formation in the organization: Business Principles of CauxRoundTable, OECD regulations on the transnational corporations, the UN Global Compact, Principles of the Interfaith Centre for Corporate Responsibility, and the Global Initiative for account reporting (Zankovsky 2011; Schumacher 2014).

The analysis showed that, despite the apparent differences, most of the documents are largely consonant with the generally accepted management style and ethical standards, especially standards of work ethics. The selected documents, firstly, are universal for all companies, regardless of business specifics or market sector. Secondly, they cover a wide range of corporate activity, not just a particular problem, function, or group. Thirdly, the analysed directives are globally recognized. From this standpoint, the corporate codes of the world's largest companies (taken from the Financial Times list), all DAX-listed companies, as well as the largest companies in China, India, and Russia, were studied. For example, the organizational culture of German Siemens AG is epitomized in three principles, which are:

1. Responsibility: a commitment to ethical and responsible actions. Staff members of the company are determined to meet the highest judicial and ethical requirements. We do our business in accordance with the highest professional and ethical standards and procedures: We do not tolerate any manifestation of behaviour that is not compatible with the requirements of corporate ethics. Principles based on this value serve us as a guide in making key business decisions. We are out to make sure that our business partners, suppliers, and others, interested in working with us, are committed to the ethical behaviour standards mentioned.
2. Perfection: a constant striving for effective activity and superb results. Staff members set themselves ambitious objectives, based on our vision of the organization's mission and verified with the planned indicators, and do their best to achieve them. To the benefit of our customers, we strive to provide the highest quality, offering solutions that exceed expectations.

   The pursuit of excellence requires us to find ways of continuous improvement and constant revision of existing processes. It also requires changes, so that we can be in the right place when new opportunities open. Excellence also means attracting the most talented employees and providing them with the skills, knowledge, and abilities to achieve the highest results. We are deeply committed to a culture of high achievement.
3. Innovation: focus on innovation for sustainable profit. Innovation is the corner-stone of Siemens success. We closely align scientific research activities with our business strategy. We are the holders of key patents and we have solid positions in both already developed and emerging technologies.

Our goal is to be trendsetters in all business areas where the company operates. We enable our employees to use all their energy and develop their potential, rushing to the new and unusual. We are looking for creative approaches in all that is manifested in originality, ingenuity, and resourcefulness.

We are entrepreneurs, whose focus on innovation brings success on a global scale. We measure the success of our innovations by the success of our clients. We are constantly updating our portfolio, seeking to meet the most pressing challenges of modern society. It allows us to achieve sustainable and excellent results (Siemens AG corporate website).

Bayer's corporate code includes four values. Having "Science for a better life" as their slogan, Bayer interprets the word LIFE as *leadership, integrity, flexibility*, and *efficiency* (Bayer AG corporate website). Some companies do not limit themselves to 3 or 4 values and put forth a dozen or more values that are most important and fundamental for them.

Gazprom corporate values are: *Professionalism*—profound knowledge in the area of expertise, timely and high quality performance of tasks, continuous improvement of professional knowledge and skills; *initiative*—commitment and independence of all staff members within the process of production optimization; *thriftiness*—a responsible and careful approach to the use of the company's assets; *mutual respect*—team spirit in work, trust, goodwill, and cooperation in solving tasks; *openness to dialogue*—open and honest exchange of information, willingness to work together to develop an optimal solution; *continuity*—respect for the work and experience of elder generations, contacts with labour veterans, professional training and mentoring; *reputation*—the use of certain techniques and strategies to create a positive opinion about the company (Gazprom corporate ethics code from Gazprom corporate website).

Despite the fact that there are so many ways to name values and principles, many of them are quite similar in content. Thus, the three above-mentioned major corporate values—excellence (Siemens AG), efficiency (Bayer AG), and professionalism (Gazprom)—are substantially close. So the need to compress value assertions is evident. For this purpose, out of the above-mentioned documents that define the fundamental aspects of corporate culture in the organization, we marked the 43 most frequently mentioned corporate values and principles, which after grouping and summarizing have turned into a list of 24 basic values, which include: efficiency, success, quality, knowledge, power, initiative, justice, honesty, active position, respect, reliability, loyalty, responsibility, team spirit, client-oriented attitude, innovativeness, leadership, pursuit of excellence (development), creativity, respect for tradition, reputation, rule of law, partnership with shareholders, and commitment and professionalism. Values were identified based on the analysis of psychological literature and management studies, as well as on discussions with experts, and were given operational definitions. These definitions formed the basis of the questionnaire which assesses the degree of importance of a particular value for the establishment and functioning of an ideal organization, capable of delivering exceptional results.

The questionnaire was spread within a sample of 226 managers from Russian and international companies. Factor analysis (main component analysis with Varimax rotation) revealed five basic factors, describing 74 % of the total variance. These factors were named after values, having a larger fraction. These values are:

1. *Trust—The confidence of a person (group or organization) that behaviours and attitudes to him of other people (groups or organizations) will meet his reasonable and positive expectations, even in the most unexpected and adverse situations* (Kupreychenko 2008; Hosmer 1995).

Trust is the measure of the quality of relationships between people, between groups, and between the individual and the organization. In totally predictable situations, the question of trust arises very rarely: people know quite clear what to expect from the organization and what is expected from them. High uncertainty, mergers, restructuring, changing business models, and globalization are creating an unfavourable soil for the development of trust. Trust in their leader is especially important when employees faced the complex problems without sufficient experience, competence, and resources to solve them. Not trusting the leader and fear of criticism and sanctions from his side, they often hide the problems or simulate its decision, what later brings serious losses, violations of technology, and accidents. Only effective leaders are able to form a stable managerial situation even under a condition of permanent change. If the leader has successfully won and maintained the trust of his followers and colleagues, efficient corporate culture will be inevitably formed. The ability to generate trust in the team strongly depends on leader's general vision of human beings and their nature. It is impossible to establish trust if the leader is convinced that people are inherently lazy, dependent, vain, dishonest, and selfish. Conversely, belief in the decency of people, confidence in their abilities and talents, and a sincere desire to help them fully realize their potential inevitably help a leader to build trust from his followers and within the organization as a whole. To trust people, the leader must also trust himself, his own professionalism, his own position in life. One must also remember that trust is mutual, symmetrical in nature: if a leader does not give his trust to the followers, he cannot await the trust on their side. Several key points that enable a leader to form and maintain trust in their units should be mentioned.

1. A leader should be very careful with his attitudes towards mistakes and success. Everyone makes mistakes and leaders are no exception. However, they have much more possibilities to reject and hide their mistakes by blaming others and ruining their trust. To avoid this situation, one must follow two rules: subordinates' errors are the leader's errors, but the leader's errors are only his own errors. At the same time employees' success is solely their success and the leader should not steal his followers' achievements. Even speaking about success achieved solely through his personal efforts, the effective leader will always emphasize the collective nature of the success.
2. A leader should be very careful with his ability and desire to listen. Effective leaders do not put people down, criticize them, do not impose their opinion and temper on subordinates, do not interrupt them while talking, allowing them to express and convey their ideas.
3. A leader should keep his word, be honest and consistent. In order to trust and be trusted it is necessary to follow rules and principles that are valid under any even the most adverse conditions.
4. The leader's trust should not be blind. The leader should periodically review, analyse, ask himself questions, and make sure that his trust is not abused.

Even in those organizations, where the level of trust is very high, everyday life is not filled with joy and happiness: disagreements, dissatisfaction, and conflicts arise quite often, but they do not matter much as long as there is a trust within the team and organization.

2. *Fairness—Real equality of everyone before the law, as well as the correspondence between the actual role of the individual in organizational life and his position in the organization, between his rights and responsibilities, between work and reward, between merit and its recognition, between offense and*

punishment. The discrepancy in these relationships is estimated as injustice (Beugre 1998).

Research convincingly shows that the effectiveness of any organization largely depends on how fair management actions are from the employees' point of view. The more the employees are sure that they are treated fairly, the higher their motivation; with more enthusiasm they follow all management instructions and regulations. Fairness is closely associated with job satisfaction, commitment, and responsibility of staff as well. The researchers often distinguish three types of organizational fairness: distributive, procedural, and interactive. Distributive justice concerns how employees perceive the ratio of efforts expended and rewards received. Comparing oneself with other organization members, they can assess the situation as fair or unfair. Other grounds of distributive justice can be equality (give a little bit, but to everyone) and needs (give more to those who are more in need). These grounds depend on the organizational context, but always pursue the same goal, i.e. to make the distribution fair. Procedural fairness has attracted the attention of researchers after the discovery of the "fair process" effect in decision making. The essence of the effect is that the more participants engaged in the discussion and preparation of a decision, the more they consider it fair, while putting minimal attention to the final decision itself. The perception of organizational procedures as fair is largely due to the attitude of the employee towards their job and organization. If people aim to receive from the organization some personal gain or appreciate a comfortable atmosphere and friendly relations, any organizational procedures that violate these terms will be considered unfair. The researchers have identified six conditions that must be followed to ensure that the organizational procedure is perceived as fair:

1. The procedure must be executed by all members and in all designated cases.
2. It should serve to the interests of the organization members themselves not to the third parties.
3. It should provide the collection and usage of accurate information for decision making.
4. The procedure should be provided with a mechanism for correcting erroneous decisions.
5. The procedure should correspond to personal or prevailing moral and ethical standards.
6. The procedure should ensure the interests of various groups affected by the procedure.

The interactive fairness reflects the importance of the quality of relations, which accompany the execution of organizational procedures. Recent studies have shown that interactive fairness has two components: interpersonal and informational fairness. The first reflects the degree of politeness, dignity and respect for subordinates on the part of management. The second is expressed primarily in the management explanations: why certain procedures are implemented this way and what the grounds are for employees' reward or punishment. It is very important to note that management and employees have different criteria for measuring organizational fairness, which requires targeted work to reduce this discrepancy.

3. *Integrity—A sustainable orientation to tell the truth responsibly, appropriately, and specifically, avoiding deception, allusions, and uncertainty. At the organizational level integrity is reflected in the transparency of organizational goals, processes, and relationships* (Radoilska 2008).

Integrity is openness and avoidance of deception in relationships with others and themselves. Integrity can be a personality trait or learned behaviour, when a person always tells the truth and tries to avoid lying under any circumstances. It is a constant intention to admit one's own mistakes, to avoid the justification of one's weaknesses and striving to be sincere in any situation. A truthful man has internal regulators that control all his deeds and actions in accordance with his principles and values. There are two kinds of integrities—integrity towards other people and integrity towards oneself. At first glance, being completely truthful to oneself is an easy task. However, very often people get into self-deception created by their own fears and illusions and can stay in this virtual world for a long time. The trap of self-deception is particularly dangerous for managers. Occupying a higher position in the organization than their subordinates, managers are often deprived of regular and objective feedback about their actions and decisions, shaping them as their own very subjective and often exaggerated picture. Over time, this leads to a dramatic mismatch between the manager's self-picture and his actual behaviour. The preconditions for real truthfulness are in liberation from self-deception, in desire for honesty to oneself, in abstinence from self-indulgence and recognition of their mistakes, in abandoning the wish to assign subordinates' ideas and success, in the habit to evaluate one's own actions by the same yardstick as the actions of others. The leader's truthfulness with others is expressed primarily in keeping his word. A truthful man will always fulfil his promise and will help a partner in difficult times. He could be trusted as you. He always speaks to the point and prefers not say anything that will flatter and tell the half-truth. A truthful man tries to help others to not tell a lie and he will ensure that in any situation justice is followed. In practical life truthfulness requires tact and should meet several requirements. Thus, an unwritten moral code limits the truthfulness in cases where information might hurt the partner's feelings or cause harm to his health. Similarly, many people prefer to hide their personal troubles, to relieve others from excessive anxiety. Therefore, it is necessary to distinguish between honesty and excessive straightforwardness, or even rudeness. An honest man is always correct, even while speaking an unpleasant truth. A straightforward person says everything that he thinks, even in the case when his words are not in place and can injure his partners. Well-mannered people pay attention primarily to their truthfulness to themselves and respect other people's feelings. At the organizational level, truthfulness reveals itself in transparency and is manifested in the open and complete information flow within the organization. It is also manifested in the availability and completeness of information about the company, the transparency of its structure, and the transparency of management procedures.

4. *Commitment—The identification of the individual with his organization, manifested in the full acceptance of organizational goals, striving to contribute to organizational success and a wish to remain with the organization under any conditions* (Ermolayeva 2008; Mowday et al. 1982).

The employees' commitment to their organization is a mental state that defines their expectations, attitudes, work behaviour, and their perceptions of management and organization. Commitment involves identification, involvement, and loyalty. Identity is the pride of the organization and full acceptance of the organizational goals. Identity depends on the extent to which organization members are informed on the state of affairs in organization and the prospects for solving important organizational challenges, how they see the correlation of their goals and the goals of the organization, and how fair they consider the assessment of their work by the management. Involved personnel strive to bring personal contribution to the achievement of organizational goals and works if required beyond job descriptions exercising extra effort. To generate involvement, the organization should do its best in elevating employees' professional self-esteem, stimulating interest in achieving meaningful business results and widening responsibility for the results of their work. Loyalty is an emotional attachment to their organization, the desire to remain its member under all conditions. Organizational loyalty implies that employees are satisfied with the content of their work and careers, feel attention and care on the part of the organization, and are confident in the feasibility of long-term work in the organization. In real organizational life commitment takes specific forms and has various causes. Hence, employees can identify themselves not with the whole organization but only with some component of organizational life: formal rules, traditions, work results, or the benefits that the organization can provide. Commitment may range from complete identification with the organization and a sincere desire to make the maximum contribution to its success to the simple emotional attachment to people, fear of uncertainty, or banal fear to be fired and be unable to find a new work. Employees often do not realize the distance that separates their real attitudes from organization to the real, sincere commitment, and that is why high organizational commitment so often declared by management, is, in fact, quite week and shallow.

5. *Responsibility—Organizations and all their employees are responsible for their actions, they seek to enjoy fair remuneration, to stay committed to the rules, to observe commitments, and to comply with existing national legal and administrative acts* (Zhuravlev and Kupreychenko 2003; Turker 2009).

Responsibility is the obligation—placed upon someone or taken by someone himself—to execute and report any actions and take the blame for their possible consequences.

Responsibility is directly related to fulfilling contractual and other obligations or promises that require their host for absolute performance. Responsibility always refers to a specific subject and reflects the limits of his obligations. Obligations are the duty of the subject to someone or to his own conscience, which is conscious understanding and feeling of one's responsibility for execution of obligations. An individual, group, and organization as a whole may be a subject of responsibility. Responsibility may be political, legal, moral, professional, social, etc. Conscious understanding of one's responsibility is determined by a whole range of factors, which include cognitive, motivational, characteristical, situational, etc. In the process of their lives, people develop internal control mechanism providing them with the ability to conduct responsible behaviour without external regulation. People start to be responsible for their actions primarily to themselves rather than to external authority. The psychological precondition of responsibility is the possibility to make one's own choice, i.e. consciously choose a certain line of conduct. This choice is especially difficult in conflict situations, where the interests of an individual, organization, and society may come to contradiction. Of special importance for an individual is the problem of choosing his own position, the problem of "to be or not to be". For a person "to be" means to be human, to assert one's position in life and take full responsibility for one's behaviour. People tend to ascribe responsibility to either external forces (case, fate, etc.), or their own abilities and aspirations. Depending on one of these approaches certain strategies of human behaviour are formed. The responsibility of a leader is revealed in his ability to make reasonable decisions in his professional activity, in the persistence and integrity implementing the decisions and the willingness to be responsible for their results and consequences. The leader's social responsibility is revealed in his strive to behave in accordance with the interests of other employees and organization as a whole, to adhere to accepted standards and fulfil his responsibilities at best. On the organizational level, social responsibility is not only the implementation of the organization's economic interests and goals, but also consideration of social impacts of its business activities on employees, consumers, partners, local communities, and positive contribution to the solution of social problems in general.

The crucial role of these values is confirmed by numerous studies in the field of organizational psychology and management (Sheppard et al. 1992; Zhuravlev and Kupreychenko 2003; Kehne 2009; Turker 2009; Caldwell et al. 2010; Lane and Bachmann 1998; Schumacher 2014).

These principles can be seen as the core of a perfect corporate culture, as benchmarks that indicate the direction of organizational and personal development. The operationalization of these values in the form of a questionnaire allows scaling with one of the poles, being close to ideal values, and another one on the contrary extreme. This makes it possible to assess the real situation of the corporate culture or the personal values system with regard to these poles.

In recent years, organizational psychology actively developed the concept of person-organization fit, which increasingly serves as the basis for modern staff selection procedures. In search of work, people consciously, and more often unconsciously, are looking for organizations that would comply with their notions of fairness, integrity, power, leadership, and harmonious relationships (Westerman and Cyr 2004).

This compliance is rarely found at a superficial behavioural level, emerging from the deep structure of the personality, consciousness, and unconscious. The importance of person-organization fit is confirmed by significant correlation with personnel labour turnover (Westerman and Cyr 2004). Robbins and Judge point out that modern organizations operate in a dynamic, ever-changing environment, which requires the willingness and ability of employees to shift tasks and functions, working in various teams. This context implies employee's full compliance with overall corporate culture of the organization, rather than with a specific narrow function (Robbins and Judge 2009).

Person-organization fit is defined as the compliance between the staff and the organization, which is possible in case they share the same fundamental background and are in need of each other (Kristof-Brown et al. 2005). Among the most important fundamental qualities, researchers specifically mark out individual goals and values that must be mutually "matched" (Van Vianen et al. 2007).

Organizational leadership as a form of organizational power is the core of organizational process. This makes a leader's compliance with the organization a key to organizational efficiency. To assess the compliance of the leader's basic value orientations with corporate culture, a cultural value scale has been created, which is based on five principles of the ideal corporate culture. Out of this scale, aligned with two traditional behavioural subscales ("concern for people" and "concern for production") a S^3-questionnaire has been formed that enables to evaluate leadership in three-dimensional space. The overall reliability of the questionnaire is $\acute{a} = 0.87$.

Factor analysis confirmed the theoretical model, identifying three factors that corresponded to a given theory. Identified factors explained 77.8 % of the variance. Correlation analysis of the identified factors showed the following regularities. The minimum correlation was present between the "concern for people" and "concern for production" factors ($r = 0.15$, $p > 0.05$), the maximum correlation was present between "concern for people" and "cultural value orientation" factors ($r = 0.47$, $p < 0.001$). The correlation between "cultural value orientation" and "concern for production" factors was $r = 0.39$ ($p < 0.01$).

These results show that the factors traditionally regarded as inherent to leadership behaviour, apparently, are independent, while the cultural value dimension appears as a certain unifying and integrating factor. Correlation analysis between the identified factors and integral indicators of activity of the departments, which were under the managers' direction, showed significant positive correlation of all three factors with cultural value dimension ($r = 0.517$; $p < 0.001$). Thus, the criterion validity of each factor and interconnectedness of the factors, which can provide effective leadership only conjointly, was confirmed.

The data obtained strongly highlight the dominant trend: as the career develops, the role of the cultural value factor increases, and, on the other hand, the "concern for production" factor declines.

Fig. 2.6 Three-dimensional leadership cube "Synercube"

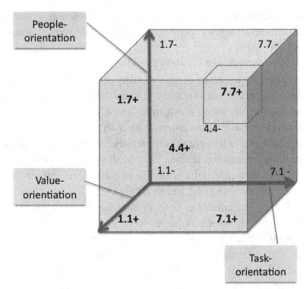

The results of clustering allowed singling out 10 groups of managers with different manifestation rates of the three factors. The principle of group, based on these manifestation rates, allows us to consider each of the selected groups as individual leadership styles.

The results can be presented as a three-dimensional leadership model (Fig. 2.6). In fact, the three-dimensional model can be represented as a combination of two 2-factor models, which differ in their cultural value content: in the first case this content is as small as possible; in the second case it is strongly marked.

2.8 Leadership Typology

Due to the fact that the questionnaire is based on a 1–7 scale, leadership styles may be shown in numerical form, denoting the extreme "concern for people" and "concern for production" factors (ranging from 1 to 7). In order to make it more clear, not encumbering style names with figures, extremes of cultural value content will be designated as − (minimal intensity) or + (maximum). Thus, we have singled out 10 leadership styles—here are their sketchy descriptions (in further chapters we will examine each leadership style in detail):

1. 1.1 – *Indifferent, cynic.* A low focus on the outcomes and on people, indifference, and negative attitude towards everything. Tendency to distance oneself from responsibility for the outcomes, desire to avoid organizational problems and any involvement in organizational activities. Being pressed by organizational requirements, he adopts a protective and aggressive attitude that

emphasizes the uselessness and futility of any action. His role, performed within the group/organization, seems quite satisfying to him.

2. *1.1+ Inhibited, unfulfilled.* A low focus on the outcomes and on people. Interest is concealed behind the mask of indifference, unrealized desire to contribute to the common cause. Disappointment associated with the inability to provide benefits, the desire to avoid political games and conflicts. Withdrawing into oneself. In a critical situation, possesses the ability to discard doubts and fears and to take an active and constructive attitude, aimed at overcoming the crisis. His role, performed within the group/organization, seems depressing to him.

3. *1.7— Adulator* (How can I help you?). Low focus on the outcomes, high focus on people, and indifference towards the work of the organization, the desire to please everyone. The desire to get along with people at all costs, adjusting to the situation. Avoidance of conflicts and tensions, lack of sincerity, flattery, and servility for their own personal purposes that man himself is not always understood.

4. *1.7+ Weak-hearted enthusiast.* A low focus on the outcomes, a high focus on people. He is not indifferent to the work of the organization and wants to create an atmosphere of friendship and encouragement. The prevalence of fantasies over real plans and actions. All kippers and curtains. He motivates colleagues to focus on positive aspects of work.

5. *7.1— Dictator, authoritarian.* High focus on the outcomes, low focus on people, indifferent or negative attitude towards people, who are regarded by him as tools to achieve results. Expecting obedience and diligence, total control and constant pressure onto subordinates. A rigorous and strict adherence to the rules.

6. *7.1+ Paternalist.* High focus on the outcomes, low focus on people, not indifferent towards work and organization. Treats subordinates as immature and in need of care. Mentoring, protective position.

7. *4.4— Conservative, formalist.* Average focus on the outcomes, average focus on people. Indifferent, formal attitude towards work and organization, the fear of change and innovation. Contentment with the status quo, defending the usual views and approaches. A rigorous and strict adherence to the rules and procedures that ensure stable and smooth functioning of the organization.

8. *4.4+ Tradition-oriented patriot of the organization* (a backbone). Average focus on the outcomes, average focus on people. Concerned with the work of the organization, desires to create an atmosphere of stability and reliability. Respecting and upholding organizational traditions and values. Devotion and loyalty to the organization.

9. *7.7— Opportunist.* High focus on the outcomes, high focus on people. Indifferent, pragmatic attitude towards work and organization. Ability to work with people and to achieve results that provide personal benefit. Lack of sincerity, declarative adherence to higher values, the ability to manipulate.

10. *7.7+ Ideal, visionary.* High focus on the outcomes and on people as well as a positive attitude towards work and the organization. A desire to create an atmosphere of commitment and involvement. Recognizing the importance of

each employee, striving to achieve the highest standards of performance. Search for and adoption of optimal solutions that are supported and shared by everyone. Committed to development and improvement, while respecting organizational traditions and values.

The criterion validity of these leadership styles was analysed. As a criterion, a standardized procedure for expert assessment of leader effectiveness was used. The most valid were 7.7+ *Ideal, visionary* and 7.1+ *Paternalist* ($r = 0.69$, $p < 0.01$ and $r = 0.57$, $p < 0.05$, respectively). Currently, fast analysis and processing of the obtained data is still underway.

2.9   Stability and Flexibility of Synercube Styles

The Synercube styles are permanently manifesting themselves in human behaviour in both short- and long-term perspectives. Regardless of the particular situation, leaders tend to react to conflict and implement other interaction skills in a way that is characteristic exclusively of this or that particular style. At the same time, interacting with senior managers, line managers, or ordinary employees, the leader, first of all, is behaving in accordance to his regular life values.

These values constitute the basic guideline for behaviour in various organizational situations and can therefore be considered as a terminal dimension of leadership style. Therefore, in order to change it, one needs an integrated system of training and development activities.

These examples show how personal values are manifested in the individual behaviour. These values often stay out of the leader's sight, retaining their powerful influence. Minor changes may occur if a person receives feedback about his behaviour, but significant changes occur only when he rethinks his values and attitudes. For example, usually people with high concern for production and low concern for people are tough, regardless of the particular context or situation. After getting feedback and rethinking the values that underlie their behaviour, people can change their behaviour as a whole.

Behavioural style factors can be extremely solid and determine a certain behaviour style. However, this can be greatly optimized through training. They can be regarded as instrumental measurements of leadership styles that should be regularly practiced.

The *dominant Synercube style* is the one that is most characteristic of the individual. This is his most typical way of interaction that begins to emerge from the first moments of joint activities and relationships.

Identifying the dominant Synercube style is not a matter of a single event or a selected conscious behaviour in one particular situation. In fact, the main style is based on firmly established behaviour patterns and it fully manifests itself only after prolonged interaction. It can only be determined on the basis of direct and multi-faceted cooperation, having its most characteristic behaviour patterns recognized.

For all the constancy of people's behaviour, their relationships with each other are determined by organizational and personal factors that have influence on them. Work in the organization is often accompanied by stress, overloads, lack of time, and force majeure. In addition, personal problems and circumstances may also cause certain specific changes in behaviour, but usually they do not lead to a radical change in personality or serious reassessment of the basic values. Such temporary shift from the basic behaviour style can be called a *back-up*. Once the difficult situation is over, the person inevitably comes back to his basic style of behaviour. Therefore, every person in addition to the basic behaviour patterns has a peculiar back-up leadership style.

The back-up Synercube style is the second type of human behaviour style, manifested in daily interactions. In certain circumstances, when the dominant style does not help in achieving the desired result, a person can temporarily switch to the back-up style. For example, a soft-tempered person, who is usually adapting to others, may suddenly bawl his subordinate out. A sudden change like that will shock both of them, and most likely this will be followed by a lapse to the usual behaviour style, accompanied by apologies and explanations. This person's dominant behaviour style has not changed, as it was just interrupted for a moment.

There are no fixed combinations of main and back-up styles. Some people show persistence in manifesting the main style, while the back-up style is used sporadically. This consistency shows the strength of the main style. A man with a strong main style is consistent in his actions, regardless of circumstances. Others shift to the back-up style more often, in certain typical circumstances, e.g. in the case of conflict or erroneous actions. Thus, the main style is characterized as fragile, since switching takes place regularly.

2.10 Synercube Coordinates as a Basis for Organizational Activity Efficiency

The Synercube leadership theory invites us to take the first step towards the effective self-development and to reach those changes that will lead to effective synergy on the organizational level. This concept provides a method for studying the quality of relationships at the individual, group, and organizational levels, using the models of 10 leadership styles (or types). Each style is a well-known pattern of behaviour, which can be encountered in daily discussions, meetings, telephone conversations, and other forms of interaction with other people.

The Synercube model is fundamental for organizational studies, since it engages dialectical thinking in any attempt to change behaviours and analyses the very aspect of interaction and change, which shows "how to do it properly". Attempts to change something rarely lead to success, if you do not set a clear goal and define a clear image of the real situation. These two points help one to stick to the right path and achieve the desired results. A clear reference system enables a person to determine the quality of real interaction and to set a goal, understanding what kind of interaction he would like to achieve in the future.

The Synercube leadership styles constitute the real point of reference for determining individual and collective improvement standards. Few would question the need for personal development and the development of effective relationships, but most of the efforts in this area remain too vague and inconcrete to encourage and support personal and collective changes for the better. To work with higher efficiency, a person or team must be able to define the very notion of efficiency clearly. The Synercube model allows us to focus on specific behaviour patterns (initiative, decision-making). It can be used to gain the support of those who can really help you to change, those who deal directly with your behaviour, namely, the immediate work colleagues, friends, family members, and others.

Once a common definition of what is effective and what is not is articulated, it becomes possible to use the Synercube model as an effective tool for identifying and changing ineffective behaviour. For example, as soon as the team members agree that the "correct" initiative must include an active search for information, without waiting for someone, it will be easy to identify "wrong" steps and decisions. People will feel more comfortable to comment on someone else's behaviour, if they already agree on what kind of behaviour is effective. Such a common understanding of effectiveness will provide, e.g., an opportunity to say: "I know that you have a lot of experience in marketing, but at today's meeting you suggested almost nothing. Can we discuss why?" If you act like that without the prior notion of effectiveness, your interlocutor can lapse into self-defence or even feel offended. In this case, a simple phrase like that will interrupt or even block the progress towards the goal. If there is a common notion and understanding, this comment will not be perceived as an insult, but as a means of moving forward. And the answer would be: "You are right. I held back from suggestions as. . .", followed by a comprehensive discussion.

The Synercube leadership theory provides a ground for changes, offering individuals, teams, and organizations a way that allows discussing what kind of behaviour is effective, and what is not. Following a natural impulse, many individuals and groups start working immediately, without examining and discussing the effectiveness of their work and interaction.

People tend to act guided by what is familiar. To work out of habit is much easier than to force yourself to develop a strategy, to discuss standards of excellence, and to set forth criteria for the desired result. If these necessary steps are omitted, people begin to think that all problems will be easily resolved during the process, implying that everyone will work effectively. This approach is similar to the situation in which a group of blindfolded people in the room are asked to show where the north is. Of course, everyone will point in different directions, and each one will be confident that he is right. The same thing happens when a group of people begins to work on a project without defining the agreed algorithm of that work. The without-a-second-thought approach is the reason for upcoming misunderstandings, wrong assumptions, and conflicts. And the longer staff members keep working like that, the more frequently they will face destructive criticism and wrong planning.

The Synercube theory points towards an understanding like that, when staff members discuss and agree on a model of effective behaviour before they start working on a task. This common understanding increases the level of commitment, and the team starts to work efficiently, developing strategies, discussing quality standards, and establishing performance criteria. Using theoretical knowledge, necessary for setting standards, the Synercube strategy gives organizations an opportunity to undergo successful changes and to achieve significant progress.

There is always someone who questions the validity of the theory, even without starting to implement it for organizational activities. By using the theory as an impulse, the team can begin to discuss various hypotheses and criteria for their changes, based on individual values and attitudes. Reaching understanding and defining clear criteria, staff members become more willing to seek changes, since their opinion is squared up, and they are involved in the decision-making process. They can act openly and honestly, as their doubts and fears are dispelled, and they are able to put forth their ideas. If an open discussion like that is not present, changes start with misunderstandings and alienation that only become more intense as time passes.

This theory also provides a starting point for individual change and development. The behaviour styles presented may help people understand how their personal fears block all attempts to change, why discussions aggravate conflicts and strengthen barriers, and why results may be worse than expected. The better a person uses methods of early detection, elimination, and prevention of inefficient behaviour patterns, the more chances he has to contribute to the attainment of synergy in the team. By eliminating all the interaction problems, the team gets the freedom to search for creative solutions, increase individual possibilities, reasonable risks, and impressive outcomes.

References

Literature

Bass B (1960) Leadership, psychology and organizational behavior. Harper, New York

Bennis W, Nanus B (1985) Fuehrungskraefte: Die vier Schluesselstrategien erfolgreichen Fuehrens. Campus Verlag, Frankfurt

Beugre C (1998) Managing fairness in organizations. Quorum Books, Westport, CT

Blake R, Adams McCanse A (1992) Das GRID Fuehrungsmodel. ECON Verlag GmbH, Duesseldorf

Blake R, Mouton J (1964) The managerial grid. Gulf Publishing, Houston, TX

Creusen U, Bock R, Thiele C (2013) Fuehrung ist dreidimensional. In: Crisand E, Raab G, Crisand N (eds) Arbeitshefte Fuehrungspsychologie, vol 69. Windmuehle Verlag, Hamburg

Durkheim E (1924) Sociologie et Philosophie. F. Alcan, Paris

Durkheim E (1950) Leçons de sociologic. Presses universitaires de France, Paris

Ermolayeva EP (2008) Psychology of social realization in occupation. IPRAS Publishing House, Moscow (Russian version)

Fiedler F (1967) A theory of leadership effectiveness. McGraw-Hill, New York

Filley A, House R, Kerr S (1976) Managerial process and organizational behavior, 2nd edn. Scott, Foresman and Company, Glenview, IL

Hersey P, Blanchard K (1993) Management of organization behavior utilizing human resources, 8th edn. Prentice-Hall, Englewood Cliffs, NJ

Katz D, Kahn R (1966) The social psychology of organizations. Wiley, New York

Kehne T (2009) Laesst sich Verantwortung normen? Ueberlegungen zu Rolle und Funktion von Standards im Themenfeld Corporate Social Responsibility. In: Aßlaender M, Senge K (Publ) Corporate Social Responsibility im Einzelhandel. Metropolis, Marburg, pp 209–236

Kupreychenko A (2008) Psychology of trust and distrust. IPRAS Publishing House, Moscow (Russian version)

Lane C, Bachmann R (eds) (1998) Trust within and between organizations. Oxford University Press, New York

Lawler E (1992) The ultimate advantage: create the high involvement organization. Jossey Bass, San Francisco, CA

Likert R (1961) New patterns of management. McGraw-Hill, New York

Locke E (1991) The essence of leadership. Lexington Books, New York

Mayo E (1933) The human problems of an industrial civilization. Macmillan, New York

Misumi J (1985) The behavioural science of leadership: an interdisciplinary Japanese research program. University of Michigan Press, Ann Arbor, MI

Mowday R, Porter L, Steers R (1982) Employee-organization linkages: the psychology of commitment, absenteeism, and turnover. Academic Press, New York

Parygin B (1973) Management and leadership. LGPU, St. Petersburg

Reddin W (1970) Managerial effectiveness. McGraw-Hill, New York

Robbins S, Judge T (2009) Organizational behavior. Pearson Prentice Hall, Upper Saddle River, NJ

Roethlisberger F, Dickson W (1939) Management and the worker. Harvard University Press, Cambridge, MA

Sheppard B, Lewicki R, Minton J (1992) Organizational justice: the search for fairness in the workplace. Lexington Books, New York

Steiner I (1972) Group process and productivity. Academic Press, New York

Stogdill R (1974) Handbook of leadership: a survey of theory and research. Free Press, New York

Yukl G (1994) Leadership in organizations. Prentice Hall, Englewood Cliffs, NJ

Zankovsky A (2011) Psychology of leadership: from behavioural model to value/cultural paradigm. IPRAS Publishing House, Moscow

Zhuravlev A (2005) Psychology of collective performance. IPRAS Publishing House, Moscow (Russian version)

Zhuravlev A, Kupreychenko A (2003) Ethics in psychological regulation of business activity. IPRAS Publishing House, Moscow (Russian version)

Journals

Bass B (1990) From transactional to transformational leadership: learning to share the vision. Org Dyn 18(3):19–31

Blake R, Mouton J (1982) A comparative analysis of situationalism and 9.9 management by principle. Org Dyn 10(4):20–43

Caldwell C, Hayes L, Long DT (2010) Leadership, trustworthiness, and ethical stewardship. J Bus Ethics 96:497–512

Conger J (1990) The dark side of leadership. Org Dyn 19(2):44–55

Fleischman E, Harris E (1962) Patterns of leadership behavior related to employee grievances and turnover. Pers Psychol 15(2):43–56

Hersey P, Blanchard K (1982) Leadership style: attitudes and behaviors. Train Dev J 36:50–52

Hosmer LT (1995) Trust: the connecting link between organizational theory and philosophical ethics. Acad Manage Rev 20:379–403

Ingham A, Levinger G, Graves J, Peckman V (1974) The Ringelmann effect: studies of group size and group performance. J Exp Soc Psychol 10:371–384

Kristof-Brown A, Zimmerman R, Johnson E (2005) Consequences of individuals' fit at work: a meta-analysis of person-job, person-organization, person-group and person-supervisor fit. J Pers Psychol 58:281–342

Kravitz D, Martin B (1986) Ringelmann rediscovered: the original article. J Pers Soc Psychol 50 (5):936–941

Larson L, Hunt J, Osborn R (1976) The great Hi-Hi leader behavior myth: a lesson from Occam's Razor. Acad Manage J 19(4):628–641

Lewin K, Lippitt R (1938) An experimental approach to the study of autocracy and democracy: a preliminary note. Sociometry 1:292–380

Misumi J, Shirakashi S (1966) An experimental study of the effects of supervisory behavior on productivity and moral in a hierarchical organization. Hum Relat 19:297–301

Moede W (1927) Die Richtlinien der Leistungs-Psychologie. Industrielle Psychotechnik 4:193–209

Nystrom P (1978) Managers and the Hi-Hi leader myth. Acad Manage J 21(2):325–331

Radoilska L (2008) Truthfulness and business. J Bus Ethics 79:21–28

Ringelmann M (1913) Recherches sur les moteurs animes: Travail de l'homme. Annales de l'Institut National Agronomique, 2e série-tome XII, 1–40

Tannenbaum R, Schmidt W (1973) How to choose a leadership pattern. Harv Bus Rev 51:162–180

Turker D (2009) How corporate social responsibility influences organizational commitment. J Bus Ethics 89:189–204

Van Vianen A, De Pater I, Van Dijk F (2007) Work value fit and turnover intention: some source or different source fit. J Manage Psychol 22(2):188–202

Vroom V (1973) A new look at managerial decision making. Organ Dyn 1(4):66–80

Vroom V, Jago A (1978) On the validity of the Vroom-Yetton model. J Appl Psychol 63:151–162

Westerman J, Cyr L (2004) An integrative analysis of person-organization fit theories. Int J Sel Assess 12(3):252–261

Yammarino F, Bass B (1990) Transformational leadership and multiple levels of analysis. Hum Relat 43:975–995

Master Thesis

Schumacher S (2014) Leadership dimensions: an empirical integration. Master Thesis, University of Osnabrueck, Osnabrueck

Others

Misumi J (1972) An empirical study of political leadership. In: Bulletin of the Institute for Industry and Labour. Kyushu University, S. 57 (Japanese Version)

3

3.1 New Corporate Culture

The efficiency of the organization, as already noted, is a crucial factor for its survival. That is why efficiency indicators are always in the focus of the top management and are used as the main criteria for assessing the success of any manager. Government bodies indirectly monitor organizational efficiency as well, by assessing and controlling tax-related, social, or other liabilities.

These assessments are formalized, executed in a standard way, and are used as objective criteria, developed by the human community in the long course of history. For example, there are international and national standards of accounting and financial reporting, which preset how the organization should report its financial results, cash flows, capital, assets, income, and so on. The same applies to resources: the organization must assess them and provide detailed information on buildings, equipment, land, mineral deposits, and so on. There are also standards of human resources assessment, which consider the level of education, professionalism, experience, motivation, and so on.

These criteria are formal and objective, hence, widely understood and recognized. Although their discussion can lead to certain difference of opinion, the overall understanding of them is universal for all countries and organizations. Ideas about high or low efficiency, right or wrong information, and level of professionalism or motivation are common everywhere.

However, it is pretty evident that all these evaluation standards can be reduced to resources and outcomes (R and O). Yet the I-ZONE criterion is a different matter. Staff members of the organization, including senior management, do not have uniform standards of right or wrong relationship or interaction patterns. Assessment and discussions here are subjective, based on personal experiences, opinions, ideas, habits, and stereotypes.

Such views and preferences are pretty diverse and rarely agree, even among people who have known each other for a long time. However, in management there exists a firm conviction that if a man is hired to perform certain functions, and signs

© Springer-Verlag Berlin Heidelberg 2016
A. Zankovsky, C. von der Heiden, *Leadership with Synercube*,
DOI 10.1007/978-3-662-49052-5_3

an employment contract, it is assumed that he will interact productively with other staff members. Nothing to argue about: everything is clear. However, spontaneous and productive cooperation is the exception rather than the rule, and the I-ZONE often proves to be the field of problems and losses. Therefore, people are used to working "as luck would have it".

Why then is it so hard to shape a harmonious synergy in the I-ZONE? These difficulties are due to: the lack of attention to the importance of behavioural interaction skills, and heterogeneity and diversity of values, attitude, and interests of all the organization's staff members. People have different attitudes towards the organization, its work, themselves, and also towards each other. They have different interests and views on the importance of various aspects of organizational life. Being hard to notice, these differences can be enormous and are likely to block effective interaction. That is why the most important task of the leader is to create a common space of values, shared by all staff members.

There are three main means that can help the leader influence the values of others:

1. Moralizing.
   What is good and what is bad is stated. Any kind of authority is used to back one's viewpoint.
2. Personal example.
   The leader tries to act in accordance with his beliefs, hoping that others will learn from this experience and use it as an example.
3. Help in clarifying the values.
   The leader helps the members of the group or organization in adopting the values that are more consistent with the objectives of the organization. The leader pays attention to their importance, usefulness, and adequacy to specific organizational situations, rather than to the need to follow familiar, traditional ways.

Help in their attempts to conceive organizational values gives staff members an opportunity to understand their own basic values that are close to the values of the corporate culture. Thus clarified, values become more personal and persistent.

However, before dealing with the changes in the value orientations of subordinates, the manager must clarify his own values. The process of clarifying personal values includes the study and re-evaluation of existing values and uncovering one's view on matters that previously were out of focus. Sometimes this task is hard to fulfil, since value judgments affect feelings, emotions, desires, and interests of the individual. Self-analysis of the clandestine and unconscious attitudes which determine a person's behaviour requires considerable effort. However, clarification of personal values can become a means of improving the efficiency of administrative activity.

The systematic clarification of values can be regarded as a kind of self-understanding. Colleagues can help an individual to clarify his values, but the final choice is for him to make. The value-conditioned self-analysis encompasses the following five steps:

1. The decision to be sincere.
   To change oneself is to decide to be as honest with oneself as possible. To neglect this obligation means to resist real change.
2. Articulation and open discussion of viewpoints.
   Common values can be discovered only with the help of candid discussion. Assessment and analysis become possible if values are articulated.
3. Analysis of value alternatives.
   It is important to identify and analyse all possible alternative values that underlie behaviour and to correlate them with the values of a perfect corporate culture.
4. Searching for contradictions and overcoming of the values-prompted conflict.
   Further analysis of values reveals inconsistency and contradictions, which are the basis for new thoughts and behaviour assessment.
5. Comparison with the practical line of action.
   Comparison of real human behaviour with the declared values often reveals significant discrepancies. This may point to unresolved conflict of different values or to the lack of understanding of basic values. In any case, the fact that behaviour does not coincide with the declared values highlights the need for further work.

The clarification of the personal values allows the manager to fully realize his responsibility. Nevertheless, we must admit: actions that contradict the declared values are pretty frequent. The leader should turn to his colleagues and subordinates for the information on a mismatch like that, as they are the ones who are carefully observing his behaviour in different organizational situations. Stable value changes occur only when the old values fully reveal inadequacy to the situation and lead to failure. Showing his values system, the manager can get the necessary feedback without waiting for the hard lessons of life.

3.2   Corporate Culture and Cooperation Skills

When a manager sees a need for change, he asks himself, "what has to be changed?" Therefore, their efforts are aimed at changing the strategy, products, and processes. However, even the best strategy begins to grow stunted, as the culture of the organization does not allow embodying it. And more often in order to get something moved, you must first change the culture and values. But even those who understand that do not usually know how to change something as elusive and amorphous as the organizational culture.

The Synercube theory focuses on "how to change?", rather than on "what is to be changed?" Synercube offers a specific way to build a culture of mutual trust, respect, and sincerity that helps to release the latent creative potential of the organization. The emerging new culture, in turn, enables the organization to show its full potential and to run operations on an unprecedented scale.

The Synercube approach offers a method of assessing relationships as precisely and objectively as the methods of assessing resources or results. The method includes the following scheme:

1. System of coordinates with three axes: cultural value dimension, concern for production, and concern for people.
2. The "right" and "wrong" behaviour division, according to clear common cultural values and criteria.
3. Acquisition of Synercube skills that allows us to assess behaviour in objective terms and, more importantly, to offer meaningful measures for teambuilding (excluding "attack" and "defence" methods).

The Synercube approach turns theory into applied method by defining relationships through simple and clear criteria of the efficient and inefficient behaviour at work. The Synercube styles framework helps people to lay a foundation for objective discussion of their activities in terms of "what is right?" and not "who is right?" With the proper standard of effective behaviour defined, one can create a model (a pattern) for making a comparison between actual and proper behaviour. As soon as it is possible to see the difference between these two kinds of behaviours, there emerges a motivational field of tension. Having the right plan, people can understand what has to be changed in order to develop more effective behaviour.

Motivational stress is the first step towards a change in behaviour. And since most people have an urge for change and perfection, mere motivation is often sufficient to start changing for the better. If a person's desire to improve is also supported by colleagues, individual efforts are transformed into a collective strive to improve the common cause. Thus, the person gets motivation, an action plan, and support from other people who are willing to tell him when he is wrong.

According to the Synercube theory, the common process of achieving organizational goals reveals five relationship skills (or elements). They do not necessarily manifest within each and every moment of activity or interaction. Some of them are more frequent than others, but over time we use all of them.

Try to answer the following questions in order to understand your own behavioural skills in the context of relationships in the I-ZONE:

1. Conflict resolution
   What do you do when your interests are violated or ignored? How often do you find yourself in situations of conflict, without understanding the reasons for it? How do you respond, if you do not agree with others or are displeased by them? Do you feel it is imperative to prove another person wrong if he does not agree with you? Do you prefer to retreat in order to stay away from the looming conflict? Do you try to spare others' feelings and to maintain the atmosphere of

agreement? What principle—"What is right?" or "Who is right?"—do you use when looking for solutions?

2. Communicative competence

How do you share information? Is it easy for you to establish contacts with new people in the organization? What are you doing to develop a unified strategy for interaction? Do you have any difficulties in your communication with management and other staff members? How do you get the necessary information? Do you feel uncomfortable and thus dependent on others? Do you prefer to get "pure" information, without comments and opinions, or do you believe it is necessary to listen to others' opinions, even if it can draw forth new challenges? When you ask others to give you information, do you pretend that you know the point and only need to be sure, or do you frankly acknowledge your ignorance?

3. Active positioning

With what do you start upcoming activities or solutions to the problem? How do you involve others in your activities? Do you wait for others to follow you? Do you wait for others to take first steps? How openly and confidently do you share your opinion with other people? Do you invite them to discuss alternatives? Does your opinion on any question depend on the status of the people involved in the discussion? Do you impose your opinion on others, without listening to theirs?

4. Decision-making

How do you interact with other people when you need to take some steps? Do you try to push the solution that you think is right, or do you want others to take the initiative and make decisions? Do you look for solutions that are favourably received by everyone, or do you prefer those that are most effective for achieving results?

5. Constructive critique

How do you examine and assess your own interaction with other people? Do you encourage other people to comment on your effectiveness? How often do you criticize others, not expecting to hear criticism in return? Do you tend to express only positive judgments? What is your reaction to failures and mistakes? Do you feel shame and try to defend yourself? Can you take responsibility for the problem caused by your failure and try to draw a lesson from it? Do you avoid doing something because of the fear to make a mistake?

3.3   Conflict Resolution as the Basis for Successful Interaction

It is not peace or harmony that should be considered the opposite of conflict, but apathy. A method of conflict resolution demonstrates how people predict and respond to the arising problem. In a conflict situation disagreement can be expressed at different levels, ranging from casual comments to an open dispute, followed by bursts of irritation and even anger. Manifestations of conflict are the same, regardless of the specific issue—whether it be a controversial presentation of the marketing department, the late-coming development of a new product in the research department, the daily problems of the operational control, or the administrative discussion of the long-term development plan. Conflict can immediately block work. People usually do not know how to behave in a conflict situation, so they try to suppress it, smooth it, find a compromise, take personal advantage, or just state that the conflict is a manifestation of disloyalty to the organization. This kind of approach is effective, but only in the short-term perspective. Besides, it rarely helps to solve the problem, leaving it "rotting" till another time.

People usually try to avoid conflicts, instead of treating them as a source of useful energy. The clash of opinions is vital for the company's progress and growth, as different viewpoints pave the way to creative expression and synergy. The conflict must inspire people to progress, to raise their level of commitment, and to use the available resources efficiently. The conflict highlights the essence of the problem and encourages people to explore different points of view, so that new ideas and new opportunities emerge.

Studies show that 80 % of conflicts arise beyond the will of its parties, and most people are either not aware of their presence or do not attach any importance to them.

The conflict is a clash of opposing tendencies in the mind of a single individual, in interpersonal interactions, or in interpersonal relationships of individuals or groups, associated with negative emotional experiences.

The main function of the conflict is the possibility to realize what the problems and contradictions are in the life of a person, group, or organization as a whole. It also helps to identify the ways of resolving these contradictions and the necessary steps for further development.

Any conflict has a fixed structure, i.e. it consists of elements that interchangeably act as a dynamically interconnected integral system.

Conflict consists of the following elements:

1. Incident (information): an event that helped at least one of the parties to realize his interests and values, which contradict interests and values of other participants of the interaction
2. Incident (activity): casus belli, that launches confrontational actions
3. Conflict situation: the development of conflict in a particular time period
4. Actors of the conflict: parties to the conflict interaction (individuals, groups, departments, or an entire organization)
5. Subject of the conflict: specific interests and values, which triggered conflict interaction (i.e. the cause of conflict)
6. Conflict relations: form and content of the interaction between the actors and their steps taken to resolve the conflict

The leading role in the emergence of conflict belongs to the so-called conflict-producers, i.e. words and actions (or inactions) that directly contribute to the emergence and development of the conflict.

These conflict-producers imply that we are much more sensitive to the words of others, rather than to what we ourselves say. This particular sensitivity to the words originates from the desire to defend oneself and one's dignity from possible attacks. But we are not so sensitive when it comes to the dignity of others. So, by not paying proper attention to our words and actions, we carelessly shell others with conflict-producing "bombs".

However, a conflict-producer alone cannot lead to a conflict. There must be "a chain of conflicts", leading to the escalation of the conflict: to the conflict-producer of others we try to respond with an even stronger one. When hearing or experiencing a conflict-producer, a "victim" wants to compensate for the psychological defeat, thus parrying an insult. This response cannot be any weaker, therefore he tries to exaggerate it. It is difficult to resist the temptation to punish the offender in order to wan him away from doing it again. As a result, the intensity of conflict-producers is rapidly growing.

There are three main types of conflict-producers:

- The pursuit of excellence
- Manifestations of aggression
- Manifestations of selfishness

How to avoid conflict-producers in the course of communication and interaction with other people?

1. It is necessary to keep it firmly in mind that any careless statement (following the escalation rule) can lead to conflict.
2. It is necessary to show empathy for others (to predict how your words and actions could be perceived).
3. You should always look for an answer to the question "what is right?" first, instead of seeking to figure out "who is to blame?"

The development of conflict includes several phases:

1. The pre-conflict period
   Different interests are present, but no one is aware of their interaction.
2. The launch of the conflict
   One of the interacting parties becomes aware that his interests differ from the interests of others. This awareness is often combined with the start of unilateral actions to secure one's interests. Tension becomes the major symptom of this phase.
3. Incident
   Casus belli for the start of confrontational actions.
4. The subject of the conflict
   Specific interests that trigger conflict interaction.
5. The crisis
   A type of interaction, when phases no longer go one after another (e.g. a long delay or destructive anchoring within one phase, stagnation, or even a return to a previous phase).

6. Successful development of the conflict
   Activities that ensure the crisis-free running of the conflict interaction.

Conflict resolution is a development of conflict interaction, i.e. the gradual transition from the current phase of the conflict to the subsequent one. Thus, the supreme art of responding to a conflict implies not the struggle but the development of conflict relations in a constructive way.

Successful conflict resolution requires to the analysis of its parameters:

1. To establish conflict's actual participants
2. To study their characteristics
3. To identify their relationship in the pre-conflict phase
4. To identify the major differences of interests that led to the conflict
5. To learn the intentions of participants and the conflict resolution acceptable to them
6. To gain insight into all possible ways to overcome the conflict

Factors of origin and development of conflicts: Some researchers believe that the human conflict is based on biological programs, aimed at survival in the struggle for existence (individual competition with a hostile world, with other species, with neighbours). Even herd animals, which follow certain behaviour rules, are expected to compete for the best food, for the female, for leadership in the pack. Thus, the desire to compete acts as a genetically predetermined program.

A number of researchers see the violation of social justice as the main cause of human conflicts, with justice regarded as the correspondence between the individual contribution to the solution of a problem and the received reward (moral or material). This correspondence is determined by the developmental level of a particular community, group, or individual. For this reason, a conflict can be triggered either by a violation of the existing and generally accepted norms of justice, or by the clash of different ideas about the standards of justice.

As stated by M. H. Mescon et al. (1985), among the main causes of business and organizational conflicts are:

• Problems of resource allocation in an organization (the problem of unfair distribution)
• Different goals and objectives (the developed specialization within the organization leads to misunderstandings, as each structural unit has its own goals and interests)
• Different ideas about values (e.g. about the right to express one's opinions in the presence of the chief)
• Different behaviour forms and life backgrounds (especially if people are working in the same unit)
• Poor communication facilities, often leading to misunderstanding among fellow workers

We must also take the personal characteristics of all staff members into account, provoking or aggravating the conflict.

The so-called problem personalities are characterized by the following features:

- A number of individual traits that come into collision with personal characteristics of others (e.g. if we are slow and thorough, then we will be annoyed by a hyperactive and hasty person)
- Low level of culture, including psychological culture of dialogue
- Proneness to conflict

The conflict situation is often aggravated by erroneous actions. Among the common mistakes in responding to the conflict are:

- The delay in taking action to resolve the conflict
- An attempt to resolve the conflict without identifying its true causes
- The use of force and punitive measures or, on the contrary, only diplomatic negotiations
- Efforts to settle the conflict using conventional universal means, regardless of particular context and situation
- An attempt to gain one's end with the help of a political intrigue that provides immediate benefit and leads to negative consequences

R. Kilmann and K. Thomas (1977) identified the main conflict behaviour styles, which allow diagnosing the conflict-handling behaviour:

- Confrontation: the desire to satisfy one's interests at the expense of others (individual actions and steps)
- Adaptation: sacrifice of one's own interests for the sake of others (passivity and inability to meet and serve one's own interests)
- Evasion (avoidance): the strategy of denying contradictions and the desire to avoid conflict at all costs, including any organizational and personal expenses
- Competition: competitive cooperation that is carried out according to the rules adopted by the parties, without any harm to others or the organization
- Compromise: a method of mutual concessions
- Cooperation: decision-making that fully satisfies the interests of both parties

All behaviour styles, with the exception of cooperation, ultimately imply one party's win and another party's loss. The following points can help us to shift from the principle of winning at any cost to cooperation, providing win–win solutions:

1. A consensus, based on clear objectives
2. A dialog to achieve sincerity, which supports the principle: What is right?
3. Constant awareness of the negative effects that accompany the win-at-all-costs principle
4. High standards and clear criteria of conflict resolution

5. The presence of "outsiders" (helping to solve problems) that leads to commitment and synergy
6. The search for an ideal relationship model both within the group and between
   groups
7. Comparison of the ideal relationship model and the actual one, which helps to
   define a strategy to narrow that gap

The Synercube approach does not contain recommendations on how to prevent
conflicts in the organization. An organization without conflicts can hardly be
imagined. That is why Synercube provides methods of conflict management and
resolution, focusing on "what is the right solution" principle (as opposed to the
principle of "who is right"). Conflicts are an inevitable part of the interaction
process, and different viewpoints should not block communication or goal fulfilment. The conflict is like an iceberg with only the tip being visible above the water
surface, while most of it is hidden underwater. Many people are mistaken, as they
believe that no arguments and bursts of anger means no conflicts at all. There is a
strong tendency to neglect comments or problem situations, as people are afraid of
would-be quarrels and conflicts. If managers avoid conflicts, they certainly create a
potentially explosive combination of alienation, frustration, and indifference of
staff.

If the conflict is resolved in an atmosphere of openness and focus at finding the
most effective solution, the results will be much better than when it is resolved
using superiority, authority, methods of suppression, or avoidance. The ability to
achieve objectives through effective conflict resolution results in the best way to
attain synergy and presents the key to successful leadership.

The Synercube approach shows how one can get the most out of conflict to
achieve the ultimate goal, gain insight, and analyse the problem. Within efficiently
organized relationships, people learn and use the skills of conflict resolution in
order to achieve mutual understanding and strengthen the commitment to the goals
of the organization. This means that the conflict can be managed and that its
resolution can be constructive.

Even within proper interaction, conflicts rouse anxiety and apprehension, but
people are not afraid, as the benefits of the proper way to resolve conflicts have
become apparent. So the fear subsides, giving place to confidence and support of
others, as in the past there already was a positive experience of such conflict
resolution. Any organization or unit that has successfully overcome a crisis situation feels a burst of energy and creativity. And that is possible only when problems
are identified, analysed, and successfully solved.

3.4   Communicative Competence

Organizational communication is the complex, multifaceted process of establishing and developing contacts between people. It results from the organization's need for activities and includes the exchange of information, development of a common communication strategy, perception and understanding of each other.

We spend a significant part of our life in various forms of communication—writing, reading, speaking, listening—and therefore it is hardly an exaggeration to say that communication can be both a source of success and the cause of many troubles. The manager spends 90 % of his time communicating. It is for a reason that communication is one of the most complex organizational problems, and its inefficiency is the main obstacle in achieving good results. No group and no organization can exist without adequate communication, ensuring the transmission of information, the exchange of ideas, and coordination.

Communication in the organizational context includes the diversity of interactions between staff members. It is necessary for planning, decision-making, coordination, control, implementation of effective leadership, conflict management, training, and other functions of leadership. Thus, having a communicative competence is essential for the efficient leader.

Unfortunately, there are a lot of barriers on the way that leads to effective communication, most of them psychological. Such barriers may arise from the fact that there is no common understanding of communication, not just because different people speak different "languages", but because of much more profound reasons. When the staff of the organization is multicultural, there may be social, political, religious, or professional differences, which not only give rise to different interpretations of the same concepts used in the communication process, but to different attitudes, outlooks, and worldviews.

These barriers do not stop the communication process completely: even military adversaries are negotiating. However, such barriers can dramatically reduce the effectiveness of the group and organizational activities in general.

Barriers in communication can occur as a result of individual psychological features of communicants (e.g. uncommunicativeness, excessive shyness or reticence), or because of enmity and distrust between certain staff members, and so on. These barriers can lead to the misinterpretation of initially adequate and useful information.

Even if the message is understood by the addressee, he can distort its meaning if the information received is contrary to his beliefs and values. For example, if one staff member offers another a more efficient way of solving the problem, the latter, instead of considering this advice, may take it as a hint at his incompetence and ignore this important information.

Efficiency of communication also depends on the emotional state of the current participants in the dialogue. When angry or depressed, one is less able to listen carefully and take another's sensible advice.

Interpretation and acceptance of the message is largely dependent on how the addressee perceives the message. For example, praise from someone who clearly wants to make a good impression and win favours is perceived as less sincere than a positive assessment from an unconcerned person.

Chances to accept the message are higher when one person treats the other with decency and respect. On the contrary, the message communicated by a stranger or an enemy will be rejected almost in any case.

The fundamental rule of interpersonal communication states runs as follows: the meaning of the message, decoded by the recipient, never exactly corresponds to the meaning inherent in the sender's intention. For example, one study found a huge discrepancy between the doctor's message and the patient's perception and understanding of them. The doctor's "It will hardly hurt" in almost a quarter of cases was interpreted as "It's going to be very painful".

To learn how your message was understood, you need to enter into a dialogue and establish a feedback. One not only listens attentively, but also informs the speaker how he understood the message. The speaker assesses that understanding and, if necessary, revises the story, striving for more accurate understanding of his words.

The role of the sender is more active by its nature: he has an intention to convey information to the addressee and invites him to be the one who listens. He is the one who speaks, who defines the subject of the conversation and its content. If the speaker is active and articulates the message clearly, the recipient needs only to be attentive to understand the meaning of the message properly.

Another problem arises when you need to obtain the necessary information, while the potential sender does not show initiative and is talking dimly on minor topics. To solve a communicational problem like that one usually uses questions.

The question often serves as a motivational drive. Asking the question, the person, in most cases, expects to receive an answer. Thus, asking questions, one can influence the course or the content of the conversation, i.e. take over the position of a leader.

However, excessive questioning can freeze speaker's enthusiasm, especially if the questions imply curt or "yes/no" answers. Excessive questioning should be avoided for three reasons.

First, the "question–answer" scheme implies the speaker's authority and listener's being immature or incompetent.

Second, it is assumed that, after hearing the answers to the questions, the speaker would tell him what to do to solve the problem. And this will obviously do no good to the listener's ability of displaying initiative.

Third, the question usually serves as a specification, what to speak about next. Guidelines like that undermine the dialogic nature of communication.

If you really need to ask the question, you must decide on how to ask it, and what about. All questions can be divided into open and closed.

Closed questions require a simple one-word answer ("yes", "no", "uh-huh", "fifteen", "I do not want", and so on) or choosing one of the alternatives proposed.

Quite often it is tacitly assumed that there are "right" and "wrong" answers to the question, assuming that this is determined by the one who is asking.

The use of questions in a conversation of this kind can make your interlocutor feel pressed, checked, and examined.

Questions "How much?" and "What?" require a simple answer as well.

In order to establish mutual understanding and trust one should not ask too many closed questions. In addition, all closed questions are inducing and suggestive. The one who asks them virtually controls the topic of conversation, assuming a directory position. As a result, the conversation loses its bilateral two-way nature.

Open questions do not imply ready-made answers. It is assumed that the answer to this question may surprise us, but we do not see anything wrong about it. If you need to understand the partner as clearly as possible, questions must be open. Open questions fall into the following categories:

1. Expanding (a request to expand the answer): "Would you tell me more about that?" "Maybe you have something to add?"
2. Narrowing: "You said you have problems with your sleep. Has something happened?"
3. Confronting: "I'm not sure I've understood you correctly. You said that you didn't want to do this work, and now you say that you're offended, as you are not invited to do it. There is a contradiction here, isn't there?"
4. Clarifying: questions that make the issue more clear both to listeners and to the speaker himself.

The correct formulation of the question may be the best way to set the tone for effective discussion. Questions initiate the discussion, because they imply the answers, that is to say a two-way interaction. The very form of the questions asked can either cause enthusiasm and sincerity of the speaker, or trigger mechanisms of defence and resistance. Groups that have "What is right?" as their guiding principle usually use questions and answers to get more information. Their motto is: there are no "untouchable" topics for discussion; the world is changing, so you need to keep asking and receiving new information.

The effective search for information and its acquisition, based on the "What is right?" principle, are characterized by the following:

- It is possible to predict all potential consequences of activities; that leads to a new level of understanding of the problem.
- People are able to share their thoughts openly and at any time; there is a guarantee that all the important information will be considered during the decision-making.
- A search like that is pushing people to dialogue and exchange of information without fear of making a mistake or getting punished.
- A framework for an objective assessment of facts is set.

If the group's principle is "Nothing matters, but who is right, not what is right", a limited number of people gain access to the information. The main task of the people in these groups is to save their face. The information in this case is selective, since the main point is to emphasize advantages, not to solve the problem. Anything that does not fit into this image is generally not taken into account. In contrast to this method, an effective search for information is based on all the specified criteria: the study of the problem and the formulation of questions, discussion, and the development of further strategies. Thus, anyone who is involved in this process understands what is happening and feels responsible for the required results.

The key point in the proper search of information and its acquisition is a two-way process of both asking questions and listening.

Using the feedback strategy, one shows his interlocutor that he has understood him, and also checks whether he grasped the message correctly. Thus, we can adjust our understanding all along.

Our understanding can be inaccurate for several reasons. The first reason is the polysemy of most words. All words of the human language have more than one meaning. Furthermore, the meaning can change, depending on the context.

The second reason is the speaker's intentioned distortions of the message's original meaning. When we share our ideas, attitudes, feelings, and assessments, we choose our words carefully, we exaggerate or underestimate, often using ambiguous words, trying to look convincing and present ourselves, and turn the words in our advantage.

The third source of difficulties is the problem of open expression. Conventions and the need of approval prevent people from speaking frankly and substantially.

Finally, a fourth source of difficulties is the presence of subjective meaning. Over a lifetime every person accumulates a huge amount of unique associations with different words. Certain words can touch adverse memories and cause pain, although the speaker would not mean any harm.

Perhaps it is no exaggeration to say that everyone is pleased when he is understood. We instinctively feel sympathy for those who do not condemn, but accept us understandingly. Therefore, communication can help us influence the relationships with our interlocutor.

As F. Schulz von Thun (2006) states, we can call a message any phrase, question, non-verbal action (e.g. the slamming of a door, an angry look, a polite bow) intended to be perceived by the audience. This audience may consist of one person or many. But if you want a message to be clear, you must first and foremost determine potential recipients.

Within the four factor model, any message can be represented as a quadrangle. Each of its faces has one out of four aspects of a message (Fig. 3.1).

The *substance* of the case is the main content of the message, the subject of the conversation. The *call* is the information about the listener's expectations. Each message is used by the speaker to reveal certain information about himself: about his feelings, psychological qualities, values, and so on, i.e. speaking to a certain extent is a *self-revelation*. Directly or indirectly the speaker shows his *attitude*

Fig. 3.1 Four factor model
of a message

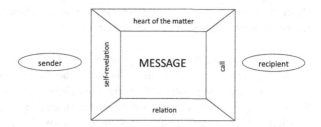

towards his listeners. Misunderstanding occurs when none of these four aspects is decoded.

It is important to point out that our internal speech (when we speak to ourselves in our thought) differs greatly from the normal speech. Internal speech is fragmentized, incoherent, and irrational: one must not be plain and clear. It is something entirely different, when we are trying to tell another person what happened to us. Willing or not, we have to frame our words in an intelligible sequence. That is why mere listening can be useful: only by articulating the problem can one find a solution that would never occur to him otherwise.

Thus, we can help our interlocutor not only by showing support, but also by influencing the course of his reasoning. The general principle of assistance in this case can be formulated as follows: trying to describe the problem or the task more clearly, an individual himself begins to understand it better.

As a part of this approach, you can use the technique of active listening, which helps the speaker to understand his words and thoughts more precisely. It is very important to be an engaged listener, who gives the speaker an opportunity to feel his interest.

Misunderstanding The first technique, aimed at improving understanding, at first glance looks paradoxical: it is a demonstration of your misunderstanding. However, it may be useful to say: "I do not understand what you mean". It is important to show your willingness to wait for more accurate rendering of the entire message, without expressing irritation or pain.

Echoing It is a repetition of the speaker's words or phrases. Usually it takes the form of verbatim repetition or repetition with slight modifications. It is important to repeat only those words that are relevant to solving the problem or fulfilling the task. Reflection should not be used too often, so that the speaker would not think he's being imitated.

Paraphrasing (paraphrase) To paraphrase is to formulate the same idea differently. Within the conversation, paraphrase means the listener's rendering of the speaker's words. The goal of paraphrasing is to check the accuracy of the listener's understanding of the message. When paraphrasing one should pick only essential elements of the message, inviting the interlocutor both to state the problem more clearly and to clarify its meaning to himself. The main function of paraphrasing is to see whether we understand the speaker properly.

Summary To summarize is to sum up a significant part of the conversation as a whole. The basic rule of a summary is that it should be very simple and clear. You emphasize the key moments of conversation, choosing as lapidary form as possible. Summarizing is particularly appropriate for discussing the differences, resolving conflicts, and handling claims. Summaries allow us not to spend much time responding to the superficial statements, which distract from the key point of the discussion.

Clarification If all the above-listed techniques failed to help the listener to understand the statement, he can directly ask the speaker to clarify the obscure or incomprehensible fragment of his story, to give examples or to dwell on something. Clarification is a reference to the speaker for explicitness and specifications.

An important element of communicative competence is the ability to defend one's opinion. This ability can prove useful as soon as someone tells others about his point of view on an issue. Everyone knows how hard it is to take someone else's opinion, even if it is correct. Therefore, it is particularly important to follow the "Always find out what is right" principle, using open and objective discussion with an eye toward the coveted outcome. One should defend his opinion only if everyone else has an opportunity to express his opinion. This requires a climate in which team members will be willing to share their personal experiences, ideas, and concerns, to discuss the problem from all angles. Finally, the most proper viewpoint must win, no matter who was the first to articulate it.

Defending one's opinion can be a collective process, when all parties are pursuing the common goal. In groups where this process is organized correctly, everyone is encouraged to express his opinion, and a detailed discussion of all views expressed necessarily takes place. In this case, silence can be as expressive as a slam fist on the table. Of course, the owner of the loud voice is more likely to be heard, but we all know that loud does not mean right. And if someone is silent all the time, then you need to freeze the discussion and stir the "Man of Few Words" up by saying: "For some reason you prefer to keep silent. What's your opinion on the problem?" Eventually, collective efforts will help everyone to learn to express his opinion. This will ensure the most efficient use of the organization's resources, as the personal involvement of each and every staff member in resolving collective problems will be enhanced.

The key point in the effective communication is the criteria set for the discussion's efficiency and orientation for results. Criteria set a direction for further exchange of views and opinions.

Here are examples of such criteria:

- We need to identify three possible options for further action.
- Each proposal must be supported by at least two specific examples.

- Before the decision is taken, everyone should give his opinion.

From the very beginning these criteria define the outcome of the discussion (three options), limit the number of proposals to those that can be backed up by examples (at least two), and involve everyone in the discussion. In this case, it is much easier to deal with empty verbiage: "You've been presenting your point for 10 minutes already, but we had no examples yet". Everyone immediately agrees that it does not meet the specified criteria, and they pass to the discussion of the next suggestion. If someone is keeping his nose out of the discussion, he will be said: "We have agreed that everyone would have an opportunity to express his point of view, but we haven't heard yours yet".

The possibility of constructive and sincere expression of one's opinion can greatly enhance personal involvement of each team member. In such circumstances, many will want to express their views and contribute to the overall result. The ability to speak relieves stress, highlights the deep-seated problems, and clarifies concerns, if any. Personal involvement increases the significance of the contribution to the common cause, raises the level of awareness and interest in achieving results, ultimately leading to success.

3.5   Active Positioning

People exert their activity in different ways. The activity depends on individual temperament, character, motivation, psycho-physiological state, characteristics of the profession, and the specific task. Thus, choleric will be more expressive, loud, and flaunty than phlegmatic; and the overworked staff member will be less active than the one who has just gotten to work. However, when we talk about an active standpoint, we do not mean individual manifestations of activity or behavioural manifestations, such as the desire to express one's opinion at every given opportunity. The active standpoint is a stable form of manifestation of values, beliefs, knowledge, and skills that have an impact on human behaviour and activities.

The organizational world is not static. It is constantly changing under the influence of external and internal factors, as well as the organization's staff members, their effort, and behaviour. Every one of them, if interested in professional development and efficiency improvement, is able to influence organizational performance. The active standpoint requires internal motivation for action, genuine orientation towards the goals and values of the organization, and a sense of personal responsibility for the work of the entire organization. It is manifested in purposeful and conscious activities.

The person who takes a proactive standpoint tends to be a leader in solving important problems, showing independent and constructive behaviour.

There are three main types of active standpoints: passive, reactive, and active.

Passive standpoint implies a passive performance to the usual plan. A person with the passive position is not involved in reaching organizational goals and sharing organizational values. He does not feel any responsibility for his work. A person like that always finds a reason not to make an effort, going with the tide.

Reactive standpoint means that the person shows his active stand only when he is being directly involved. Reactive standpoint is characterized by the pretentious personal involvement in reaching organizational goals and sharing organizational values. The staff member feels responsible only for tasks entrusted to him and takes any action only as a response to this or that problem. Reactive standpoint does not imply the analysis of the situation and efforts made in order to find new solutions, as the staff member does not care or feels lazy.

Active standpoint is oriented towards the constructive solution of problems and the control over the situation. A sense of deep personal involvement gives rise to a continuous search for solutions that will allow overcoming difficulties and conflicts for the common good of the organization. The motto of the active standpoint: act and waste no time. An active person believes that everything in this world can be achieved with only his own efforts and hard work.

The active standpoint is manifested when the person takes up a new activity or continues his current work. Initiative is the way a person takes up a new job or uses a new opportunity. A personality with a strong active standpoint is steadily moving forward, determining the necessary course and managing his activity. In turn, activity is embodied in the specific course of action, strategy planning, involving other people and immediate intervention in cases in which the activity deviates from the direction set. A person with active standpoint does not need supervision and regulations, he is confident to take the risk and to make the first step towards a new goal.

The type of the person's activity sets the tone for the interaction in general, as the initiative is the starting point for activity. The nature of the initiative is important when a person wants to involve other people. Properly expressed, the initiative can involve different kinds of people, giving them enthusiasm and confidence. If a team member has taken part in the very first initiative actions, he will feel that the result obtained is in some way his achievement.

If personal activity is unreasonably high, it prevents the involvement of other people and causes resentment and defensive stance. This usually happens when the initiator is "galloping ahead", ignoring other participants and skipping the discussion-of-the-plan step. Team members can also be unhappy if the leader, though showing interest in other people's opinions, never takes them into consideration. He pushes forward as the icebreaker with his own idea of right direction and does not need other opinions.

If on the contrary personal activity is low, the level of people's involvement is also low, as they do not feel confident enough to act independently. This is particularly evident when the leader's initiative is feeble. A leader's weakness is as contagious as its opposite's enthusiasm and confidence.

An active standpoint can be naturally developed within cooperation based on mutual trust and respect. One no longer needs to look for additional ways of gaining acceptance of his colleagues.

When the initiative is manifested properly, the fear of failure is replaced by the confidence that everyone is doing his best and using all available information. If people trust each other, activity is focused on "what is right?" rather than "who is right?". Team members tend to get as much information as they can and share it with others, they are not afraid to discuss their weaknesses and hardships openly. Having all the information available to everyone and starting to act, the team is ready to work purposefully and enthusiastically.

3.6   Decision-making

One of the primary tasks of leadership is decision-making. Experts believe that only the one who can make decisions can be called a leader.

The most serious and widespread mistake concerning decision-making is to reduce this complex process exclusively to the very moment of decision-making.

However, as research and practice show, a proper decision can be made no sooner than a number of consecutive steps are taken (Malik 2006):

1. Defining the problem precisely
2. Making a list of requirements for the decision
3. Identifying all possible options
4. Analysing the risks and consequences of choosing each option, as well as the constraints
5. Choosing the decision itself
6. Determining the conditions of the decision's execution
7. Establishing feedback by monitoring the process and its conclusion

The first step in the decision-making process is the thorough and complete definition of the problem. Any phenomenon depends on a number of reasons. Thus, the drop in sales can be caused by the poor quality of the products sold, or the change in market conditions, or the decline in the solvency of the population, or by untrained staff, etc. It is not a matter of opinion or past experience, as careful analytical work is required. At the same time, the biggest challenge is the realistic definition of the problem, which is always incomplete and partially right.

In determining the problem, it is important at least to understand whether it is an incident or a fundamental problem. Making a decision on an incident is not usually crucial, and here we can improvise, because a problem like that may never arise again.

The fundamental problem requires a different approach and a fundamental solution, which implies the necessity to identify certain principles and laws.

The most important is to discern the essence of the problem. One of the common errors is to answer this question quickly and without due consideration. The effort involved at this stage is repaid many times. Improper understanding of the problem prevents us from finding the right solution. However, even if the problem is assessed adequately, errors may occur at the stage of decision-making, but in this case they can be detected and corrected. Therefore, the analysis and definition of the problem should be verified, reckoning all the facts available. If all the facts are not taken into consideration, this step cannot be considered accomplished.

The second step—"Making the list of requirements"—implies the most accurate formulation of the requirements to be met to make decisions. The key question here is: What is right?

The third step of the decision-making process is finding options. At this stage, there are two possible mistakes: (1) to stop after finding only a few first available variants; (2) to choose to make a decision, even if all the options found are improper.

The fourth step is usually the most time-consuming: a systematic, thorough assessment of all the consequences and risks associated with each option. Here the time period required to implement each option is defined, as well as the would-be risks for the group and the organization. Of course, the options that can lead to serious adverse or even irreversible consequences should be considered with great care.

Moreover, within this step the so-called constraints for each option should be determined. Even after a thorough analysis, there will remain unrecognized factors, so we have to deal with the assumptions for these issues. These assumptions form the basis for limiting conditions. They are to be properly defined and documented, as they will be used in the search for the answer to the question: why a decision that had been right initially became insolvent and unsuitable under new circumstances?

If one of the limiting conditions emerges and there is a possibility of serious consequences, the original decision must be discarded. In this case, we face a completely different situation, which usually requires admitting the inadequacy of the old solution and the adoption of a different one.

If all previous steps have been properly performed, we can (and must) make a decision, as we did our best to prepare the ground.

The sixth step includes the identification and enumeration of the necessary activities required for the chosen decision, the appointment of the person responsible for each activity, and the setting of deadlines. In other words, you need to determine what to do by whom and when.

The last stage is the monitoring of the process up until it is accomplished.

Within the process of decision-making all staff members analyse the available resources and determine further action. Two key factors in reaching proper, effective solutions are:

- Proper interaction and support for every solution, no matter who proposed it and under what circumstances.
- Defining the criteria for the efficiency of the decision.

Consensual and efficient solutions are the result of the joint, open, and objective examination of all the facts and other data, past experience, as well as the criteria for evaluating the desired result. Only in this case do we have a solution that is supported by all team members. This does not mean that everyone must be involved in the final stage of the decision, or that everyone should agree with this decision unconditionally. The main thing is that all support the chosen path.

The idea of "collective decision-making" often evokes a false idea that every preparatory stage on the way to the final solution must involve each and every member of the team. But this kind of work would take a lot of time and organizational resources, burdening team members with additional work. The decision-making process should involve only those people who have the relevant expertise and experience. Another common misconception is the idea that one person cannot make the right decision. This is also not true, all the more so in the rapidly changing circumstances of the business world, the ability to react and make decisions quickly is becoming a vital one.

The right decision can be the result of various forms of cooperation that can be chosen depending on the size and structure of the organization, distribution of power, as well as the fundamental nature and complexity of the would-be decision. Effective solutions can be suggested by a single person, or by two, three, or more people or the entire group as a whole. The key point is to involve all the necessary resources.

Most right decisions are taken in organizations wherein there is mutual trust and respect. Even if someone does not agree with the decision, he still supports it, as he understands that the decision in the long run agrees with the basic goals and values of the organization, and he—directly or indirectly—contributed to the process of its adoption. The direct involvement of people provides more effective decision-making. However, the need to act under time pressure does not allow most companies to ensure such involvement. Mutual trust and effective cooperation based on personal involvement call off the need for direct participation of all employees in decision-making. People are different in taking action. For example, one can make a decision only after a detailed study of the entire case. For others, on the contrary, the main thing is the estimated figure of future output and trade, and the third just likes any new creative idea. The team takes all this into account and gives ear to everyone's opinion before making a decision.

If the team works in a stable atmosphere of mutual trust, respect, and sincerity, the person who makes the decision is fully informed. He has got all the necessary information from all potential experts and made a decision, knowing everything about the issue. This means that if the solution can cause a negative response of a certain team member, it is necessary to inform the decision-maker immediately and explain everything to him. For example, if someone makes a decision without taking into account the history of the issue, then you need to discuss this decision with those who regard the history of the issue the most important aspect. This simple but wise way—taking into account everyone's point of view—helps to keep effective interaction even if the decision was individual. The concern of a "history lover" will be less intense if the management presents him a rational explanation. If such a decision turns out to be false, then the "opponent" will be less tempted to say maliciously, "Well, I warned you!"

It should also be kept in mind that staff members will quickly understand when the "collective" decision-making lapses into window dressing and formality. It is not sufficient just to gather people and ask their point of view. People must believe that their opinion has really been taken into account. For example, if the manager organizes regular monthly meetings, wherein new ideas are expressed, but decides only on the basis of his own ideas, staff members will no longer share their thoughts and suggestions.

To achieve a long-term agreement, managers and staff members should honestly and openly share information and assess it in objective terms. If the leader simply collects the ideas of others, without taking into account their decision-making, it will cause resentment, as (1) the idea was ignored and (2) its author wasted time to present it. In the atmosphere of mutual support, it is much easier to analyse any fact or idea from the point of view of common sense, drawing the necessary lessons for future actions. If one mentally analyses a problem from the perspective of each and every team member, he will more likely make the right decision, even without discussions of the issue.

3.7   Constructive Critique

Critique (derived from the Greek *kritike*—"the art of argument") is an interaction skill, aimed at changing behaviours, thoughts, opinions, or attitudes of another person. Critique, intentionally or spontaneously, can be used for the following purposes:

1. Constructive change (optimization) of behaviour, opinion, or attitude
2. Implicit or explicit proof of one's superiority
3. Causing another person to go through unpleasant experiences
4. Discharge of the nervous tension and a way of channelling the uncontrollable

Unfortunately, for many people, critique is associated with the three latter objectives and is therefore perceived as an unpleasant and generally negative phenomenon.

Constructive critique is, in our terms, the critique aimed at structural changes (optimizing) of behaviour, opinion, or attitude. Other types of critique are not constructive, because they are not directed at optimizing behaviour, improving communication, and organizational performance.

In order to draw a clear line between constructive and non-constructive critique, we should look through the most common types of non-constructive critique. Polish psychologist E. Melibruda (2009) identifies the following types:

Rhetorical Questions A question like that is an indirect way of expressing indignation; the answer is not expected. The goal is not to encourage your opponent to correct or improve something, but to make him apologize, "Why are you always coming late?"; "How dare you call me?"; "Why do you have this mess here again?"

Orders and Prohibitions Such critique is expressed in the form of categorical prescriptions, without revealing what exactly is wrong. It is expressed in the form of direct and precise instructions: "You must apologize immediately!"; "Stop shouting!"; "Do not worry so much! Easy!"; "You need to be patient. . ."

Even when orders are delivered by the senior manager, they are perceived negatively, usually outraging a staff member. While obeying the order, he will work most likely reluctantly and subversively.

Swearing and Cursing A "critique" like that has several forms: the use of bad language, without addressing a particular person; curses, wishing harm to your opponent; the use of words and expressions which injure, belittle, or threat someone. Swearing would not inform a person about the essence of one's claims, but merely convey the negative attitude.

Reprimands and Rebukes Here the emphasis is made on personality, rather than the behaviour of others. Reproaches often contain improper generalizations that cause controversy and disagreement: "It is beyond your abilities to do at least the minor job well and on time". Reproaches often provoke reactive accusations.

Irony and Sarcasm This kind of critique does not imply any positive response, as the goal is to cause embarrassment or shame and to demonstrate one's own intellectual superiority, "Needless to say, you're the most intelligent here!"; "You are very insightful!"; "Very funny" (in a serious tone).

Dispraise The manager not only points at the subordinate's mistake but also makes negative conclusions about his behaviour. At the same time his personal opinion and assessment of the facts are presented as facts, "You have performed your task poorly"; "You don't know the simplest things".

Attributing non-existing characteristics to others The one, who is criticizing experiences certain feelings and tries to explain their origin, attributing certain features or qualities that could be the cause of those feelings. For example, he is concerned about the result and explains this feeling, accusing a staff member of indifference and slapdash attitude.

These non-constructive critique methods are particularly damaging when they are used with a scornful tone and ambitious facial expressions, accompanied by aggressive gestures and postures. Relying on the four-factor model of the message (Fig. 3.2), we can single out the most important distinguishing features of unconstructive critique. First, the critique is aimed towards a certain personality which is being criticized, negatively assessed, and causing troubles. The attitude is always extremely negative. This often causes a defensive response from the criticized.

Constructive critique does not contain regulations and policy guidelines; the critic relies on the common sense and good will of the criticized. Not feeling the pressure, an individual makes his own decision and feels free from pressure, so

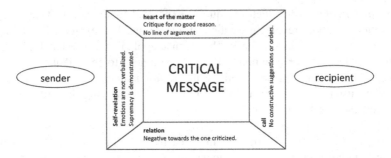

Fig. 3.2 Unconstructive message

constructive critique makes it possible to choose, make decisions, allowing the staff member to feel independent.

1. Constructive critique includes detailed and objective descriptions of what is to be necessarily changed.
2. Constructive critique reveals the real feelings of the one who is criticizing.
3. Constructive critique contains suggestions for improvement of a situation and helps the criticized one to understand what everyone expects from him.
4. Constructive critique contains the positive relation to the one criticized, it implies the belief that he can find forces for the necessary changes.
5. Constructive critique describes the behaviour's impact on others.

In the course of constructive critique, there is a possibility to discuss any phenomenon in order to understand it better and gain new experience. It represents an important relationship skill, helping to increase the organization efficiency. The critique "sets information free" and gives the chance to reach synergy (Fig. 3.3).

If the group is able to analyse not just facts, data, and figures but to discuss how they can be used more effectively, productivity will surely increase. In particular, such discussion can become a necessary step on the way to decision-making or an algorithm for the solution of arising problems. When staff members can openly state the creative ideas or doubts, and also everything that is usually held back, it will allow the group to predict the outcomes more precisely and to solve problems more quickly. Four elements of critique can be distinguished:

Preliminary Critique The preliminary critique is necessary at an early stage of preparations for activity. It represents the main question: "What are we going to do and how?" On this stage the strategy is preliminarily defined. Many people got used to rushing into work, especially if work is well familiar and rushing seems quite productive, while planning is considered a waste of time. Thus comes the principle of "shooting without having aimed", when the group is too busy with work to stop and look at how this work is being performed. Preliminary critique can be short and take a couple of minutes. For example, it is very important to define the agenda at

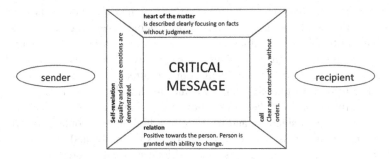

Fig. 3.3 Constructive message

the very beginning of a meeting, or to specify what both parties eventually want to reach when the telephone conversation has just started.

In addition, planning of further actions during preliminary critique helps to define the schedule of their realization and implementation. It makes everyone be realistic about the objectives and their fulfilment. We have to take into consideration the additional work, necessary resources, planned time to finish the work, and so on. If the preliminary critique is effective, one can clearly define the way of achieving the result that had been, in turn, clearly predicted. If everyone agrees on the final result, it is much easier to stay on the right track. And in this case it is easy to stop the speaker who is deviating from the main issue by saying: "We have strayed from the topic of discussion."

Regular Critique Regular critique is a set of fixed reference points of the control over determined activities, which are to be agreed upon during the preliminary critique stage. These predetermined points allow the team to stop the work and discuss the quality of its execution. Regular critique can be associated with a specific time interval (e.g. once a week) or to certain stages of activity (e.g. at the beginning of each new stage). These can be weekly meetings, wherein the progress of the project is discussed, or the 10-minute planning brief at the beginning of each working day, or quarterly meetings on the issue of sales. Thus staff members can stop, leave mundane problems behind, and analyse the work as a whole. Regular critique allows people to evaluate what has been done, in case you need to adjust and improve further activity.

Spontaneous Critique Spontaneous critique takes place when someone interrupts the working process and calls everyone to discuss and analyse it. A discussion like that is focused on emerging problems, unplanned changes in processes or procedures, arising new ideas or any concerns or doubts. Spontaneous critique is important in detecting problems that were out of sight at the stage of preliminary or regular critique. Spontaneous critique requires greater flexibility, since it is necessary to interrupt the process without waiting for the planned regular critique. Spontaneous critique is a vital step towards synergy, as problems are identified and solved at the very moment they arise.

Spontaneous critique can be the most effective when the statements focus on results and are based on clear criteria of their achievement, agreed during the preliminary critique. For example, if a staff member undermines the work as a new software product with new features appears, everyone must compare these features with the desired outcome, and with the already established criteria for quality. The team must quickly decide whether to shift their deadlines and implement this software, or if it is better to continue working with the same software.

In groups in which sincerity and trust are at a high level, spontaneous critique gives the opportunity to assess the necessary results regularly, and to minimize the possibility of any deviations. In this case, critique is usually perceived appropriately, since the team operates with a high level of efficiency. If the level of trust is low, then someone's remark such as "Let's stop and compare our progress with the original task requirements" may seriously disrupt the activities, causing bursts of anger or resentment. In the team with a high level of trust, the reaction is the following: "Of course, let's do that." In this case, the remark cannot jeopardize the work.

Subsequent Critique Subsequent critique, as a rule, is the only type actually used in teams. People tend to wait until the operation is finished, and only then do they start to discuss positive or negative implications. In teams with the lowest level of trust and respect such critique is usually used to shame and punish others. With good results being achieved, it can also be used for praise and rewards. In both cases, the group loses a valuable opportunity to use the experience gained to improve operations and enhance its efficiency. Within the subsequent critique stage, it is very important to be able to assess what caused work efficiency. In this case, the team can actively promote effective methods and push aside inefficient activities leading to problems.

Subsequent critique should be carried out immediately after the work is finished, while all the details are still in mind. The most valuable are the remarks given in the previously defined terms and concepts and related to a method of performing the work. At the same time there should be no personal orientation.

Like other kinds of critique, subsequent critique is effective only when the comments are based on the criteria agreed upon during the preliminary critique. The criteria are equally important for the discussion of both successes and failures. Critique will achieve its goal if the team starts the discussion with a clear understanding of what is necessary. The team that reached lower results than expected can concentrate on what went wrong and why, and develop measures to improve interaction. The team that has managed to achieve greater success than expected can understand the reasons for this, rather than to immerse in celebration or complacency. It is necessary to detect this new resource that has led to greater success to use it in the future. It may well be that the excess of the expected outcome is the result of setting goals too low, and in the future they should be reconsidered. And of course, in any case, the subsequent critique is very important for the continuous improvement of team interaction.

A well-known method of receiving feedback in the absence of sincerity is the anonymous critique, which is opposed to the direct and open one. Often the argument for anonymity is the following: people are more inclined to criticize objectively and without bias, when they do not know who the target is. In this case, the one who is criticizing is often telling the truth.

However, anonymous comments reduce the possibility of drawing benefit from the comments received, as there is no opportunity to discuss and clarify the problem and understand its essence. People can learn from the experience of others only when they discuss it. Without discussing, personal opinions cannot be developed, remaining just one man's opinion. This reduces the possibility of synergy, since the problem is not discussed and new experience is not acquired.

The grounds for critique are the criteria set before the activity. They define goals and ways to achieve them. These criteria are the result of setting short-term or long-term goals, strategic planning, and scheduling tasks. Once such criteria are identified, they will form a framework for reaching a common goal.

Criteria can be improved or changed in the light of new facts or new experiences. Their accuracy and reliability are checked during each and every phase of critique. Criteria give a clear idea of where we are going, what we are doing, and how we should act.

Principles of Effective Critique Effective critique should contain specific examples illustrating the critical comments. "I think that you are not qualified", is an unspecified point. "It is the third time today that you are asking me to help in the fulfilment of your duties. Maybe you need some additional training?" This saying is specific, objective, and imbued with the desire to help.

"Here and now": In any situation, the most effective feedback and critique are those that relate to "fresh" events that have taken place here and now. Such critique has an absolute advantage, because it uses specific examples that are still remembered. For example, by saying: "This morning your valuable comments helped me concentrate on a certain aspect of a new project", we are giving immediate feedback on our partner's effective behaviour. There is one more obvious advantage of this principle, namely, the appeal to the feelings that are still "fresh" and can help better understand the impact of one's behaviour on other people. Fresh memories of experiences help to focus the discussion on what exactly caused these emotions. For example, if a person says, "When you were arguing with me, without having studied all the information on this issue, I felt that I wasn't understood", he feels immediate relief, and his addressee understands that he caused a reaction like that.

The "here-and-now" principle is not effective in a situation when the atmosphere is so tense that it is impossible to discuss the issue objectively. If the conversation partners are angry or irritated, the discussion may do more harm than good. In this case, time is necessary for the dust to settle, so that participants can collect their thoughts and restore the ability to speak more objectively. This may take an hour or even a day, depending on human personality and context. The main point is to use this time effectively, to think everything through, and get ready for an objective discussion. Emotions constitute an important and valuable element of interaction, provided that they contribute to mutual discussion.

The Absence of a Personal Orientation: Feedback and critique are the most effective when they do not include any attacks on the personality and if they are expressed exclusively in behavioural terms, and include the reaction of the speaker to this behaviour. "When you broke my speech off at the meeting so roughly, I was shocked, and I was no longer able to speak". This method makes the attacks on the personality impossible, as it does not imply any judgments, but merely makes it clear what the effect of his behaviour was on other people. At the same time, the tone of the speaker expresses a sincere desire to help the criticized.

Basing on Criteria: Many groups intentionally oppose intra-corporate critique, as they consider it tedious and fruitless. Even one critical comment at the meeting provokes a murmur of indignation, as the agenda is violated. However, if critique is used effectively, long and fruitless discussions turn into something quite the opposite. Effective critique increases the efficiency of all components of the interaction. And then, a long conversation with each member of the group can be replaced by a personal 5-minute phone call or a brief meeting with the two or three team members. Critique can be short and concise, if criteria were predetermined. Team members should be able to compare the actual results of their activities with the plan that was drawn up and make the appropriate adjustments, if necessary. Then a critical discussion becomes clear, task-oriented, and fact-based.

Constructive critique is necessary when individuals and groups look back and try to understand the mistakes that led to lower results than expected. Proper overcoming of failures implies a direct and open analysis of the errors, as well as the transformation of frustration and other negative emotions into a real under-standing of the causes. Even with a high level of mutual trust and respect, it is difficult to admit mistakes. The Synercube approach cannot make it easier to confess, but it gives an opportunity to learn from one's experience and to improve future efficiency. To admit mistakes and to take responsibility for them is the only way to benefit from negative experiences. In many teams that is impossible, as everyone immediately starts to make excuses, blame others, and conceal flaws. Moreover, team members can rush headlong into a new job, without having time to correct past mistakes.

Correction of errors is the most important way to succeed in a constantly changing world of business. The ability to draw lessons from the past, even bitter ones, and turn them into a valuable experience useful in the future is an extremely important quality. In such cases, it is the interaction in the I-ZONE that is effective, as it is based on constructive critique, mutual trust, and respect. It is in these conditions that decision-making is effective and consistent. Thus, the critique process starts to function effectively. In order to "recover" after a long illness, and to continue moving forward to the goal, staff members are to discuss and analyse the mistakes in a frank, objective, and constructive manner.

Failures analysed objectively and with full responsibility may become the most effective motivator for individual changes. When success is too obvious, it is possible to lapse into self-satisfaction and complacency. One can lose direction, being sure of his infallibility. Thus, the competitor who is actively analysing his failures can find a creative solution for a breakthrough and beat you. "Recovery" after the failure will be faster if the level of mutual trust and respect is high, and failure causes people to unite, to gather strength, and to move forward. The team, which sets the highest standards of quality, will be constantly thinking about the results and moving forward.

3.8   Conclusions

The team's attempts to change anything should be backed by a common understanding of the future outcomes "O" and of the recipe, how to do it. The Synercube theory makes it possible to master this way, by organizing cooperation in the I-ZONE with the help of Synercube-based skills and the underlying principles of the corporate culture. The skills of effective interaction are critical to the proper use of all available resources. In fact, it is quite easy to analyse the contribution of a staff member by comparing his daily activities, such as decision-making and conflict resolution, with the relevant Synercube skills. Thus, the value of the Synercube theory is expressed in daily interaction skills. Relationship skills can also be used to improve specific aspects of work, until the proper methods become second nature to all employees. Individual action in relation to the methods described above is based on a deep assimilation of values that is shared by all team members. People get used to working effectively, as they are used to turning off the lights before leaving home. They do not reflect, they just do it.

The study of the above-mentioned characteristics of the interaction is important, if one wants to change. Existing interaction skills are not unchangeable. Most of us simply do not know how to effectively analyse the behaviour of people in the team. However, any changes are possible only after considering all peculiarities of behaviour in its everyday interactions, as well as after a clearly stated purpose— what this behaviour should be like. Successful change of human behaviour requires three elements: a clear understanding of current behaviour, goal setting and support of others, and interacting on a daily basis.

References

Books

Malik F (2006) Fuehren. Leisten. Leben. Wirksames Management fuer eine neue Zeit. Campus Verlag, Frankfurt

Melibruda   E   (2009)   Ich-Du-Wir.   Psychologische   Möglichkeiten   für
   Kommunikationsverbesserung (from Russian: Мелибруда Е. Я – ТЫ – МЫ. М.: Прогресс,
   1986). Progress, Moskau
Mescon M, Albert M, Khedouri F (1985) Management: individual and organizational effective-
   ness. Harper and Row, New York
Schulz von Thun F (2006) Miteinander reden. Rowohlt-Taschenbuch-Verlag, Reinbeck

Journals

Kilmann R, Thomas K (1977) Developing a forced-choice measure of conflict-handling behavior:
   the "MODE" instrument. Educ Psychol Meas 37(2):309–327

Style 7.1−: Dictator (To Head and to Rule)

4

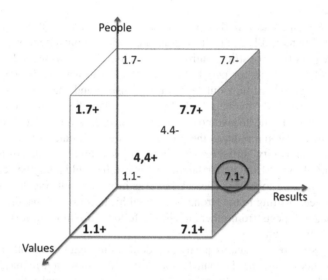

The organizational system is always right, the immutable established order must be unfailingly observed. The 7.1− style expects best efforts of his subordinates and keeps everything under control, setting a clear course of action. No rule, which helps to achieve results, can be violated.

4.1 Basic Features of the 7.1− Style

The 7.1− style leader demonstrates a high level of concern for production, combined with a low level of concern for people and disregard for the cultural values of the organization. The high focus on the outcome, typical of this style, makes the whole team focus their efforts on success. Normally, such a person is professionally

© Springer-Verlag Berlin Heidelberg 2016
A. Zankovsky, C. von der Heiden, *Leadership with Synercube*,
DOI 10.1007/978-3-662-49052-5_4

well-trained, organized, experienced, and can help an organization to achieve very good results. He is confident, demanding in observance of high standards, and is able to take risks, if they are pre-calculated and evaluated.

At the same time, the 7.1− style rarely analyses his resoluteness that makes him leave everything behind, but the result. These people are convinced that the organization is a perfect system, based on perfect principles, and man by nature is lazy and dependent. Therefore, it is necessary to constantly monitor all the staff members, as they can never be trusted. An individual is regarded as one of the small gears, which is to be properly directed, in order to ensure the functioning of the entire organizational machine. The ideal staff member must demonstrate unquestioning obedience and strict adherence to the goals, fully merging with them. Therefore, the 7.1− considers that one can trust only those employees who always strictly and accurately comply with all instructions, do not question them, and demonstrate readiness.

On the basis of these attitudes, the 7.1− considers caring about people not only unnecessary, but harmful, as it leads to greater emotional attachment, which greatly weakens the possibility of strict control and pressure. The 7.1− is not able to see that the low level of concern for people limits his ability to achieve lasting synergy: efforts to engage others turn out to be unsuccessful, and the result is achieved mainly by using force. Anyone who follows this style believes that people do not act together, each trying to overcome the resistance of another. He believes that open concern for people reduces the goal-achieving potential, so it is essential to minimize the "humanity" of all relationships. The low level of concern for people prevents the 7.1− style from understanding what results could really be achieved by all the staff working together. The 7.1− style is heavily result-oriented, seeing all other employees drifting in the strong tideway of his initiative. Thus, the 7.1− style senior manager expects from others to simply follow him, moving forward on the path towards the result.

The 7.1− style person seems pushy and demanding, neglecting other people's reactions to his behaviour. Human factor-based situations such as pay, training, flexible working hours, socially oriented activities, and personal interviews seem unimportant to him. He lacks philanthropy. All human aspects of relationships (candour, openness, mutual trust and respect, personal goals, etc.) are often seen by him as impediments on the way to high standards and important results. If he has to cut costs, the first thing he is willing to sacrifice would be his staff. Personal objectives of this or that individual employee seem unimportant to him; often, an approach like that leads to a situation in which all company's staff members are unprofessional and poorly motivated people. The 7.1− style does not necessarily imply attacks on people, but a strong belief in the need for total focus on results. The motto is: "The rest doesn't matter".

4.2   The 7.1– Style in Collective Cooperation

The following examples are typical of the 7.1– style behaviour in the organization. When a staff member cannot cope with his work, the 7.1– style reacts like this:

He speaks with the employee in a blaming tone. Critical statements may contain accusations of laziness or inability to work. There may be other attacks on the personality of the employee, including accusations of incompetence. The employee's attempts to explain anything are perceived with intolerance or partiality, accompanied by statements like, "Yeah, maybe it's true, but..." or "I can believe that this is so, but really..." or "Again excuses". In the end, the employee gets a number of tasks that must be fulfilled, expressed in the form of an ultimatum.

The reaction of the 7.1– style leader to constructive criticism from a staff member is as follows:

He immediately begins to defend himself. Even if the staff member is right, the 7.1– is trying to make him agree that his intentions were true, even if the results were negative. In addition, he immediately passes the buck to some other person, or to some external cause, which is beyond his control.

Inside the team the 7.1– stands apart, as he needs to keep the necessary distance and control over the whole situation. He works hard on the preparations, scheduling, strategy, and so on. He needs no advisors, including even those who are responsible for this work. It does not matter whether they developed the right strategy, for his individualistic actions would anyway become an obstacle to the participation of other interested people. Commitment of staff members weakens, as they are detached from the goals that they have to reach. The general attitude is: "Why should I try so hard if he's still relying only on himself? All my suggestions are ignored, and no one can hear me!"

Thus, the subordinate is exactly as effective as his 7.1– style manager. It does not matter if the leader is talented, skilful, and experienced, as the low level of involvement of other team members leads to his monopoly over the resources of the entire team; any alternative views, ideas, and even simple questions are ignored.

The motto of a 7.1– leader is "no cooperation". It implies submission with not a single question asked. Alternative views or objections are ignored or regarded as interference or deviations from organizational goals. The work is organized in such a way that team members have almost no chance to express any idea, criticism, or defend their views.

Interaction is built on solid but very one-sided basis, which nevertheless makes it possible to maintain control over the whole work. Instructions are articulated with comments like: "This is exactly what we are going to do", "You should do this or that", or "I have already designed a plan for you". The leader with the 7.1– style prefers to determine the course of action and then to articulate it, leaving no opportunity for discussion or creative participation. Others just have to start their work. This approach minimizes the possibility of synergy, as the personal involvement of other team members is excluded.

The 7.1– leader strives for the best outcomes, setting ambitious goals, which, however, are not backed by the support of others. And if a team member detects a problem, he will not inform a leader like that, even if the problem may block the achievement of major goals. Similarly, the one who has an interesting idea and knows how to put it into practice will still remain silent. Relationships are built on the principle of non-participation, "Why should I make efforts and help him?" In fact, the only way to optimize the use of available resources is to encourage people to help each other and immediately inform each other about problems. But this requires a simultaneous collective suspension of work, implying the possible improvement of its quality in the future. Even if the leader is an incredibly intelligent and experienced man, he still cannot anticipate all possible problems and offer the best solutions to all problems. Indeed, major goals are hard to achieve, even if all the team members actively exchange information and integrate efforts. If they conceal the information or even shirk, the problems begin to multiply.

The 7.1– leader loses benefits from the activity of others, preferring total personal control. In addition, he does not want to waste his time explaining something to others, discussing the problems, and assessing the performance of each staff member. And on top of that, the 7.1– leader spends a huge amount of his own resources on the continuous monitoring of his orders' execution. However, he feels fully responsible for the detection and elimination of all difficulties, obstacles, and challenges. The 7.1– style usually considers himself the most hardworking person in the team, while the quality of the overall work is low because of over-active participation of one and non-participation of others. But the 7.1– leader does not usually see the imbalance and does not understand why others do not want to work as hard as he does. When problems emerge, he reinforces the concern for results and forces others to work even more.

4.3   The I-ZONE and the 7.1– Style

The 7.1– style is an embodied contradiction to the natural human desire to communicate, share ideas, and move towards a common goal. The sense of personal commitment is the result of mutual trust and respect, as well as the possibility of contributing to the common cause. All this does not fit with the 7.1– style (s. Fig. 4.1).

If the 7.1– leader has made his decision on the activity of the whole team, any team's attempts to take the initiative stumble on his remarks: "You are incompetent in this matter" or "Your suggestion is out of the picture".

People like to feel that they are doing something useful for the common cause; but the 7.1– leader's approach divides and does not consolidate. When the manager criticizes or brushes aside any idea, staff members begin to think, "Well, okay, I don't want to know, what's going on here. Anyway, my ideas are paid no attention" and to look for a different job. Moreover, indifference and non-participation can cause feelings of opposition.

In the worst case possible team members begin to oppose the 7.1– leader, undermining his efforts and experiencing pleasure when their queering of his pitch is successful: "Serves him right. We all warned him that it was not going to

Fig. 4.1 7.1–

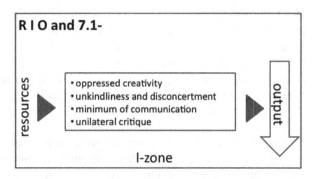

work, but he wouldn't listen". With an oppositional team like that, the 7.1– leader will lose any support, having no chances to create an atmosphere of mutual trust and respect.

4.4   7.1– Culture and Values

Culture of Control, Pressure, and Fear. Basic Feature: Production and Good Results at any Cost

Trust The 7.1– style leader believes that people are inherently lazy and dependent. They cannot be trusted and are to be constantly forced to work. He finds reliable only those employees who always comply with all instructions strictly and accurately, not questioning his instructions and orders and showing obedience. The 7.1– leader is suspicious about people who try to act independently. In his case, trust in people is replaced by confidence in organizational processes and procedures. Subconsciously, the 7.1– style does not fully trust oneself, associating one's own image exclusively with the results achieved and the relevant organizational procedures and requirements. His fear of not fulfilling the task, of making a mistake, or of being helpless creates an atmosphere of nervousness, stress, and anxiety that can hardly be resisted long.

Fairness The 7.1– style is convinced that justice should be associated with results. Those employees who diligently execute orders and get results may rely on his appreciation and attention. But even in this case, they must respect his commands and should not question his instructions. Those employees, who do not achieve the desired results, or those who displease the 7.1– leader, do not have any right to express their opinion or human relation. All measures that help to achieve results are considered justified and fair.

Commitment The 7.1– style perceives his commitment to the organization as unquestioning obedience and strict adherence to goals. According to the 7.1–, staff members should identify themselves with the goals of the organization; they should completely merge with them. Whatever the objective, psychological and moral aspects for achieving the goal, the result would justify anything. Personal identity is reduced to the result, while all the achievements are attributed solely to the manager, who, from the point of view of the 7.1— leader, is the epitome of the entire organization. Thus, organizational commitment and identity is ultimately reduced to rigorous commitment and identification with the boss and should be expressed in a willingness to do lots of work in accordance with his instructions.

Responsibility The 7.1— style is highly reliable in situations where the objectives, procedures, and processes are clearly defined and authorized by management or fixed tradition. Over-concentration on the given orders often comes along with neglect of all factors that are not directly associated with the achievement of results, but can disrupt the reliability of the entire organization. The 7.1— style's responsibility is selective: the focus is on the results that have something to do with his career and the performance measurement from the part of the chief. The 7.1— leader internally opposes the philosophy of social responsibility, which requires the organizational cooperation and involvement in solving social problems. In terms of 7.1—, these problems should be solved differently: reinforcing control, pressure, and power. As a rule, questions of social responsibility are considered by the 7.1— style only as a response to the demands of senior management.

Integrity Openness and honesty, according to the 7.1—, are to be expressed in the fullness, accuracy, and timeliness of instructions, orders, and requirements that must be followed by employees. Strict compliance with these conditions should make interaction simple and effective. Any other information is hidden, as the 7.1— style regards it as useless and even harmful. The open exchange of information is out of the question, as it can damage the manager's authority and power. Feedback is given in the form of punishment and condemnation. The 7.1— style does not consider it necessary to discuss goals with anyone or attract someone to take action. Therefore, the overall picture of organizational activities, its meaning, and development are completely unclear to employees. It expectedly results in low involvement, anxiety, and mistrust.

4.5   7.1— Culture and Power

Focus on Punishment and Job Title

Punishment The 7.1— style uses punishment as a main tool to influence and change the behaviour of employees. The range of punishments varies widely from frowning and harsh remarks to raising the voice during a feedback session, fines, and dismissal. This kind of power is constantly pressing on staff members, even when they do everything in accordance with the 7.1— leader's requirements. The punishment is often inadequate to the degree of the employee's misconduct or error. Serious "addressing" may be caused by even a minor fault.

Reward   The 7.1– style considers reward as an inefficient and optional means of influence. Assuming that all men are lazy and passive by nature, the 7.1– leader does not believe in the efficiency of reward. Subconsciously, the 7.1– thinks that even those employees that achieve good results can reduce their effectiveness when encouraged and rewarded. A good employee, according to the 7.1–, will be working well without any reward. Therefore, when the 7.1– rewards and thanks a staff member for good work, he does that reluctantly. Even a simple "thank you" for the work is extremely rare and insincere. Assuming that the result is the most important and that he is the only one responsible for it, the 7.1– leader considers himself the only one to be rewarded.

Position   The 7.1– leader considers the position in the organization very important, and his career ambitions are very high. So he emphasizes his status by all means and always keeps a distance with the staff. Facing disagreement, he would definitely say or think: "I'm the boss, so you do as I say!" Trying to deal with employees' objections or unwillingness to submit to his orders, the 7.1– style often emphasizes his authority. Position, according to the 7.1–, gives the right to control any step of any staff member. Orders of senior managers are perceived as right and require immediate fulfilment.

Information   Information exchange is reduced to setting tasks and instructions that the 7.1– leader gives to his subordinates. The volume of information is strictly limited to the content of the task. As a rule, information is accompanied by an indication of how and what to do. Being sure that this amount of information is sufficient for the job, the 7.1– leader does not like questions, as he regards answering to them a waste of time. Important organizational information is left for his personal use only. Often he uses important information to strengthen his influence and control. The information given is dry and concise, highlighting the status distance and underlining the impossibility of disagreement and distrust.

Expert   As a rule, the 7.1– style is well organized, highly professional, and is aimed at achieving good results. He enjoys emphasizing his superiority in knowledge and skills. The idea of his professionalism and the desire to dominate prevents him from perceiving and acquiring new knowledge, especially from his subordinates. He is convinced that he knows everything better than others, and is stubbornly doing what he thinks is right. Being afraid of losing control, the 7.1– leader is scarcely inclined to teach others, passing on his knowledge and skills.

Referent   The 7.1– style tries to create an image of a business-like, successful executive, who is the champion of the organization (department, group) in pursuance of common goals and shared results. His faith in the fact that by virtue of his personal and professional qualities he is able to act correctly and always pick up the right decision can make a strong impression on colleagues and subordinates. However, this attitude is often negatively perceived by staff members as arrogance and conceit. The intolerance to the opinions of others and the unwillingness to engage in constructive dialogue and cooperation make the 7.1– style a reference figure, which is used only in force majeure situations.

4.6   Cooperation Skills of the 7.1– Style

Conflict Resolution

Any individual or joint activity is inevitably connected with overcoming of difficulties, problems, and contradictions. However, even individual activity constantly throws one into dilemmas: what, how, and when should it be done. That results in inner doubts and internal conflict, when one cannot decide what is proper, better, and more useful. When many people are working together the situation is complicated by the fact that each person is unique and has his own goals and interests. In other words, conflict is omnipresent, and the way a leader tries to resolve it largely determines his effectiveness and compliance with the spirit of the corporate culture of the organization.

Effective conflict resolution includes the identification of problems and contradictions in the activity of the individual, group, or organization, and the search for ways to resolve these contradictions. The leadership style largely determines how a person uses this skill in everyday work. The 7.1– style considers any conflict as a negative, unacceptable phenomenon, since it reduces effectiveness. He believes that the main cause of conflict is the lack of control from the part of the manager. The 7.1– leader's solution is to bring the situation under his control and cover up or suppress the conflict, so that it does not interfere with work.

Conflict threatens the ability to control, so the 7.1– style does the same as in other dangerous situations: namely, he immediately rushes to attack the conflict instead of searching for ways to resolve it. The 7.1– style leader inhibits the conflict, making the decision single-handedly and actively defending his viewpoint. This approach leaves no room for doubts and questions, providing the 7.1– style with tight control over the situation.

The 7.1– leader tries to put down the conflict as soon as possible in order to keep the productivity. Doing this, the 7.1– style stubbornly rejects any counterarguments, firmly and rigidly defending his point of view. Even if the 7.1– leader understands what is wrong in a conflict situation, he will never agree with his opponent because of the fear to show his weakness.

If the conflict cannot be suppressed at once, the 7.1– may try to use the whole range of reliable means: all his position powers (with the emphasis on the negative consequences that await those who do not agree), his personal and professional authority (to shame the opposition), and the need to follow the instructions and regulations, strictly sticking to duties. He also uses the situation to warn others about similar actions. Demotion, reprimand, or denial of a reward can be used as a penalty. Doing all this, the 7.1– is convinced that he regained his prestige and achieved consensus, even through intimidation. The 7.1– leader often backs off and tries to avoid conflict, when he sees that he cannot use his power and his authority to force others to accept his solution.

Typically, the 7.1– leader detects a conflict at a fairly late stage, when the confrontation over the different interests and values has gained an explicit form. However, the 7.1– rarely analyses the causes and history of the conflict. As a rule, he does not care about the reason of the conflict, i.e. the problems and contradictions that caused it. The 7.1– style is immediately looking for a culprit. None of the interested parties is involved in the resolution process and, as a rule, staff members simply find themselves informed of the leader's decision.

Due to the fact that the cause of the conflict is not found, its resolution turns out to be superficial. The 7.1– leader avoids systematic work to overcome conflicts, eliminating every possibility to learn from them. If the 7.1– leader acts as an arbitral referee in a conflict, he prefers not to focus on the details, but to separate the conflicting parties, while the discontent are moved to other positions.

Within a conflict, the 7.1– style follows a strategy of confrontation, aiming to satisfy his interests at the expense of the other side (on the basis of his own activity and individual action). The 7.1– style's behaviour in conflict eventually implies his win and the loss of all other employees.

The 7.1– style is not able to get positive energy out of the conflict, overcoming it constructively. He does not try to clarify or discuss its possible causes. Instead, in order to identify differences and discuss solutions, the 7.1– focuses on the suppression of the conflict for a prompt return to work. Besides, he ignores the personal aspect of the conflict and often solves the problem by giving rise to painful experiences and insults.

Communicative Competence

The high concern for production makes the 7.1– style use mostly a downward, one-way communication model, which does not imply dialogue and feedback. This kind of communication, although focused on the task at hand, at the same time leaves behind the information that, at first glance, may seem unnecessary, but is often critical to the success of all activities. The 7.1– leader is convinced that access to critical organizational information must be given to a limited number of people.

The 7.1– style is convinced that in communication the most important is to articulate the problem, explaining *what* must be done, *when* it should be done, and *who* the performers are. Therefore, the 7.1– believes that he has the highest communicative competence, so he can properly and clearly formulate tasks to his subordinates. Attention to the feelings and concerns of subordinates, faith in their abilities, and the need to reassure and encourage them, all this is considered by the 7.1– leader as something unnecessary and even harmful, because it can distract from the main thing, which is the achievement of goals.

The necessary information for matters that concern other employees is solely gathered by the 7.1– leader. For example, if he is responsible for finding the new office, he talks to the experts to find the best location for the future office, but it would not occur to him to talk to the people who will be working in this office. What do they need? What are the problems they may have in this office? What could they recommend? But these are the people who will work there and are expected to bring the company's success. Nevertheless, the 7.1– leader considers it unnecessary and even harmful to consult co-workers, thinking the following: "There's no need to consult with them. They, as always, will complain, but I already know what they need."

The 7.1– style controls the work process by constant monitoring and asking everyone about the work done. However, the 7.1– leader's approach to communication does not encourage people to discuss anything with him. This type of one-sided communication involves only yes/no answers, or mere repetition of what had already been said.

The 7.1– style leader cuts out the possibility of discussions in advance, using phrases like: "This is exactly what we have to do" or "You should. . ." In order to intercept unnecessary questions and discussions, the 7.1– leader likes to add: "I hope everything is clear!" Such statements do not encourage new comments or ideas. This is especially true if the 7.1– style has major position powers. In this case, all staff members have to obey and follow him without a word.

This approach to communication does not suggest an atmosphere of mutual trust and respect among people. Everyone is cautious and afraid of asking questions; the whole team suffers with the consequences of this kind of interaction. What the 7.1– leader calls "information exchange" looks more like an interrogation. This approach becomes an obstacle on the way towards the effective circulation of information within the organization. People start to hide vital information that could improve the efficiency of the entire team. People's relationship towards the 7.1– style is based on a principle: "You think you're so smart, so pick up the pieces yourself."

In communication, the 7.1– leader does not see and ignores the barriers that can impede or distort understanding. It seems to him that his instructions are so simple and clear that only the lazy or stupid employee would not understand them. The dialogue and feedback mode with employees is unacceptable. So when he realizes that he has not been understood, he treats the words with a grain of salt and will be careful to say, "And now for those who are less attentive, I repeat once more what is to be done".

In conversation, the 7.1– style often uses closed questions. Thus, employees often feel that they are expected to give "right" answers. They feel as if they are passing an exam, so their initiative is suppressed and a trusting relationship fails to be established. The very form, with which the 7.1– leader asks his questions, often causes a reaction of defence and resistance, instead of enthusiasm and sincerity.

When defending his opinion, the 7.1– leader tries to establish performance criteria in advance and focus the discussion on the results. Thus, the ability to push one's opinion at any price becomes the main criterion for the effectiveness of any discussion. The 7.1– style leaves no room for constructive and sincere expressions of opinion, thereby reducing the personal involvement of each and every staff member. In circumstances like that, many of them are reluctant to express their views and to contribute to the overall result. The inability to speak strengthens the tension, pushes serious problems deeper, and reduces commitment and loyalty of employees. Alienation and the loss of the significance of their contribution to the common cause reduce the motivation and could eventually have a negative impact on organizational performance.

Active Positioning

The 7.1– style has a strongly pronounced active standpoint, based on the following assumptions:

1. I know the best way to achieve the goal.
2. If I ask others their opinion, I will show weakness and lose control.
3. I cannot trust other manifestations of initiative.

Enthusiasm and desire to throw himself headlong into the work without any hesitation are characteristic of the 7.1– style. He usually has high professional skills and, as a rule, is self-confident and not afraid to take responsibility. The 7.1– style usually comes to the meeting not to discuss some ideas with colleagues and subordinates, but to put forward ready-made suggestions, as he is willing to implement them immediately. Such behaviour shows a low level of concern for people. The 7.1– leader presents his individually designed plans with confidence and conviction. He never tries to hide his attitude towards others, expressing it with the phrase: "Well, everything has been decided, now let's work".

Too much initiative of the 7.1– often adversely affects others. He usually rushes to implement the project before others have an opportunity to learn the necessary information and develop a common understanding of the working process. The team members may not even understand what he had presented as a project, but they feel uncomfortable asking questions. The 7.1– leader usually knows the topic well enough, while others stay uninformed. Planned activities may require unknown procedures and a new level of responsibility, which leads to more and more questions. Regardless of the reasons why people feel bypassed, the 7.1– style does not see and does not want to see what effect his active standpoint has on others. The low level of concern for people does not allow the 7.1– leader to understand the involvement in activities, necessary for every staff member. Naturally, everyone wants to understand the new task and perform it well.

Arguing his position, the 7.1– leader categorically emphasizes the correctness of his views, which cannot be discussed. He points to others' weaknesses and makes them find excuses and worry about their real or imagined mistakes. The 7.1– leader avoids even the well-deserved praise, as he fears that it could cause complacency in the future and adversely affect the results.

The 7.1– style is at his best when it comes to defending his views. He exhibits the same characteristics as when he's taking the initiative. The 7.1– leader articulates his arguments confidently, making it clear that his opinion is the only right one and cannot be changed. One will not see any shadow of uncertainty or doubt, when the 7.1– leader expresses his point of view. His opinion is presented very logically and scientific-like; it is based on facts and evidence. Statements are made in an unconditional and even passionate manner that does not imply a different opinion: "This is the only possible way", "It is impossible", "Everyone knows that...", and so on.

The 7.1– leader cuts out all attempts to challenge his views. Other opinions are rejected categorically and firmly. Other suggestions, opinions, and alternative views are perceived as a provocation and are refuted by irrefutable arguments, and a torrent of criticism. The 7.1– style does not pay any attention to their importance and validity. Those who dare to express them often become morally destroyed under a stream of arguments or criticism. They usually give up, feeling that it is useless to struggle. This is particularly true if the 7.1– style has position powers. Thus, others are reluctant to speak or to ask a question even more.

The 7.1– style's method of defending his views looks more like a fight where you either win or lose. This taste for competition leads to a situation in which even right observations and opinions have absolutely no chance to change the 7.1– leader's point of view. Deviation from the original position is seen by the 7.1– leader as weakness that he avoids at any cost. He is often too passionate defending his opinion, never accepting reasonable arguments against it. In those rare cases when the 7.1– leader is forced to change his mind, he shows his displeasure and refers to the circumstances: "Okay. If you think that it is really necessary, I give up." The 7.1– style rarely changes his mind, even if a more efficient alternative point of view is at hand. Exceptions are the viewpoints of the higher authorities, which are generally accepted without a word.

The 7.1– leader is sure enough about his abilities to take the risk and to make the first step in solving problems of any complexity. The 7.1– style's initiative sets a powerful push to the group interaction in general, but the dominant, peremptory nature of this initiative blocks the involvement of others, reducing their enthusiasm and confidence. Team members do not feel their personal involvement in achieving the result if they do not participate in the initial actions.

Decision-Making

Decision-making, as we have noted in the previous chapter, is a complex process that involves many steps. However, when the 7.1– leader takes a decision, it seems very fast and simple: "I have decided that we will do so!" Thus, employees see that the complicated process of decision-making paradoxically consisted of only one stage, the decision itself, adopted without discussion, consultation, and involvement of others. They are simply reported on what they are supposed to do in this situation.

The 7.1– leader's approach to decision-making is one-sided and unconditional. But it does not mean that this style of decision-making is always inefficient. The 7.1– style often achieves success due to his ability to make tough decisions quickly. This is particularly valuable in times of crisis and force majeure situations.

The 7.1– leader's decisions are accepted almost without discussion and then are declared as final, with subsequent transfer of clear guidelines for their implementation to each team member. All the rest have to make do with some guidance on the implementation of the forthcoming decisions. A couple of questions on the implementation can still be set, while any doubts or alternative suggestions are not allowed.

The 7.1– style leader prefers to make decisions alone, based on his own experience, knowledge, authority, and delegated responsibility. He comes to make decisions with a high focus on the subject and is sure to perform the required number of consecutive steps. But he does everything alone, without attracting any of the staff members. This individualistic and direct approach often suffers from lack of completeness or realism in the perception of the problem, which subsequently prevents its effective implementation.

The 7.1– style leader usually does not involve any employees in the process of preparation, even those who are to implement it. He can ask a few questions or ask for a report, which is required for the preparation, but he never involves others in discussions or tells them why he needs this or that information. His logic is the following: "I know what is better." From his subordinates he needs facts, not opinions. This approach leads to incomplete knowledge of the matter in question, while staff members can give all the necessary information only when they know what is happening and know why are they actually asked to do this or that.

Most good decisions are taken in teams where there is mutual trust and respect. The lack of trust and respect leads to a situation in which even the right decision fails to trigger motivation and involvement of employees; thus, it becomes "stalled".

The 7.1– style sincerely believes that the decision is the exclusive prerogative of senior managers, while attempts to discuss their decisions and alternative solutions provoke his jealousy. At the same time, in order to emphasize his right to make decisions, the 7.1– style would say, "Sorry, you don't know all the details", alluding to his status position and possession of information available to a limited circle of persons. According to the 7.1– style, only top management can know everything or almost everything.

Constructive Critique

The 7.1– style's criticism is one-sided and unconstructive. He is always pointing at the mistakes and weaknesses of others. Thus, according to the 7.1– style, he helps others to learn from the mistakes made and to boost the quality of work; but the categorical, convicting manner of the 7.1– style usually does not take into account other people's feelings, expectations, and motivations. Thus, the criticism does not work, producing the opposite effect: people take up a defensive position and lose their desire to work better.

He can make a blame storming on the general meeting, "so that everyone could learn his lesson". The 7.1– style sincerely believes in the effectiveness of a method like that. His logic is simple and straightforward: all employees will recognize their errors, so there will be no need to explain each case separately, and everyone will make the right conclusion for himself. More often, however, this approach has a destructive effect, humiliating the human dignity of employees and causing fear and anxiety.

The 7.1– leader's approach to criticism does not allow others to take part in the discussion. The 7.1– leader prevents others from expressing their viewpoints, giving the final explanation: "You are wrong, and I'll tell you why..." or "I'm not interested" or "You don't understand what you're talking about". In the same way, positive results are either ignored or commented through clenched teeth. Successful result is the only kind of result the 7.1– leader expects, so he considers positive comments as a sign of weakness and a distraction from work, leading to complacency.

The 7.1– style believes he has the right to ask others, but nobody can ask him. The 7.1– leader asks meaningful questions to find out whether he was understood or not. He gets only the information he needs at the moment. He does not need to get acquainted with ideas that do not coincide with his view on the subject.

Of all types' critique, the 7.1– places special emphasis on the subsequent criticism, when work is already done and it is impossible to fix anything. The 7.1– leader rarely tries to find out the causes of failure, and he pounces with all his indignation on employees who have not been able to achieve good results and, in his opinion, are to blame for the situation. After such criticism, employees are often discouraged. In general, the 7.1– style leader criticism is unconstructive: "I ask others, but don't like when others ask me. I only ask meaningful questions to find out whether I was understood or not, and I only get information that I need at the moment. I don't need to get acquainted with ideas that don't coincide with my view on the subject."

The 7.1– style leader likes to use rhetorical questions that do not imply any response and indirectly express his negative attitude, leaving employees with the only option to explain themselves and make excuses. Hearing the words "Why do you never do anything on time?" the staff member does not fully understand what exactly had not been done properly and what he needs to do to change the situation. Thus, the employee does not know how to improve his performance, but rather sees the 7.1– leader's hidden superiority and negative attitude.

Expressed in the form of categorical prescriptions, the 7.1– leader's criticism does not disclose in what the employee was wrong and contains a direct indication of what should be done: "You have to be smarter!", "I will not allow frustration of department's plans!" This form of criticism usually discourages employees, causing a feeling of inner resistance. The 7.1– leader often uses other forms of unconstructive criticism: reprimands, accusations, sarcasm, and blames that are particularly unhelpful, when expressed in a contemptuous tone and accompanied by aggressive gestures and facial expressions.

4.7 Conclusions

The 7.1– style leader brings determination, focus on goals, and opportunities to the group. He is reliable as far as achieving results is concerned, particularly in the context of force majeure and the shortage of time. However, his limited way of regarding people as a means of achieving goals produces negative effects on the efficiency of the interaction. The low level of concern for people often turns out to be against him and his organizational potential. The 7.1– style demonstrates courage, he is not afraid to say anything or to make a tough decision. He is well organized, usually shows the solidity of action, and defends his opinions with confidence which is close to passion.

However, his attitudes, his conviction that people are lazy and passive, and his exaggeration of his own role in the organization can nullify his high concern for production for two reasons. Firstly, the 7.1– style leader does not understand the importance of other people's involvement in the interaction process, which is called the "team". His main concern is the conversion of resources (R) into output (O). He does not understand that not only himself, but other people can bring creative ideas, mutual trust, respect, and support to the I-ZONE. This means that the determination and dedication of the 7.1– style often have a limited view of the mission and values of the organization and a simplified, one-sided view of the way of achieving the output (O). Secondly, the low concern for people and reduced understanding (at times, the neglect) of the corporate culture values can neutralize the productivity, as staff members will be reluctant to blindly implement someone's individual decisions. Thus, instead of commitment, interest in the outcome, and the desire for more efficient cooperation, employees lose motivation and feel an internal resistance towards any indications of the 7.1– leader. And all this inevitably affects the final result.

Style 7.1+: Paternalist (To Assign and to Manage)

5

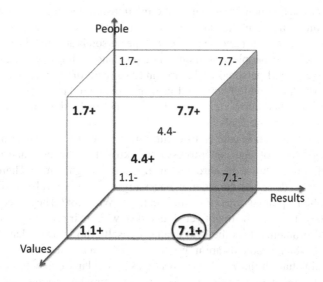

High concern for production, low concern for people, positive attitude towards work and the organization, patronizing the treatment of subordinates that are perceived as immature and in need of care. Doesn't accept objections, assumes mentoring, and protective position. The 7.1+ leader clearly defines borders of behaviour and takes initiatives both for himself and for others. He appreciates and is grateful for the staff members' support, but does not accept any objections.

© Springer-Verlag Berlin Heidelberg 2016
A. Zankovsky, C. von der Heiden, *Leadership with Synercube*,
DOI 10.1007/978-3-662-49052-5_5

5.1 Basic Features of the 7.1+ Style

The 7.1+ style perceives the world as ordered, stabled, and developed according to long-known models, including a family model that sets parents a main task—to care, to teach, and, if necessary, to punish their children. The identification with staff members' parents allows us to characterize the 7.1+ style as paternalistic (deriving from the Latin word *Pater* that stands for "father"). The 7.1+ leader is convinced that his subordinates, regardless of their age and professional skills, are yet immature and dependent. They still remain children that are in need of kind, understanding parental supervision and guidance. They can define and decide some unimportant issues for themselves, but for the key ones they need an experienced, wise mentor, who tells or indicates them what to do.

At first glance it may seem that the relationship between the paternalistic leader and his colleagues, which is similar to the relationship between father and child, should be valued much higher on the "concern for people" scale. However, the highest level of concern for people means that the person is able to take into account and understand other people's opinions, thoughts, and feelings, listen carefully to their professional and personal problems, and take care of their development and well-being. The high level of concern for people, expressed in the right way, gives people confidence and allows team members to trust each other and communicate their ideas openly and honestly.

The 7.1+ style notion of care is different. The 7.1+ leader is patronizing towards everyone regardless of age and professional skills, treating his subordinates as immature children who need parental supervision and guidance. Therefore, the 7.1+ style really does not consider it necessary to treat carefully and to try to understand their opinions, thoughts, and feelings. What for? They need direction and help. They themselves are not yet able to deal with their priorities, professional and personal problems. It is the 7.1+ leader himself who knows what they need, what is right, which problems are important, and which are not.

The actual nature of the 7.1+'s care becomes particularly evident in cases when others do not agree with the role of dependent and immature people. They want to be taken seriously and treated with respect, they want to be heard, they want to have their professionalism appreciated, and they want trust, not control. In a situation like that, the 7.1+ leader often instantly turns into a strict father, who can give his kids a tough kick in the pants.

The 7.1+ leader may feel frankly and deeply outraged, as he cannot imagine why someone rejects his fatherly care. His slogans are: "It's for your own good!" "Following me is the best for you!" And as the caring parent often feels a grudge against the growing-up children seeking independence, so too can the 7.1+ leader give a negative emotional response to staff members' attempts to shift to parity, partner-like relationships.

Paternalism is the most common and pronounced leadership style in prosperous companies. This style is a kind of "new and improved" version of an authoritarian leader. The 7.1+ style leaders show strength, confidence, and courage that allow the company to achieve the desired results, and at the same time they take care of people who work with them. Paternalists are often regarded as benevolent autocrats, people who seek not only to control the behaviour of others, but also to make them smile and say "Thank you". These leaders usually have a lot of experience in their field and want to share this knowledge by taking part in every event or project that could be useful for business. The paternalist helps others, even if they do not ask for help or it is evidently needless. The problem is that, by doing that much, the paternalist creates a sense of dependence among others, ultimately limiting their participation in a common cause.

The 7.1+ style leader aims at high standards of work and expects the same from others. Anyone who meets these requirements receives remuneration in the form of awards, benefits, and payments. The 7.1+ style believes that a team member who accepts his rules must show good results at work; and the 7.1+ leader actively supports and encourages these results. For those who do not want to obey, the 7.1+ style leader applies quite a different attitude, which is expressed in more frequent inspections and in statements like: "Prove to me that you are worth of my support" and "I'm doing this for your own good".

Good intentions do not allow the paternalist to realize that his behaviour suppresses others. This blindness further leads to the fact that people start to say to the paternalist only the words he wants to hear: "I think that's a good idea, boss!" Paternalists often interrupt employees to voice their suggestions and impose their ideas. As a result, they have no desire to speak their minds, especially if the paternalist holds a higher position. Those who are being helped by force grow tired from the permanent overseer's presence and interference in their lives; they do not like to see all decisions being made and all fruits being reaped by their boss. They feel like children who have long grown, but whose parents did not want to admit that they are already adults.

The 7.1+ leader tries to create an environment wherein he would have been revered and respected as a strict, smart, and caring leader. He also wants to be seen as a mentor, care-taker, and "nice guy" (e.g. senior manager paternalists usually speak to lower-status employees in a deliberately caring, friendly, and attentive manner). The paternalist seeks to ensure that people are dependent on him, so that he can decide for them: "They themselves are waiting for me to control this project." "With my help they will be able to do a great job on this project." The paternalist's favourite expression is: "I think you should. . ." and the phrase he often hears from others is "Please tell me what you think about this".

The standard of excellence established by the 7.1+ leader can be summarized as follows: "Everyone should try to be like me." He sets work and behaviour standards that reflect his own values and expresses disapproval when employees deviate from these standards. So, if the 7.1+ leader prefers any particular form to formalize suggestions, he expects that employees will praise this form and will formalize their suggestions this way as well. If he does his presentation using only a certain pattern, others adopt it, as this will be praised. The 7.1+ leader can even expect his subordinates to have the same interests, dressing taste, or speech manner. The independence and individuality of others are regarded as challenges to the paternalist's perfection; so he resists it saying: "The idea is fine, but you'd better do it as I said". This kind of remark can be put either in a polite or in a tough manner, if they imply disapproval: "You are determined to do it your way, am I right?" His standpoint is nevertheless positive as the values he is imposing are the ideal values of the ideal corporate culture.

5.2   The 7.1+ Style in Collective Cooperation

The following examples show typical 7.1+ leader responses to different situations.

If a team member fails to do his part of work: The 7.1+ leader expresses disappointment and disapproval. The consequences of failure can range from remarks intended to induce a sense of guilt—"I thought I could count on you for this"—to a warning—"we have to talk seriously about your future in our company". The degree of punishment depends on the nature of relations between the paternalist and the employee. Anyone who is out of favour is condemned and penalized more severely. To those who are in favour, the 7.1+ leader applies less severe sanctions, perhaps even encouragement or praise: "I believe that in the future you'll do all right."

The 7.1+ style's response to a piece of constructive criticism from a team member is as follows. Although the 7.1+ leader does not show it, he always feels offended by any kind of criticism from other employees. He takes a critical statement as a personal attack and tries to defend himself. If the majority of employees support the paternalist, he may call his opponent a dissenter and apply a punishment. However, most often the paternalist simply expresses his dissatisfaction, his attitude becomes cooler, he stops to smile politely, and even pretends that he did not notice the employee in question. The 7.1+ leader must make sure that his actions have produced the desired effect on the "culprit" and on others who may want to question his authority. When the paternalist sees that a lesson has been learned, he lapses into the usual warm relations. If the paternalist's neglect of the critical remark leads to negative results, he may start blaming others, to instil in them a sense of guilt: "That's what happens when I do not get all the information that I need in advance" or "I work too much, and I can't correct all the mistakes by myself".

The 7.1+ leader channels the team's energy in a false direction, diverting people's attention from the fact of *what* would be appropriate in this situation, and focusing on *who* is right. The true standard of excellence is substituted by the paternalist's personal view. The 7.1+ leader's team is effective only when he is effective, as the paternalist controls the resources (R) and the relationship in the I-ZONE. The 7.1+ leader takes the control of the information and coordinates the team activities; he also monitors the critical speeches of colleagues and their response to them. This is the same unilateral control over people we have seen in the 7.1− style, but paternalism is more attractive in the short term. In contrast to the 7.1− style, paternalists seem friendly and caring people. Paternalists appeal to people's needs for security by offering them care, encouragement, and support, which makes a confrontation with him much more difficult. After receiving such support, accompanied by sincere intentions, nobody wants to hurt the paternalist's feelings.

This limitation of opportunities ultimately causes team members' resentment and indignation, because they cannot fulfil their full potential. Moreover, if the paternalist is the leader of the team, the staff regards this as an additional disadvantage, because the paternalist can use and even abuse his position. Although his approach is a little more attractive than the 7.1−'s, it is still a primitive control. The pressure of the paternalist does not allow employees to be frank and open with each other. Over time, team members get tired of the disbelief, the patronizing tone, and the manipulation and start to perceive the paternalist only as an overseer and egotist. This eventually leads to their indignation.

If the 7.1+ leader has his "much fancied" ones, it contributes to the collective sense of injustice and leads to strained relations between those in favour and those who are out of it. Team members who do not belong to the "inner circle" are irritated by the fact that they are imposed a higher standard than those who are in favour, and they have to work harder to meet excessive demands, without having the support and remuneration. And "favourites" feel superior and let themselves have a "holier-than-thou" behaviour towards other employees, because they know that the 7.1+ is on their side. These polarized relations create bad working conditions within the team. Employees are more concerned about the fact that they are in unfavourable conditions than about work and promotion.

For the team, the standards of excellence are limited to the paternalist's objectives. If the 7.1+ leader makes a wrong decision, other employees will not only suffer the consequences, but they can also be to blame, as the paternalist cannot admit his mistake. And instead of being engaged in their duties, increasing efficiency, and trying to feel personally involved in a common cause, employees are focusing all their attention on how to please the 7.1+ leader and not get into trouble.

If the problem is solved successfully, since all other alternatives were ignored, the 7.1+ leader gets all congratulations and praise for the result achieved, though all this seems insincere. "Favourites" also get their part of praise, though paradoxically they were the less resourceful. Similarly, the work done by the "dissenters" is often downplayed or completely ignored, causing further resentment.

The 7.1+ leader treats others more as family members than as employees, and that makes the relationship too personal. As a parent, the paternalist wants to teach his "children" how to work, and he uses incentives and penalties in order to influence their behaviour. Employees are encouraged to take initiative and responsibility, but only to the extent that is outlined by the 7.1+ style as acceptable. Thus, people stop analysing the situation and do not know how to assess it properly. In the end, when there is a need to express their own opinions, they feel helpless and defenceless. They ask in confusion: "What do we do now?" and wait for guidance.

5.3   The I-ZONE and the 7.1+ Style

The hierarchical pyramid with the paternalist sitting on top of it is the basis for a paternalistic relationship model. The paternalist regards himself responsible for everything and for everyone, and sees other team members as his subordinates, whose work directly affects him personally. This leads to the fact that he has an attitude like "If I want something done right, I must do it myself". This feeling of exceptional responsibility does not allow him to grant others with it. The only exceptions are those people whom the paternalist trusts like himself (see Fig. 5.1).

The paternalist feels most comfortable when he is in full control of the relationship. For example, if the paternalist works in the police department and the police need to carry out an operation, he behaves very aggressively, instructing the rest. During the operation, the paternalist considers it his duty to control everything: "When you are ready, we will check everything together" or "Inform me about each and every step of yours". He will try to be there to be sure that everything is done as had been instructed, and immediately intervenes if the employee begins to do something differently. He does not give any opportunity to do anything beyond instructions and prescriptions.

The 7.1+ leader's attitude can be difficult to recognize, because the external control and dominance may seem unobtrusive, and the casual observer can consider relations quite normal. People working with the paternalist quickly understand what they must do to avoid punishment. A dissatisfied paternalist will at first show his dissatisfaction nonverbally, then he will articulate a warning in the form of a brief analysis of what is happening or soft remarks which on the surface do not seem to be oppressive or controlling. The paternalist can smile and say in a friendly and caring voice: "I was surprised when I learned that you do not agree with my plan. It's interesting why you have not used the opportunity that I gave you." Such a quasi-benevolent tone creates the impression of a friendly, sympathetic leader.

Another reason why it is difficult to recognize a paternalist under the guise of benevolence is because his pressure becomes a positive driving force for the organizational working process, apparently everything looks well, and people seem happy and interested. But in such an atmosphere team members become

Fig. 5.1 7.1+

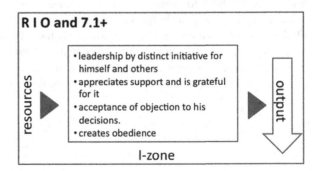

dependent on praise and compliments, they experience discomfort. Once these relationships are established, the paternalist does not need severe punishment to get the desired results, as the lack of praise in itself is a sufficient punishment.

If an individual cannot be manipulated by the paternalist, he uses the help of his loyal followers and takes action aimed at persuading the naughty one and making him comply. Depending on the current relationship, such actions may range from soft to very hard ones. In some cases, it is sufficient to refuse the friendly support, in other situations a remark will do. Sometimes the total control can be punishment, or an exclusion from participation in the project. If the paternalist is not sure whether he can count on the loyalty of a staff member, he can move him to another department or even fire him. Such tough measures are regarded as useful, because they also intimidate the rest in case they suddenly decided to question the paternalist's hegemony.

Ultimately, the 7.1+ leader's behaviour is destructive, because team members develop a sense of dependence. Over time, they stop striving to do what is necessary to do what the boss wants. They feel overwhelmed and they develop an attitude towards work which can be expressed this way: "I know what I need to do to survive here" or "It doesn't matter whether or not I'm right, if my rightness can lead to a conflict".

5.4   7.1+ Culture and Values

Patriarchal Culture

All work is being performed in order to serve the interests of the organization. The 7.1+ leader sets an example of personal working efficiency and expects high motivation and best efforts from the employees. At the same time an average result is not welcome. The 7.1+ leader delegates tasks but he does not leave space for the actual implementation of these tasks. He supervises and warns about possible mistakes and thus makes any spontaneity in the behaviour of employees impossible. The 7.1+ leader is convinced of the infallibility and infinity of his knowledge, and relies entirely on himself. The 7.1+ leader demands and praises good work, encourages team members to act according to his expectations, and expects a response of gratitude in return. People who contradict the 7.1+ leader, or question his recommendations or criticism, are warned about the inadmissibility of such behaviour. The 7.1+ leader expects admiration and approval, and he does not allow people to contradict him. The 7.1+ leader is even willing to forgive mistakes, but not opposition. The 7.1+ style focuses on the success of the company and all his efforts are devoted to this. The high concern for production and values and at the same time focus on the weak people are manifested in daily work in the form of selective behaviour with people and selective perception of these people. The 7.1+ style wants to show his authority, he likes to play leader, he expects praise and honour from others, and believes that this is the only way to achieve good results. The 7.1+ leader is convincing, informing, confident, generous, demanding, and rigorous.

Trust The main characteristic of the 7.1+ leader is his identification with the parents of the staff members, who are perceived as immature and independent. Regardless of age and professionalism, they still remain largely children for him, who need kind, understanding parental supervision and guidance. Therefore, they must fully and completely trust the 7.1+ leader, while he cannot trust immature people. They can be trusted to solve and define some unimportant issues, but for the key ones they need an experienced, wise mentor, who tells them what to do. Only those employees who would come to the 7.1+ leader for advice and support are fully trusted. Thus, trust is replaced by immature dependence on an authority figure and fear not to justify his goodwill and care. Asymmetrical "parent–child" relations do not allow establishing real trust, creating a climate of uncertainty, anxiety, and fear, which is partly neutralized by the 7.1+ leader's sincere desire to achieve organizational goals and to provide full support to the staff.

Fairness The 7.1+ style is convinced that he is an eminently fair man. His solutions and approaches are certainly fair as he, better than the employees, knows what they need and what they deserve. The 7.1+ leader sincerely wishes only good to his subordinates. For the sake of higher justice, team members must not only follow his advice but also feel gratitude for him. Those employees who are diligently doing their job may deserve special gratitude from the parent and become the boss's pets. But even in this case, they must comply with the rules of good behaviour set by the paternalist. Those who do not want to take the role of children deserve a "just" punishment.

Commitment The 7.1+ style regards commitment to the organization as unquestioning obedience and strict adherence to the instructions and advice of an authority figure. According to the 7.1+ leader, employees must perceive their organization (department, group) as their own family and identify themselves with the roles determined by the pater familias, i.e. by the 7.1+ leader. Moreover, if the ideas, interests, and individual goals of employees reflect the views and opinions of the 7.1+ leader, they will be taken into account and supported. In a different case, the 7.1+ leader clearly explains all the drawbacks of his position to the staff member and suggests the only right way. Thus, the identity of the person in the organization is reduced to the role of an immature, insecure person who needs constant care. Nevertheless, employees who have accepted these roles experience a sincere commitment to their leader and their department.

Responsibility The 7.1+ style is characterized by orientation on stable, reliable goals and values of the organization. Particularly, it concerns the situations and departments where employees are willing to accept the role given by the 7.1+ leader. As a rule, such a role is not accepted by staff members with high professionalism, experience, and the need for independence and autonomy. In this case, serious conflicts are the inevitable; overcoming them requires considerable effort from both sides. The 7.1+ style is committed to high social responsibility, based on the basic attitude to help and support others (according to his own subjective understanding). The 7.1+ leader is inwardly convinced that the organization is obliged to cooperate with the public institutions and to participate in solving social problems.

Integrity Integrity in the 7.1+ leader's understanding is expressed in an open and sincere desire to support staff members and help them to become more efficient (according to his own subjective understanding). If a staff member assumes the role given by the 7.1+ leader, the attitude is highly oriented to openness and honesty. Why hide and be ashamed of if we are a good family? However, the lack of real trust and keeping of important organizational information only for personal use negatively impact transparency and openness in relationships. In the case of a conflict that is inevitable when the role of the child is rejected, the situation changes dramatically: the openness and transparency are transformed into closed and secretive actions of the opposing sides. Therefore, the overall picture of organizational performance becomes quite controversial, causing anxiety and stress.

5.5   7.1+ Culture and Power

Focus on Position and Expert Power

Punishment The 7.1+ style rarely uses punishment as a necessary evil that must be tolerated and used for good purposes of education. The range of punishments is quite narrow and is generally limited to relatively soft means: disapproval, comments, and fatherly "dressing-down". The punishment may be expressed in the 7.1+ leader's deprivation of his care and attention. Often the 7.1+ leader explains what is good and what is bad, and thus the offender gets a second chance to behave properly and to be forgiven. A behaviour like that leads to the fact that team members avoid expressing their own ideas for fear of falling out of favour. This type of power is to a greater extent represented potentially: "Well, if you don't understand the easy way, we can talk seriously." The degree of punishment depends not on a real scale of error or misconduct, but on the "offender's" willingness or unwillingness to assume the role of a child and to come back to the usual role system.

Reward The 7.1+ style considers reward as an effective means of education. Based on the belief that all employees are immature enough and are not ready to work independently, the 7.1+ style makes the reward of employees his exclusive prerogative: he defines who is worthy of reward and what this reward will comprise. Therefore, the criteria for rewards are often poorly linked to the real achievements of employees. When rewarding an employee for a good job, the 7.1+ leader does so with some subtext: it is not just for the results but also for the correct behaviour and respect. He rewards and sets as an example only those who unconditionally accept the role of a child and strictly follow his instructions.

Position Status position in the organization largely reflects the 7.1+ leader's parental position in life in general. Therefore, he is not trying to emphasize his position, as he considers it something unquestionable. He does not try to keep a distance with the staff, claiming a close, almost family-like relationship. He has to emphasize his authority only if a "parent–child" role-playing system is not accepted by a team member. The cogency of the 7.1+ leader's position is that, imposing his opinion, he is basing it on his knowledge, experience, and sincere desire to help, to find the best solution.

Information Information exchange with the 7.1+ style may seem like a dialogue, but really it is a top-down pattern primarily used for the transmission of instructions, advice, and guidance to subordinates. The volume of information is not limited to the content of organizational tasks and often includes extra-organizational topics and questions, even personal life. Believing that personal information is not relevant to the organizational environment, some employees explicitly or implicitly reject such an intervention in their personal lives. The 7.1+ style prefers to leave important organizational information for personal use, assuming that the employees are not quite ready to take it properly. Some information is sometimes deliberately distorted in order to strengthen the paternalist's position. Information that does not correspond to the views and intentions of the 7.1+ leader is ignored or rejected. Counter-arguments are usually subjected to reformulation in order to comply with the original idea of the 7.1+ leader.

Expert As a rule, the 7.1+ style has high professional competence and experience, he is well-organized and aimed at achieving high goals. He sincerely shares the objectives and values of the organization. He does not try to show his supremacy. The idea of his high status, experience, and professionalism reduces intrinsic motivation to seek new knowledge. The 7.1+ leader does not consider his subordinates as a source of new knowledge and skills. He is constantly focused on the training and personal development of his subordinates, but only if it accords with his idea.

Referent The 7.1+ style tries to be a paragon of the experienced, wise, and successful leader, who is concerned with a common cause and shares the results more than anyone else in the organization (department, group). It is by virtue of his experience and personal and professional qualities that he becomes a wise mentor who can help all team members to do well not only in work, but in life in general. This mind-set can be perceived by employees both positively and negatively. A sincere desire to help and support and the great experience and professionalism allow the 7.1+ leader to act as a reference figure for those employees who agree with a given role. Reluctance to assume such a role entails conflicts and the loss of referent influence.

5.6   Cooperation Skills of the 7.1+ Style

Conflict Resolution

For the 7.1+ leader the world is a respectable family with traditions, which lives happily without inner conflicts and serious contradictions. Conflict threatens the 7.1+ leader's authority and the ability to achieve good results, so the representative of this style tends to overcome the conflict by force, unilaterally deciding and explaining the destructiveness of conflict situations for all. The 7.1+ perceives conflict as a misunderstanding: the staff just does not fully understand what is right and how to behave.

He believes that conflict is a sign of weakness for the organization, himself, and others. Good staff, according to the paternalist, quickly realizes that by following his instructions, imitating him, and feeling a deep sense of gratitude, they choose an optimal strategy. That is the only way they can ensure the success of the organization. If they resist, argue, express criticism and doubts, it is regarded as childish, immature behaviour which will only harm everyone. The 7.1+ leader considers conflict inadmissible, since it violates the harmony of the patriarchal culture. The 7.1+ leader's response is to bring the situation under his control and to resolve the conflict on the basis of his vision and status.

The 7.1+ leader considers himself responsible for reducing all contradictions among team members. He encourages employees to be loyal, and he is ready to punish or reward them in order to provide common cooperation and mutual support. The 7.1+ leader resolutely blocks any objections and doubts concerning his instructions.

Settling conflicts is based on the 7.1+ leader's authority and a system of rewards and punishments that helps to control the behaviour of employees. The paternalist presents himself as a paragon and feels entitled to lead people where they, in his opinion, should be. Praise, privileges, and rewards are used to establish the order, and the members of the team soon realize that they have no other way but to support the paternalist. This usually leads to the fact that the team creates an atmosphere of insincerity towards the paternalist. They pretend they express support to the paternalist and approve of his actions, even though they often internally do not agree with him. It gives him a false sense of confidence that all he's doing is right. The paternalist's ego is even stronger without proper feedback, because no one wants to express his disagreement to the paternalist and thereby provoke a conflict with him.

When conflict arises, the paternalist tries hard not to lose his authority, not to distort his image of "a respected leader". Since the 7.1+ leader does not like to get involved in conflicts that could cast doubt on his authority, the first attempts to solve the problem, as a rule, are mild: comments made in a polite manner and expression of disapproval. This technique often works, because employees understand their boss's mood well and know what is coming next. Therefore, they are often commenting on his mood and plan behind his back: "Today, stay away from him, he is in a bad mood" or "He's in a good mood today. Try to approach him with your suggestion, surely he will approve it."

If the mild disapproval of a conflict does not work, the 7.1+ leader begins to act more decisively. There may be open remarks or covert disapproving comments made during a general meeting. The paternalist does not like to make disapproving comments, because it violates his model of organization as a tight-knit patriarchal family. Therefore, he sincerely expresses his concern and regret about the conflict and "terrible problems", hoping to make employees regret what happened, as well as realize all misconducts and mistakes.

If this fails to extinguish the conflict, the 7.1+ leader adopts more stringent measures to punish the "perpetrators". The punishment is usually expressed in the stigma attached to those who cannot calm down and stop the conflict, so perpetrators become deprived of the paternalist benevolence. If the conflict assumes the stage, the 7.1+ leader is forced to use the last argument and publicly punish the culprit. The paternalist is unlikely to quickly forgive, holding a deep grudge. The culprit of the conflict will have to work hard to restore the former boss's attitude.

If the 7.1+ leader comes across conflict between his subordinates, he willingly serves as an arbitrator, figuring out the position of the opposing sides and urging them to peace based on compromise. He uses every opportunity to explain and convince the staff of the inadmissibility of the conflict and possible harm for both the organization as a whole and for each of the conflicting parties.

Communicative Competence

The high concern for production and low concern for people makes the 7.1+ style use one-way, top-down communication, which does not imply dialogue and feed-back. However, the high focus on a common cause, ideals and values of the corporate culture make the 7.1+ leader's communication with employees more efficient, compared to the 7.1−: the paternalistic model of a family organization to a greater extent expresses the interests and values of the majority of employees than the authoritarian model. The commonality of values and care for the common cause is partly compensated for the one-sided communication. However, the lack of feedback makes it impossible for an adjustment of the 7.1+ leader's own behaviour and leaves the information from employees, which is necessary for achieving good results, on the periphery of attention.

Communication, according to the 7.1+ style, performs two important functions:

1. Setting and achieving the goal.
2. Strengthening the paternalistic structure ("parent–child") which, as the 7.1+ leader believes, is the only proper one.

The first function is to provide a clear statement of goals and objectives, coordinating interaction, management, and control; the second is to convince employees that only the willingness to follow the instructions, deep respect, and confidence in the boss's words and actions can ensure the success of the organization as a whole and of each employee individually.

The 7.1+ style tends to implement these functions successfully and therefore genuinely believes that he has an extremely high communicative competence: he can always appropriately and clearly formulate a goal and convince others that this goal is the right one. Perceiving others as immature and dependent, the 7.1+ leader implicitly scorns their opinions and feelings; he believes that their ability and professionalism can be displayed only thanks to his support.

The 7.1+ style needs information from other people in order to achieve good results and, at the same time, strengthen and consolidate his position. He encourages and supports the search for such information and avoids discussion of issues that are not related to the results, or may threaten his authority. The paternalist tries to influence those whose opinion differs from his viewpoint and will do his best to convince them to discard their views and share his opinions.

The 7.1+ leader usually does not seek an intensive informational exchange and does not consider it necessary to clarify the situation in its wholeness. He takes a keen interest in the results of the work and people, but his questions are not objective and thorough, thus they do not contribute to the common development (synergies). The 7.1+ leader is so confident on his experience and knowledge that he does not attach great importance to the opinion of others. People around the paternalist answer what he wants to hear, rather than what really must be said for the good of the cause. As a result, the interaction and communication set by the 7.1+ leader are effective only as far as resources (R) are concerned. Moreover, those are the resources that the paternalist personally brought in, while the opinion of others on any subject was never taken into account.

The communication pattern set by the 7.1+ leader suppresses the independence and creativity of other people. The goal of communication is the desire to make sure that people who "help" clearly understand what they need to do. The paternalist asks questions very thoroughly and often in a patronizing tone. They are designed to make sure once again that one understands what the paternalist wants of him: "Now repeat what I just said, and let's make sure we understand it identically" or "Let's dwell on it again".

After hearing an interesting idea, the 7.1+ leader, as usual, does not pay attention, but still takes notes in his notebook, or simply remembers it. Subsequently, he can come back to this suggestion, realizing that it corresponds to his own thoughts. The 7.1+ leader will sincerely claim his right-authorship of the idea: he cannot admit that someone is smarter, more creative, or more informed than he is. An employee-"child" offering valuable insights, according to the 7.1+ leader, is simply an imbroglio.

Questions are formulated specifically in order to make sure that everyone understands everything properly. Other ideas and opinions are allowed, but they are treated as leading to the same conclusions and ideas that have been suggested by the leader. The 7.1+ leader, ultimately, makes all decisions alone. Employees and colleagues are involved in the discussion of solutions only to better understand important aspects associated with the decision. The 7.1+ leader tries to formulate a solution in such a way that everyone who is associated with the task accepts it without further discussion, and rushes to implement it.

The paternalist's search for information is one-sided. He does not it like when someone asks him questions or expresses doubts about his ideas and initiatives. The 7.1+ leader often unloads an excessive number of questions about team members' work. However, these issues sound more like guidance and instructions. Therefore, the typical response is: "How am I supposed to do this?" or "Could you explain that one more time?"

This approach to communication reduces the level of mutual trust and respect among people. People feel cautious and indecisive, or stand in hidden opposition to their leader.

Active Positioning

The 7.1+ leader will present his ideas and views with confidence, assertiveness, and authority, expecting others to join him. He strongly defends his views and, if someone has any doubts, stresses that his position is primarily based on the common interests and aims for the employees' own benefit.

The 7.1+ style listens to the views of others, but discussions are allowed only if these views coincide at least partially with what has already been suggested by the leader. Deviations from the original idea are rare. If better alternatives are found, they are thoroughly cross-checked and taken reluctantly, and only in exceptional cases.

The 7.1+ leader immediately begins to defend his point of view and makes it with conviction. Since the paternalist feels superior to other team members, he defends his opinions and actions with confidence and power. Even if he hears the opposite point of view, he still does not see any need to seriously understand it. On the contrary, he is quite sure that his opinion only provides the desired results for the whole team. The need of being worshiped makes the paternalist constantly wait for praise and admiration from others.

Initiatives are expressed in a didactic tone, reminiscent of the parent–child relationship, "You should...", "They need to...", "We have to..." It is expected that employees should be happy to accept the 7.1+ leader's word, preferably with admiration. Moreover, the paternalist tries to make sure that employees understand his statement, emphasizing the main points: "This is very important" or "What I am about to say is very important". The paternalist can repeat this to make sure that everyone has heard him: "Do you understand what I mean?" or "Is it clear?"

When articulating his ideas, the 7.1+ leader imposes them and suppresses the initiatives of others, but this is usually done in a careful manner that does not offend or alienate other staff members, as in the case of the 7.1− leader's taking initiative. The paternalist is based on his authority and enthusiasm: "I have already reflected on this issue, and I have a plan." When the work begins, he constantly monitors the process of implementing his ideas, offering his leadership and assistance.

An important drawback of this leadership style is the dependence boosted by mentoring and active "parent" position. Team members can discuss suggestions and offer alternatives, but the paternalist has his clear vision of how things should be done, and he rarely allows making any changes. The 7.1+ leader is so sincere, convincing, and pleasant that others start to fall within his charm. Months pass before a person who had a reasonable idea realizes that the paternalist easily convinced him; and this person sadly thinks: "Well, why wasn't I able to defend my position? After all, we would have been able to achieve significantly better results!"

Employees sometimes find ways to "bypass" the 7.1+ leader's hyper-initiative, using tricks that allow the paternalist to attribute other people's ideas to himself, and thus to realize them. But such attempts are usually a waste of time and effort and, besides, you have to find people who will voluntarily pass their merits to others.

The depreciation of the active position and the dependence that the 7.1+ style brings out in others often lead to serious problems in emergency situations. Believing that team members are not able to make the right decisions in extreme conditions, the 7.1+ leader always asks to immediately inform him of what happened, so he can give guidance. At the same time, employees are patiently waiting for his solutions without taking any actions. If the paternalist is not there and cannot be reached, all work stops, because no one wants to take responsibility (as it is possible to fall from grace).

Even if the 7.1+ leader expresses valuable initiatives using his extensive experience and knowledge, ultimately his approach has a negative impact on others. People do not feel the need to exercise their activity and defend their position, feeling that their actions are always manipulated by the leader. For those who agree to be under strict control and assume the role of the immature, dependent employee, there is little chance for professional growth and work on oneself. And those who want to have more freedom and responsibility will inevitably find themselves in opposition to paternalism, thus reducing or stopping their effectiveness in professional and personal development.

Decision-Making

Decision-making is one-sided and single-handed. The 7.1+ leader sincerely believes that his option is the best. However, in contrast to the 7.1− style, the paternalist is not straightforward, categorical, and unequivocal. The 7.1+ leader asks others their opinions, discusses alternative views, listens carefully to everything, but in fact the decision has already been taken.

He has been discussing other suggestions only to demonstrate the correctness of his own decision, to feel the admiration and gratitude of employees, rather than to make an objective assessment of the strengths and weaknesses of the proposed solutions. Therefore, summing up the discussion, the 7.1+ leader says: "Thank you for your suggestions, but I think we should do the following (and explains his decision). I hope you all agree?"

During the discussion, the paternalist first of all asks those who are likely to have the same viewpoint. Those who are likely to question the decision or even reject it will be perceived negatively, their words will be ignored or even discredited. This approach enables the paternalist to feel satisfaction, as the decision looks like a collective one. In fact, the paternalist asks others only to find their support.

The 7.1+ style leader takes to decision-making with great responsibility; he carefully analyses the problem and performs the thorough analytical work necessary to identify all possible alternatives. However, the inadequate and dismissive attitude to the ideas of his subordinates does not allow to take into account all the important facts and factors that reduce the quality of decisions. This subsequently impacts on the effectiveness of joint activities.

In spite of the discussions held, those who are supposed to implement the decision do not really take part in its elaboration and do not feel involved in the work. Therefore, their motivation decreases, their helpful information is lost.

The paternalist is proud of having taken a firm and final decision; he considers such determination proper and helpful: "I have great experience, I have something to offer, and I want only the best for all the staff." Making decisions for others makes the paternalist feel comfortable and confident: "Our family is alright!"

Constructive Critique

The 7.1+ style leader's criticism is always one-sided and patronizing, while it is often presented in a rather soft, polite manner. The paternalist believes that he is doing a good job, giving instructions, advice, and guidance, and expects gratitude in return. He believes that by criticizing others, he does them only well, even if remarks are unpleasant. However, criticism of the paternalist is not allowed. Employees who stand on the lower level of the organizational hierarchy are not allowed to express their evaluation, and their observations are usually rejected or not taken into account. Such restrictions allow employees to articulate only two "critical" comments: they can say to the paternalist that "everything is alright" or "everything is just great".

The paternalist himself is extremely sensitive to criticism of any kind, and he has a defensive reaction even on a mild remark or suggestion. Even if the criticism is valid, the 7.1+ leader resists it. Then he pounces on the "prosecutor" to punish or discredit him. All this makes the paternalist a dangerous and destructive force in the group, especially if he is the leader of the team, because people are afraid to come into conflict with the authorities.

A form of criticism of the 7.1+, which is largely due to his deep identification with the values and goals of the organization, is the desire to instil a sense of guilt: "I warned you." Sincerely worrying about the success of the organization and considering that he makes a decisive contribution to its results, the paternalist is convinced that people who disagree with him are to blame for the failure or lack of effectiveness of the organization.

This kind of criticism is the reverse of the medal, which has as its face a categorical statement, "You have to do this". The 7.1+ leader radically suppresses other opinions when he believes that only his personal involvement can ensure a successful outcome. He is always willing to point to the mistakes at others and, moreover, attribute the mistake to the breach of his instruction. When this happens, the paternalist certainly uses this opportunity to convince employees to learn instructions by heart: "Maybe next time you'll listen to me and you won't make the same mistake again." Statements like "I told you that" initially do not admit the idea that the paternalist can share others' responsibility for the mistakes.

Just like other manifestations of the paternalistic style, criticism is based on the need for recognition and admiration from others. The 7.1+ leader wants to be admired as a strong and capable leader, and if he is supported and admired, he can be really strong and fearless in overcoming any problems. He feels responsible for his faithful followers, and is doing everything to help them; he will take on additional work, will work to exhaustion, sacrificing something personal.

If the paternalist, instead of support and admiration, hears at least the slightest bit of criticism, his faith in himself quickly extinguishes. Without recognition and support, the 7.1+ leader becomes vulnerable and helpless. His confidence hides an unprotected person, who expects too much from both himself and others. He needs to create an image of superiority, but in doing so he sets high and sometimes unrealistic demands. He should always make his own decisions, to exceed all expectations and achieve high results.

The paternalist lacks one of the most important components necessary for successful and constructive criticism: the recognition of equal partnership. If he admits the possibility of two-sided criticism, he will have to act with other team members on an equal basis, which in itself is fundamentally unacceptable to the patriarchal worldview.

5.7 Conclusions

As a rule, the 7.1+ style leader is a gifted and even talented individual. However, he demands too much from himself and at the same time has difficulty in taking help from others, because he is afraid to show weakness. The 7.1+ style demands devotion and loyalty of his colleagues: "You are with me or against me." As a result, he either completely controls others, or is in absolute subjection to another. Paternalists appear proud or with a sense of superiority over others, or helpless and dependent on others, which in turn prevents them from experiencing faith in people, respect and satisfaction from joint ventures.

The 7.1+ leader wants to be the best for himself and for everyone else. Of course, to meet such high demands is totally unrealistic; as a consequence, the paternalist has to balance constantly between success and complete failure. In today's organizations, when the success of the whole team should be much greater than the sum of the efforts of individual members, the paternalist is doomed. He cannot afford to go down to the level of the rest of the team and sets the distance between himself and other team members, instead of joining the team in order to fully experience all the benefits of teamwork and synergy.

Style 1.7−: Adulator (Compliant and Agreeable)

6

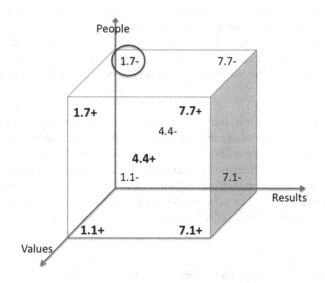

Low concern for production, high concern for people, indifference towards work and organization, eager to please everyone and enjoy positive attitude. Desire to get along with people at any cost, according to the circumstances. Escape from conflicts and arguments, lack of sincerity, being an adulator and pleaser for one's own personal purposes, which are not always realized by the 1.7− person.

6.1 Basic Features of the 1.7− Style

A 1.7− person is sure that the entire world is a stage, and all the men and women merely players. That is why you would better not trust people. The safest way of life is to wear a flatterer's mask and stay in a well-protected capsule, not letting anyone

© Springer-Verlag Berlin Heidelberg 2016
A. Zankovsky, C. von der Heiden, *Leadership with Synercube*,
DOI 10.1007/978-3-662-49052-5_6

in. In the 1.7–'s opinion, all people are vainglorious by nature, and one can rely on flattery in order not to worry too much about minor matters. Being ready to win somebody's favour is not equal to being ready to provide real support and cooperation. Such behaviour is mainly aimed at manipulation. Fear of being involved paves the way for nervousness, tension, and alarm masked with a smile. The 1.7– style is highly aimed at people, not at results. A 1.7– person is good at detecting other people's emotions, their personal goals and aspirations, and he knows the way this or that decision affects anyone. Internally, the 1.7– is quite far from real problems and organizational issues, thus he has great scope for manipulation. The 1.7– is good at telling jokes, is polite, and can always listen to anyone, expressing signs of care and sympathy, which are assumed as facts. The low priority of results highlights the 1.7–'s indifference towards the goals of an organization and its work in general. Consequently, the relations of such a person are insincere and superficial. Thus, it is impossible to achieve any significant results. Such people are bad at raising efficiency amid tough competition.

For the same reasons, the 1.7– can set up reliable and productive relations with neither their subordinates nor his colleagues. What they can set up looks prospective at the beginning, but soon everything gets worse and productivity inevitably goes down.

The key phrase of the 1.7– is: "What can I do for you? Please, tell me what you think about it." Nevertheless, the 1.7– is not able to avoid problems. But instead of concentrating on their grounds and solutions, he pays all attention to emotions and preferences of the people around him. Work is substituted with discussions, no matter the way they go. If anyone gets angry, the 1.7– tries to calm them down and displays sympathy and applause in all ways possible. If someone is satisfied, the 1.7– is pleased as well. The 1.7– quickly evaluates the mood of all those present and responds to any shifts by encouragement, support, and praise.

6.2   The 1.7– Style in Collective Cooperation

Here are some examples of typical 1.7– behaviour in an organization, when a colleague does not cope with his job.

First of all, the 1.7– does his best to avoid conflict. As soon as a conflict arises, the 1.7– shifts it into the interpersonal field. The discussion concentrates on minimizing tension instead of settling the most important matters. The 1.7– believes that to motivate everyone to take part in solving the problem, it is enough to talk personally with every member of the team. Meanwhile, the fact of not taking part is never pronounced by the 1.7– straight away. The 1.7– hopes that slight hints are good enough to make one understand. Even in case some problem arises again and again, the 1.7– will not conflict. If the team is not satisfied, he can take up some extra duties in order to reduce tension. If conflict becomes inevitable, the 1.7– prefers to abdicate and pass authority to someone else, or limits rescue measures to the most superficial ones, which cannot change anything.

Reaction to constructive criticism from a colleague:

The 1.7− immediately starts to apologize self-critically for his mistake: "I regret so much having let you down. How could I let such nonsense happen?" One should not expect any further counter-evidence or objection. Then, the 1.7− asks for advice, he is glad to receive it and goes on encouraging others to look for the best way of overcoming the difficulties.

A team build-up of 1.7− people is the perfect place to have a good time, but it does not wholly realize its potentiality. Its members do not believe that cooperation can be a good means of calming down a conflict, and they try to support a comfortable and pleasing atmosphere. They want everyone to be happy, and every discussion is devoted to each other's moods. Opinion differences are ignored, disagreements are handled with the help of positive declarations, and any agreement is to be celebrated. The motto of the 1.7− style is "If you cannot say something nice, say nothing". Such an approach might seem productive at a short distance, but it is useless in the long term. The only real and profound personal motivation is the possibility to cope with a conflict and to get over troubles. This is the only thing that makes people unite and trust each other, sincerity and open behaviour are better for improving relations than plain mutual praise.

In a team of 1.7− people attention is largely paid to the relations between colleagues. Consequently, the atmosphere of such a team lacks exactness of facts, lacks accuracy, common sense, and business-like grip. Such a team is not capable of acting adequately in the face of unsteady circumstances, or discovering problems and resolving them, because they are afraid of probable quarrels, arguments, and so on. Praising each other over and over again makes the members of such a team too self-assured, but the production of their work is not so good in fact. While non-productive activity is not evaluated properly or is ignored at all, the team can do nothing but reproduce wrong behaviour patterns and make all the same mistakes again and again. It goes on till the situation gets worse.

Another significant feature of relations in a 1.7− team is excessive kindliness. The team achieves the state of universal prosperity, when only words of applause are pronounced and heard. Any result is welcome. No one is interested in the accurate evaluation of its quality and in reaching important conclusions. Instead, the team wholly devotes itself to displays of mutual support and approval, even though the activity has been incorrect and the production has not met expectations. As soon as anyone pays attention to low productivity, he is accused of trying to destroy the team, of insulting people. Such efforts are usually ignored, but sometimes the "fault-finder" is somehow isolated from the others. Despite self-righteousness and excessive kindliness, sooner or later there come signs of depression, as no one is asked about important things and no one is motivated well enough.

6.3   The I-ZONE and the 1.7– Style

The 1.7– style creates relations that are warm and friendly, but largely superficial. Such relations are very much different from "strong" cooperation based on mutual trust, respect, and sincerity. Colleagues can work together for years and communicate every day, but they often do not become friends as the level of trust and mutual respect remains low.

A 1.7– person constantly generates praise. Even if an idea sounds at all incredible or seems absolutely wrong, he will not cancel it. His motto is "Anyway, something pleasant has to be said". Relations always turn out to be more important, and they are supported at the level of friendship and are aimed at making everyone happy. In such conditions a conflict is unwanted and seems to be something insuperable, as everyone is afraid to lose the atmosphere of kindness and friendliness. The team tries to smooth over all the controversies. They calm down those who argue and tell them arguing is no good. The stronger the personal relations, the less people want to face challenges (Fig. 6.1).

They think: "I am not going to spoil our wonderful friendship; I don't want to be offensive."

His failing to analyse non-productive behaviour and newly arisen problems leads to a decrease in production (O). The most important resources turn unclaimed, as the team does not take various opinions into account and does not analyse the whole range of scenarios. Thus, such a team never gains the necessary experience of facing challenges, which is really the best motivation in conditions of a serious job. Neither will such a team make correct decisions and synergism efforts. Instead, the 1.7– team will cooperate as if they were inside a glass house which can collapse after any wrong movement.

6.4   1.7– Culture and Values

Basic Feature: Being Complaisant and Indifferent

Trust A 1.7– person likes to say he wholly trusts his colleagues and that trust plays the most important role in the relationship between people. However, this

Fig. 6.1 1.7–

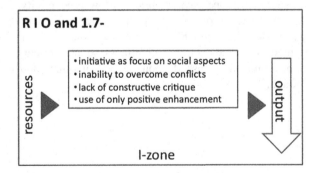

is no more than words. In fact, this style rejects trust as a value and as a principle. He thinks that people are by nature vainglorious and that one can easily live a fine life with the help of servility and flattery. One should not trust others and the safest way of life is to wear a mask of a smooth-tongued and obsequious person and to stay in a well-protected capsule where no one can enter. The open eagerness to please someone does not envisage genuine cooperation and support. It is largely aimed at manipulation. Fear of being involved leads to tension, nervousness, and alarm which is covered with a smile. The 1.7– harbours hope that a task can be completed by itself or by some colleagues, or that no one really wants it done.

Fairness The 1.7– style is convinced that fairness and justice have to do only with personal contacts and links and are not associated with the colleagues' duties in the organization. That is why the 1.7– considers it fair to stimulate activity and behaviour that help to complete organizational tasks and support a calm and comfortable atmosphere. Definitely production at least is not the top priority. Real team duties are pushed out to the area of secondary issues. They can be returned to the top only after some pressure from the front office. Quite often such pressure and control is viewed as unfair and undeserved. Besides, any step aimed at creating comfortable conditions and any prevention of actual involvement into the fulfilment of the organization's schedules are consciously or unconsciously seen as fair and well-grounded.

Commitment 1.7– people display devotion to their team, but in fact they are totally indifferent to its troubles and to organizational issues in general. They stay inside only because they are afraid of long-term unemployment. The 1.7– thinks that committing and identifying with an organization is a mask which everyone puts on in order to do his own business. In a few words, the 1.7– identifies not with the organizational business but with the atmosphere of comfort which is so attractive. Thus, devotion and identity in the end turn out to be imaginary and do not touch the genuine motives and incentives of doing this or that.

Responsibility The 1.7– style is usually unreliable in all situations, as he works only due to pure necessity and is not aimed at true high-quality production. Their reliability improves a little when something really threatens their well-being. The social responsibility of the 1.7– is purely declarative: attention is mostly concentrated on the positive image which is created to impress first of all higher executives. The 1.7– is inwardly indifferent to the philosophy of social responsi-bility, which requires some cooperation and participation from the team in facing social challenges. From the 1.7–'s point of view those challenges do not touch him. Social responsibility issues are taken into account only when he has to somehow meet the demands of higher executives.

Integrity Being open and transparent is viewed by the 1.7– as following the masquerade etiquette. The masks of polite and nice people should be accepted as real faces and are to never be taken off. The 1.7– thinks that this condition makes cooperation easier. Any other information, including the information about the job, is considered dangerous and even harmful. That is why the 1.7– style considers it irrelevant to discuss the arising problems, to share truthful news, to hold honest discussions about mistakes, and to acknowledge the mistakes. The general picture of organizational activity, its sense, development, and outcome are totally unclear to the colleagues, which leads to a lack of enthusiasm, anxiety, and distrust.

6.5   1.7– Culture and Power

Focus on Encouragement and Information Power

Punishment The 1.7– style hardly ever resorts to punishment as a means of influencing and shifting the employees' behaviour. As the 1.7– does not care for results, punishment has no substantial ground. If ever carried out, it assumes the gentlest forms and has largely defensive functions: to protect oneself from probable involvement and further problems. Employees consider a punishment from the 1.7– so unlikely that they even venture to tell jokes about it.

Reward The 1.7– style looks at rewards as the main means of influence, but they do not associate rewards with achieved results. They depart from the belief that people are by nature insincere, vainglorious, and conceal their true intentions. Thus the 1.7– is sure that the main purpose of encouragement is building warm and mild relations which allow working without too much effort, in the most habitual form. Encouragement and incentives exist and are accepted as a wholly deserved and natural form of organizational interaction, certainly not associated with achieved results.

Position Status and position in an organization are not very important for the 1.7– and come from the formal distribution of duties. This distribution is often unclear and badly substantiated. When trying to overcome the employees' reluctance, when trying to have things done and instructions implemented, the 1.7– style rarely puts a stress upon his official powers because he rarely gives any instructions. Career ambitions of the 1.7– are very moderate, and by all means the 1.7– tries to highlight that the relations in the team are based on equity and closeness. Besides, the 1.7– likes to talk about organizational democracy, when anyone does his work on his own, without any "petty" control. Consequently, anyone is content, no matter whether achievements are good or bad. An exceptional case is a situation in which the 1.7– faces categorical demands of higher officials, which have to be fulfilled within a certain time. But even in this case, the 1.7– can only say "I am your boss, I am responsible for everything. Let's do something to stop being criticized all the time".

Information The informational exchange of the 1.7− comes, first of all, for building a comfortable and quiet environment. Disturbing information of any kind is excluded from communication. The content of communication and its volume do not have very much to do with the essence of the organizational activity and set targets. Meeting minimal demands is enough. Being concentrated on creating a positive environment, the 1.7− reacts negatively to the questions which envisage disturbing responses and compromise harmony. That is why information is gathered very superficially and only in the case one can do nothing but to do it. Furthermore, the 1.7− prefers to keep really important organizational data and not to transmit it to anyone, and/or leaves it without consideration when there is no control from a higher chief and no personal responsibility.

Expert The professional competence of the 1.7− style is either quite high (sometimes too high) or rather low. In the former case, because of the low motivation and indifference to the team goals, the 1.7− cannot make even partial use of his expertise. In the latter case, being indifferent to any definite result becomes a form of psychological defence and serves to conceal incompetence, confusion, and fear from others. In both cases expertise is used not for the job but is aimed at creating a quiet and positive environment. The 1.7− style is certainly not inclined to teach others or share skills and knowledge.

Referent The 1.7− style rarely has any charismatic qualities. Under complicated or tough circumstances, when it is necessary to take responsibility and lead people and encourage them, the 1.7− looks common and undistinguished among other employees. The lack of real involvement into facing organizational challenges does not let the 1.7− be a genuine leader in getting over hardship. At social events, e.g. at corporative parties, the 1.7− behaves differently: he shines with positive energy and inspires everyone to solve organizational, financial, or any other problems. The internal indifference to the organizational objectives and the unwillingness to solve problems essentially do not let the 1.7− act as a model and as an example for other staff members.

6.6   Cooperation Skills of the 1.7− Style

Conflict Resolution

The 1.7− style does his best to avoid everything that might cause disagreement and conflicts, as any conflict threatens the peaceful and mild atmosphere of the team/ organization. If a conflict takes place, the 1.7− tries to distract attention from it. He tries to calm people down, to encourage and please them, or assumes all responsibility for the conflict. The 1.7— tends to hide the conflict under the carpet and let the employees feel safe, allowing them to avoid responsibility for their mistakes and their job. At the same time, he tries to look confident and pretends nothing has happened.

It is more typical for the 1.7— to smooth over a conflict than to resolve it. He avoids conflicts, calling for mutual agreement and mutual aid, and very rarely expresses disagreement. He looks after the others' moods very carefully and provides emotional support if needed. Even when the 1.7— disagrees, he can accept another opinion in order to preserve the harmony of relations. He rarely investigates the roots of conflicts and hardly ever evaluates them on the basis of facts or analysis. Instead, he reassures the arguing sides and considers it sufficient.

If there is no hope to avoid a conflict, the 1.7— first of all tries to calm down the quarrelling colleagues. Here he is very creative and convincing: he calls to look at the positive aspects of the situation and to stop quarrelling. He tries to shift everything to the circumstances and to understate the scale of the problem: "It was so hard for him", "I know he did not mean it." He tries to attract attention to less controversial questions, assuming a joking tone: "Well, someone is too serious here, eh?" Another approach is calling to tolerance: "It is not easy to survive in today's situation, so let's help each other" or "We can yield to each other in this matter, can't we?" Besides that, the 1.7— can make the colleagues ashamed of the conflict and then propose them to make peace in order to restore the atmosphere of friendship.

If the attempts to smooth over the controversies fail, the 1.7— keeps away from the conflict, declining responsibility: "I have nothing to do with it" or "It was not for me to decide". The 1.7— style looks at a conflict as an unambiguous threat to good relations.

According to the 1.7—, interaction cannot be improved through resolving a conflict. Even when the 1.7— knows about the conflict, he prefers to keep temporary and shaky peace rather than to reveal the conflict and resolve it. The dominating approach is: "We can deal with it later" or "All we need is to calm down, isn't it?"

Another type of behaviour for this style's is well described by the proverb "I see nothing, I hear nothing, and hence I say nothing". This way, ineffective behaviour and problems are concealed or ignored and never become an issue to discuss. The fact that later on he will be so reluctant to any analysis of the problem leads to even worse consequences.

Conflict resolution by the 1.7— is considered difficult for one more reason. There are no preannounced criteria for evaluating the team's activity. Everyone prefers to start working inspired by bare enthusiasm. They believe that planning anything in advance and having clear criteria diminish the employees' motivation. "If people are gifted and work with enthusiasm, the rest comes by itself a bit later." As long as there are no criteria, any criticism seems to be someone's arbitrary opinion. In fact, criticism should correlate real behaviour with some ideal criterion. That is why it is hard to evaluate the team's productivity: there are no standards to stick to, there is nothing to depart from when shifting behaviour patterns and improving them. In response to criticism or a remark, an employee who is bad at his duties can just say: "Is there any document saying what I shall do?"

Communicative Competence

The communicative competence of the 1.7– is fairly good. It allows him to establish and support relations that look good. He tends to be benevolent, he asks many questions, he is friendly and hospitable. He cares about every employee and is aimed at establishing harmonic personal relations with them. Such a person displays a subtle understanding of people and their needs. This allows the 1.7– to look profoundly into the behaviour of other people and to predict their reactions to these or those circumstances. However, the genuine motives of using the 1.7–'s communicative skills and informational exchange are far from improvement of organizational efficiency and from gaining best results. The main purpose of the 1.7– in searching for information is not to evaluate whether the job is done well or not, but to make sure that the current mood of the team is still harmonic and there is still place for mutual approval. The 1.7– relies on information to get an answer to the main question: "What is your attitude towards me?" He does not care so much about the question "What shall we do to cope with the task in the most optimal way?" That is why the questions asked by a 1.7– person, despite expressing approval, understanding, and sympathy, have to do with things that have only a distant relation to the team's activity. The 1.7– style spends much time on talking with people about their wishes, thoughts, and feelings and does not contribute to the improvement of their professional qualities. Furthermore, he obstructs their professional activity because he distracts their attention from its purposes.

A 1.7– person relies on his communicative competence in order to find out which measures will be accepted and which ones repelled. He puts forth an initiative only after this and according to this. The 1.7– prefers to get information indirectly. He wants to sound neither persistent nor reproaching. If someone makes a mistake in the project, the 1.7– does not carry out a straight investigation. At first he finds out how the guilty person feels, as the reaction should be a display of support and encouragement: "I hear there has been a problem today?" Such approach allows the 1.7– to conduct the further discussion on his own. At best, the one to blame admits his mistake. In this case, the 1.7– can deal without any negative words at all and can try to restore a comfortable atmosphere at once: "I'm sure things are not so bad. Only those, who do nothing make no mistakes. We all work a lot, so this is a minor inaccuracy."

This indirect way of getting information requires a lot of time as you have to wait until people start to tell you everything. They may not even know what to tell you, and then the 1.7– learns nothing or gets distorted data. Besides, such approach envisages a revelation of thoughts and emotions of other people instead of facts and arguments. As long as the situation is not absolutely urgent, the 1.7– can stay calm and complacent. He says: "We are a little upset by the results of our efforts, but in spite of that we are full of optimism and we hope for the best" or "I don't think there is something to worry about. We have no more controversies."

Active Positioning

The 1.7— actively defends only the opinions that hardly can be opposed by anyone. If it does not compromise friendly relations and influences the team well, he defends his opinion quite openly and earnestly. As soon as the 1.7— foresees discrepancies, he gives up his point of view and tries to smooth the arisen controversies, shifting to another topic. Where discussion and collision of different opinions are inevitable, where one has to take sides, the 1.7— lacks motivation, interest, and active position to articulate and defend his point of view. Generally speaking, he does not have a point of view. He does not express ideas that might cause a debate and tries to remain completely neutral.

However, the 1.7— can actively and enthusiastically stand up for his opinion in case it can encourage a friendly atmosphere of the team and diminish tensions in interrelations. He displays sympathy and compassion and carefully traces positive comments concerning himself. He is ready to offer help, but in most cases it does not go further than words.

If the situation includes controversy or leads to a conflict, the 1.7— does not feel like being active in defending his point of view. His enthusiasm can rise only if he feels support, recognition, and encouragement. Such behaviour pattern slows down his progress, as the 1.7— is always busy with the evaluation of the others' emotions in connection with the controversial issue. Another reason for the low efficiency of such an approach is the lack of attention to the criteria and standards for achieving result. Instead of formulating particular notions of what should be done and how, the 1.7— concentrates on individual preferences and emotions. Thus, he cannot organize a circumspect universal effort aimed at a determined result, as each participant relies on his own view of such criteria. The 1.7— does not know the value of the elaboration and use of universally effective criteria.

To keep a positive relationship tone, the 1.7— first asks about other people's opinion before speaking out his own: "What do you think I shall do?", "I would like to know your opinion before I say something", or "I highly appreciate your opinion and I don't want our friendship to be compromised by anything". Such declarations clearly let the others know that the top priorities are peace and harmony.

Even when there is evident support and the 1.7— feels confident, he expresses his opinion very carefully, as he is afraid to look obtrusive. As a result, he looks uncertain and evasive, a person who expresses his point of view like this: "This is a proposal, not more than that…" or "This might sound awkward, but I suppose…". His declarations often include such words as perhaps, probably, on occasion, etc. Such behaviour paves the way for easy retreat in case of a conflict.

The 1.7— is the champion when there are pleasant things to do, e.g. to report a successful breakthrough, to speak about prizes and bonuses, new appointments, or supply increase. He likes to do it and he does it with pride and great inspiration.

The 1.7– style tries not to put forward any initiatives if there is a controversy of interests. In such cases, he prefers to leave initiative to other people and to watch the conflict from some distance. Thus, he can avoid taking steps that could cause discontent or be rejected by other people. The main point of his initiative is to find out what people would like and to propose further steps according to their demands. For him the question "What do people want?" is always more important than "What's better for our business?"—no matter how it affects the final production (O). The 1.7– is ready to sacrifice production O in order to support positive relations.

The 1.7– has a positive and largely passive standpoint. If the front office sets high standards, the 1.7– tries to fulfil them by encouraging and cheering up his colleagues. He mostly ignores the demands and standards which he considers excessive. His logic is to do without overwhelming anyone with unnecessary details. For instance, if there are some corrections to be made, he will not say a word, as he thinks: "What if no one really needs our corrections, then why should we talk about it?" The lack of definite criteria and quality standards leave him without seeing someone's wrong behaviour or unnecessary initiatives. That is why the 1.7– almost does not need constructive criticism. And that is how the illusion of a good job to be praised by the 1.7– appears with pleasure.

Decision-Making

The 1.7– style tries not to make decisions, as he hopes that someone else will take over this duty, or even that there is no need for any decisions. However, he rarely makes decisions without preliminary talks with colleagues, where he can learn what they think about it.

The 1.7– makes decisions highlighting the agreement of other people, who have helped to prepare the decision as well. He postpones unpopular decisions or passes the right to make them to someone else in case such decisions compromise the existing relations.

A 1.7– person takes his time to make a decision as he waits until everyone agrees with him and until the circumstances are good for its implementation. If the circumstances are good enough, the 1.7– substitutes decision-making with lengthy discussions, where too many people take part. He has no clear criteria and no particular order of decision making. As a result, discussions become chaotic and their agenda is rather unstable. For example, a meeting dedicated to a new software can easily turn into a 2-hours' chat about a wide range of questions and there is neither a stable structure nor criteria for the meeting's efficiency. The 1.7– wants to involve as many employees as he can into the discussion, as thus he could rely on the will of the majority when a decision is to be at last made. To arrive at such an agreement he spends a lot of time asking questions. He gets answers and recommendations that are useful for him. It continues till the 1.7– makes sure that he has gained maximum support and that the forthcoming decision will not break the precious positive and friendly atmosphere of the team.

In making decisions the 1.7— is very much dependent on other people. He likes it when the criteria of decision-making are elaborated by the people above him. He does not want to be responsible for the decision and have to deal with its consequences in case it is wrong.

When making decisions, the 1.7— is torn between the wish of demonstrating power and his dependence on others. He wants to make a decision that on the one hand will please the team and his employees, and on the other hand will meet his bosses' demands. But as the request for good personal interrelations is quite high, the decisions are mostly taken in favour of the team, as with the team the 1.7— has closer and more immediate relations.

If the process of making a particular decision has some internal controversy, it slows down or completely stops. As soon as a discussion discovers new problems, the 1.7— looks for alternative solutions that would be acceptable for his colleagues. It inevitably leads to further discussions—usually face to face—aimed at some agreement. The whole process is rather exhausting, and the decision is severely delayed or given up. If there is any chance to find an alternative, the 1.7— can do the following:

- Choose the variant that is acceptable for the team, but is of no use for the result.
- Postpone further decision making and wait until everyone forgets about it.
- Pass the responsibility for the decision and its consequences to another person, washing his hands off it.

Constructive Critique

The 1.7— style avoids proper constructive criticism and adequate mutual communication. He encourages and praises other people when something positive is going on, but he never talks about anything negative. He welcomes positive "criticism" and feels uneasy when he has to say unpleasant words.

The 1.7— turns to positive criticism all the time. Being largely aimed at people, not at the result, makes him pronounce real criticism only in personal conversations. Thus, he is able to trace the emotions of his interlocutor. That is why he prefers to talk confidentially. Being a leader, he declares open-doors policy and displays being ready to talk at any time. Personal problems cannot be minor problems unworthy of a few words. The 1.7— displays compassion and offers his help, but in fact it is rarely more than words. He pays special attention to emotions and feelings of other people and believes it is necessary to support them with his sympathy. Such strategy allows him to ask for other people's help in his own private business, as he always listens to them and takes care of them.

The quality and depth of the 1.7—'s criticism are restricted by the scale of personal emotions, moods, and preferences. Usually there are no concrete criteria of task fulfilment and quality standards. Remarks come to positive words only. If a colleague raises any concerns or looks discontent, the 1.7— person becomes an "encouraging" leader. He encourages others and persuades them to concentrate on the positive aspects of the current situation and inspires them with firm belief that the problem will be overcome. The main slogan is "smile and have patience!" The efforts of such a leader come to levelling various opinions instead of analysing them.

In case such encouraging conduct is of no help, the 1.7– moves away from the problem and tries not to interfere any more. He displays compassion, but avoids any talks that could compromise peace and harmony. Therefore, the 1.7– tries to stay at a distance from the conflict and avoid responsibility for its resolution. Although he listens to the arguing sides, he advises anyone to abstain from potentially problematic actions. The 1.7– ignores the wrong steps of other people as if his motto were "See nothing, hear nothing, say nothing". He avoids any criticism.

Being ready to sound only positive adds up to the aforementioned approach as well. The more problems arise, the more efforts the 1.7– makes in order to inspire other people with self-confidence and to highlight their advantages in other spheres. Disadvantages and inefficacy are ignored, and colleagues are told about their talents, skills, and highly appreciated work all the time. There is no room for negative criticism even if it were right, constructive, and if such attitude would be shared by others, because the 1.7– can cause someone's displeasure. If the mistakes and problems cannot be ignored, criticism comes to encouraging the self-confidence of the guilty person despite his errors: "Although you've been unlucky this time, you are so gifted! If I were you, I would not worry about it." Such superficial attitude to problems deprives people of a chance to realize their weak points and improve them.

A 1.7– person is not helpful when people need support in overcoming their troubles or obstacles. Under difficult circumstances he cannot really raise their fighting spirit and give them self-confidence. The 1.7– lavishes words of praise, he always finds positive nuances even in failure, but he cannot inspire each person to overcome failure and improve after that.

6.7   Conclusions

While the 7.1– immediately tries to convert resources (R) into output (O) ignoring relations, the 1.7– ignores both resources (R) and results (O), concentrating all his attention on himself and his position in the I-ZONE. To put it short, the ideal purpose of the 1.7– style is a calm team life without conflicts and problems. This purpose inevitably interferes with the general aims of the organization. The 1.7– tries to resolve it by building friendly and positive interrelations in the I-ZONE. However, he does not succeed in it. The more efforts are made to establish such interrelations, to save himself and his colleagues from conflicts and controversies, the more disappointment they get in the end. Like spoilt children, they are satiated with constant praise and wait for more and more compliments and enjoy irresponsibility. After some time a team of the 1.7– type loses control over the influence it has on others. They get accustomed to constant applause. Usually it turns into great disappointment when the team has to face the harsh reality.

Style 1.7+: Soft-Hearted Enthusiast (Don't Worry, Everything Will Be Alright)

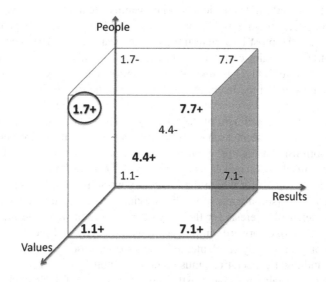

Low concern for production, high concern for people, interest in work and the organization, eagerness to create an atmosphere of friendship, trust, and enthusiasm. Dominance of unreasonable optimism and fantasies over real plans and tasks, pipe dreams. Colleagues are motivated with an accent upon the positive and socially significant aspects of labour.

7.1 Basic Features of the 1.7+ Style

The 1.7+ style has such typical features as compassionate, apologetic, friendly, careful, and cautious. The 1.7+ person, as well as the 1.7−, combines little care for results and attention to people. But the two styles are very different in their cultural

© Springer-Verlag Berlin Heidelberg 2016
A. Zankovsky, C. von der Heiden, *Leadership with Synercube*,
DOI 10.1007/978-3-662-49052-5_7

value orientation. The 1.7− style is indifferent to work, people, and the organization; he does not trust anyone, and his willingness to please anyone and to make a good impression is to a considerable extent a mask and a means to protect himself from being involved in the organization life. For the 1.7+ work, people, and the organization are of great value; he is devoted to the organization, he trusts people, and sincerely believes that everything is going to be alright and that the results will turn out brilliant. He is always positive and wants to contribute to the business of the team, though he does not always understand what practical measures are required. His top priority is friendship, general inspiration, and people's optimism. This priority is so strong that the purposes of the work are driven out to the periphery of his field of vision. He strongly believes that good relationships are sure to lead to great results. He wants everyone to be cheerful, content, and to share his firm belief that everything is being done correctly and will bring good outcome. One must not lose heart and support kind and friendly relationships. He thinks that being aimed at positive emotions, believing in the final success, and forming amicable and trustful relationships are the most important things in an organization. The successfulness of the results (O) for him correlates with the level of satisfaction and inspiration of the colleagues, so the 1.7+ is always full of optimism and busy with establishing positive relationships in the team. In addition to that, he tries to be always present in order to encourage everyone, to share energy, and to offer help and support, if needed, even to the detriment of the whole job. Thus, for a short period of time, the 1.7+ leader might seem a charismatic prophet, who can inspire people with belief and optimism in making great accomplishments. But the lack of practical orientation for results soon makes it clear that the 1.7+ is a soft-hearted optimist and an incorrigible dreamer, for whom the imaginary world is more important than the real one. A 1.7+ person always offers his services, his help, and is even eager to sacrifice his personal interests for the sake of the common weal: the organization must thrive and move forward, employees must be happy and pleased. But these righteous words are rarely implemented, because purposes are not achieved by themselves and great expectations thus come to nothing.

The 1.7+ is invariably positive, trustful, cultured, and careful. He tends to look at everything positively, his optimism often has no grounds, and he is eager to act in favour of the organization and his colleagues. All these features make the 1.7+ a nice person to communicate and to deal with, but on the other hand he is rather susceptible to manipulations, as in his inspiration and trustfulness he is not always able to interpret other people's real intentions.

The 1.7+ is a wholly positive type, but his Achilles heel is the lack of focus on results. He realizes the importance of achieving results and calls on others to strive for significant fulfilments, but his attention is all the time shifted to people and to keeping up an amicable and enthusiastic atmosphere. That is why tasks and efficiency become inferior. That is why real plans and duties largely remain dreams and hollow hopes instead of being subject of practical, purposeful work. The good sincere intentions of the 1.7+ too often remain castles in the air, and his inspiration turns into idle scheming. The 1.7+ has high organizational loyalty, he is capable of establishing good relationships, of interpreting emotions and intentions of people, but unfortunately he does not bring as much luck as he could. The lack of focus on results counterbalances the sharp attention to people, and the colleagues are distracted from the purposes of the organization. In the end, relationships are warm and friendly, but rather hollow and of no content. Such relationships are not purposeful and do not help to move the organization forward at all. Thus, there are many teams where good things are articulated all the time and people are full of hopes and enthusiasm, but these teams at the same time are not ready to face difficulties and to raise effectiveness amid tough competition.

7.2   The 1.7+ Style in Collective Cooperation

The 1.7+ style feels a constant fear of being rejected. One of the hardest situations for him is that of inevitable conflict, when he has to bear the critique and irritation of other people. The anger and critique might not be against him, but the 1.7+ suffers sharp anxiety and profound uneasiness anyway. He tries to do his best to restore peace and harmony as soon as he can.

The fear of being rejected most often becomes apparent amid critique and mutual communication. If he has to take part in a conversation about someone's weak points, he fills it with lots of words of regret and groundless optimism. Any form of critique is considered unacceptable if it does not contain clear or latent optimism and support. The same is true for critique concerning other people. The 1.7+ finds it hard to talk straight about someone's weak points and mistakes, so quite often he draws a veil of praise over his remarks and avoids the objective aspects of constructive critique.

For example, the 1.7+ talks about some not quite flawless results with the chief of the project. He can say: "You've worked a lot on the project. Nevertheless, the result turned out not so brilliant as we had expected. But I am sure that we will have many chances to demonstrate what we are capable of!" After such "critique" even the most negligent employee can conclude: "Oh yes, the job I've done is really not so bad!"

Most of all, the 1.7+ is afraid that all the efforts in building a warm and friendly team might be in vain because of his own blunder. That is why when he hears critical remarks, he does not make use of them to improve but starts to complain that he has let someone else down. After that he immediately tries to find some ground for optimism, as he is afraid of sadness. He tries to look at the situation from another angle and to restore the optimism and former relationships. He criticizes himself and takes care of others. In such cases one can hear him say: "I wonder how I could have ignored such an important thing!", "What do I think about it? I should have foreseen everything when I started this business", or "This is wholly my fault". Such declarations are made in order to make others confirm that everything is alright, as for the 1.7+ it is very important to restore his positive mood and to make sure that his colleagues share his optimism.

Problems, weak points, and mistakes are smoothed over and put away without detailed analysis, and the optimistic atmosphere and friendly relationships are immediately restored. The 1.7+ worries so much about making a mistake that he might compromise the organization's brilliant future and good relationships with other people and that as soon as he recovers no one dares to remind him of the inaccuracy or say anything critical at all. It is better not to notice the mistake at all, or to report it in an indirect way, because straight critique is so painful for the 1.7+ that he cannot accept it objectively.

The 1.7+ style knows people well, but generally is too positive in his attitude towards them and towards the organization. That is why he often cannot detect people's genuine intentions, ambitions, and motives. He thinks that they share his own interests and purposes. He is also rather credulous, and all these features may be taken advantage of by more manipulative colleagues. They can pretend to share the values and concerns of the 1.7+, silently doing their own business. If they are careful enough, they can feel safe.

The 1.7+ style does not feel the necessity of succeeding through his own efforts. He does not trust himself enough and tries to pass responsibility to all other people at once, creating good conditions for the lazy ones and hard conditions for the hard-working. The former work too little, as they see a chance not to bear responsibility, and the latter work too much, as they feel responsible for everyone.

As for his own work, the 1.7+ style tries to do it strictly within the planned volume. But he does so not due to his care about future results. First of all, he is afraid to spoil his relationships with the front office. In other words, he does not rely on good relationships in fulfilling tasks but has to achieve such results that allow him to support good relationships.

The 1.7+ rarely generates new creative ideas due to his fear of making a mistake that could damage good relationships. At the same time, the colleagues are verbally encouraged to work productively, as achieving results can guarantee enthusiasm and a nice atmosphere. However, these general instructions and calls hardly ever develop into particular tasks and actions. They remain only words. If there are no aims determined for the work, there is no ambition and no eagerness, no struggle. Goals are set within a moderate and achievable scope, because their fulfilment should be joyful for the leader and his colleagues, believes the 1.7+.

The 1.7+ style gathers information to demonstrate that things are going alright. The 1.7+ relies on mutual support to keep up a peaceful and positive mood even when a discussion takes him to controversial problems and cases. Thus, controversies are smoothed or passed over. The 1.7+ style easily accepts responsibility for his colleagues. He believes that to improve cooperation it is not bad to shift from business communication to closer and friendlier relationships.

Departing from his values, the 1.7+ style is sure that all people are equally kind-hearted and positive. If everything goes well, the 1.7+ encourages his colleagues with a lot of praise. If everything is not so well, his attitude however remains steadily positive and not devoid of some encouragement.

7.3 The I-ZONE and the 1.7+ Style

The 1.7+ style tends to create an atmosphere which is characterized not only by warmth and friendliness, but besides that by a certain degree of trust, respect, and sincerity. On the other hand, such a team is usually not aimed at definite results, and this style lacks synergism which would have appeared in conditions of "strong" and purposeful cooperation.

Colleagues can work together for many years and they can communicate every day and be friends. Nevertheless, they often feel that they lack full mutual trust and respect, as everyone suspects that despite the great potential and overestimated expectations, the real production is again and again rather moderate.

A 1.7+ person is an inexhaustible source of enthusiasm, hope, and belief. Even if the situation turns almost hopeless and some problem looks insuperable, he does not allow himself to be sad. He tries to find something positive and inspiring. His motto is "Everything will settle, everything will be OK if we cheer up and save our relationships". Harmonic relationships, trust, and the firm belief in a happy end are more important than organizational objectives and current tasks. Amid all this, there is often no place for a deliberate analysis of problems, for conflicts and mutual critique, which are replaced by cheerful expectations and weakly grounded optimism. The team tries to smooth over all opinion differences, to calm down those who argue, to convince them that there's no practical need in arguments. The stronger the personal relationships and enthusiasm, the less people want to face practical difficulties. Here the 1.7+ follows the slogan "Why shall we spoil our nice relationships, if everything ends well?"

Excessive and weakly grounded optimism minimizes the ability to analyze inefficient behaviour patterns and arising problems. Thus, it makes the results (O) worse, which in turn spoils the general tone of interrelationships (I). Despite having correct values and being aimed at people, the most important resources (R) remain unclaimed as the team forgets about organizational objectives, ignores controversies and conflicts that inevitably appear, and does not foresee alternative variants of the events' contour (Fig. 7.1).

Consequently, such a team never acquires such necessary experience of achieving definite results and troubleshooting. Without this experience, any activity loses

Fig. 7.1 1.7+

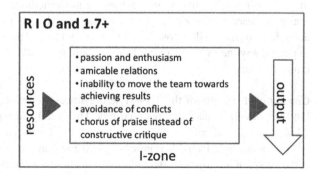

sense and direction. Besides, such a team never learns to make the right decisions and achieve synergism. Instead, 1.7+ people always cooperate as if they lived in a happy world with no problems and discrepancies, where achievements come after hopes and expectations without much effort.

7.4   1.7+ Culture and Values

Culture of Kindness, Optimism, and Pipe Dreams

Trust A 1.7+ person believes that people are decent and trustworthy by nature. Work, people, and company are of great value, he is devoted to his company, he trusts people, and sincerely believes that everything will go very well. The 1.7+ is always positive-minded. In case he comes across dishonesty and trickery, he considers it bad luck and pure trifle. He is naive enough to trust people who have let him down many times. He is eager to contribute to the business of the team, but he does not understand well enough how to contribute. Thus, he passes many key tasks to other people. He sincerely hopes that they know what to do. His top priority is a friendly atmosphere; he is trustful and full of optimism. This style is so dominated by credulousness that he often yields to manipulations. It goes so far that he is ready to excuse manipulations and does not stand up against them at all.

Fairness The 1.7+ style is convinced that such notion as fairness should be viewed only in the context of friendly and trustful relationships, where everyone gets inspired and believes that achievements will excel expectations. If such an atmosphere exists and is maintained, if there is optimism and hope for the best, realization of these hopes and plans is the supreme form of fairness. The 1.7+ is a soft-hearted enthusiast and an incorrigible dreamer; the imaginary world is more important for him than the real one. Similarly, his notion of fairness is rather artificial. They have little connection with the scale of his and his colleagues' participation in the company's fulfilments. Real company problems are shifted to the periphery of his attention and are put back to the centre only when the gap between the overestimated expectations and real achievements gets so large that it is absolutely impossible to ignore it any longer. As long as the gap is not so large, the 1.7+ style prefers to encourage even the most mediocre results. He believes that praise is deserved by every person because each one works as hard as he can according to their skills, possibilities, and eagerness. The 1.7+ considers it fair not to punish anyone even for major blunders and to excuse them due to unfavourable circumstances.

Commitment People of the 1.7+ style are sincerely devoted to their organization, but their devotion has some peculiarities. They really worry about problems of the whole team and of each of its members. But the 1.7+ style identifies himself more with personal and friendly relationships in the team and with the atmosphere of inspiration and enthusiasm than with the results of the activity. The former is what the 1.7+ always strives for. Organizational devotion and identity can be assumed by the 1.7+ only in case there is clear emotional connection with the company based on friendly relationships and cheerful expectations. Thus, the organizational commitment and devotion, as well as the identity, turn into a sort of emotional addiction in the end and do not touch profound motives and personal objectives of the organizational behaviour patterns.

Responsibility   The 1.7+ style is more or less reliable in all situations. His reliability is based on a positive culture value orientation and high devotion to the company. Strange but true, the 1.7+ style is more devoted when there is a real threat of breaking friendly relationships and spoiling the atmosphere of optimism and cheerfulness so highly appreciated by the 1.7+. In other words, the 1.7+ style gains the best efficiency and reliability not on the base of harmonic relationships, but for the sake of such relationships! Thus, the 1.7+ culture·is reliable mainly in the sphere of human relationships. The social responsibility of the 1.7+ is very high and is one of the key elements of his culture values: the 1.7+ deeply shares the philosophy of social responsibility that requires cooperation and taking part in handling social problems. From the 1.7+'s point of view, such problems are extremely important, but usually his actual participation in handling them comes to words and slogans. The issues of social responsibility as a rule come into his vision only if he has to respond to the demands of higher executives.

Integrity   For the 1.7+ style, integrity and honesty are a warm and friendly atmosphere, where colleagues encourage and inspire each other and enjoy the working process, no matter the results. Such integrity is rather peculiar: as a rule, only positive emotions are displayed, negative things remain inferior or are completely ignored. People of the 1.7+ type are eager to respond positively; they convince each other to compromise and pass their responsibility to others. In such a team, it is common practice to thank for positive critique and to bring apologies in response to negative critique. That is why the general landscape of the organizational activity and its sense and development are concentrated not only on production but also on the very process of work, and all of this leads to an unreasonable use of valuable personal and collective resources.

7.5   1.7+ Culture and Power

Focus on Reward and Information Power

Punishment   By nature, the 1.7+ style denies punishment as an instrument of influence and means of changing staff members' behaviour. He tries to abstain by all means from punishing anyone. He believes that all employees are by nature decent and try to do their best. Even if they make serious mistakes, it is not their fault but an effect of fatal circumstances. If the 1.7+ ever has to punish anyone, he does it in the mildest and most harmless way with apologies and peaceful words. The 1.7+ will also say that the punishment is neither his will nor initiative, but it comes from the front office. "I would have never paid attention to this, but you understand that I am obliged to do so. Please, take it easy, everything will settle down."

Reward   The 1.7+ style looks at rewards as a natural means of forming a warm and friendly atmosphere in the team. He firmly believes that all people are by nature decent and hardworking and deserve praise and reward no matter how they work and what results they get. That is why the 1.7+ is eager to praise people; he praises them excessively and encourages them even if the results are far from good. The lack of a purposeful orientation at definite results leads to a lack of criteria according to which one could evaluate them. Such criteria are not discussed in advance; they are simply not set. That is why employees get used to applause even if the achievements are minimal. They are puzzled when they for some reason get no reward.

Position   The importance of his position and status in the company is for the 1.7+ the opportunity to contribute to forming friendly and harmonic relationships in the team, organizing corporate parties, giving presents, and defending the employees' rights. The 1.7+ style hardly ever highlights his official authority. He prefers to achieve close and friendly relationships with his colleagues and to create an atmosphere of a united team. He does his best to lay stress on equity and understanding. He believes that all his colleagues are decent and hardworking. He rarely gives them direct instructions. He accentuates the importance of harmonic relationships and often no one is in charge of doing the job properly. The 1.7+ does not have overstated career ambitions, but at the same time he is full of hopes that the higher officials will appreciate the atmosphere and relationships formed in the team thanks to his efforts. Thus, he hopes to be raised to a higher position. The 1.7+ has to exercise his official authority only if there are categorical demands from above concerning definite production. But even in such a case he can only say: "I rarely ask you for something, but now it's a must. Of course, if you appreciate our team and our friendship and your boss as well, you don't want another person to be appointed instead of me".

Information   The exchange of information in the case of the 1.7+ comes first of all to forming a friendly and enthusiastic environment in the team. That is why the 1.7+ is eager to gather and accept positive information and is glad to inform others about the things that help strengthen such an environment in detail. Negative information is presented in such a form that it is hard to detect its real meaning. That is why information is accumulated in a rather superficial manner and takes place only if it is necessary. Information that immediately has to do with work, duties, and production is gathered only in case of insistent demands from above. The 1.7+ prefers not to pass negative information to anyone before he evaluates it well on his own. As a rule, after his analysis the negative information acquires a fairly positive and optimistic appearance.

Expert The 1.7+ style is very competent in the sphere of forming positive relationships and a prosperous organizational atmosphere. His professional competence however is not so high. Even in the process of acquiring new knowledge and skills, he is aimed at relationships more than at definite purposes of studying. That is why he lacks self-confidence concerning his own professional qualities and he tries to compensate it through shifting responsibility to other people and through forming close and friendly relationships. Consequently, he is not able to act independently. His activity is focused not on the organizational processes and their improvement but on colleagues' feelings, emotions, and moods. Departing from his cultural values, the 1.7+ style highlights the necessity of teaching and training the employees all the time, and he contributes to teaching and training them; but the lack of his own skills and knowledge does not let him teach others by example.

Referent At the cost of his cultural values, constant positive mood, and personal charm, the 1.7+ style has well-displayed referent power. But it largely depends on particular situations and has little to do with key objectives and organization tasks. Best of all his charismatic qualities are displayed in corporate meetings when the 1.7+ can encourage the team with his energy, pathos, and emotional speech and convince everyone of the brilliant opportunities that appear in front of his mind's eye. His referent power is also strong in cases when the organization's efforts bring good results amid a positive concourse of circumstances, good luck, and successful market conditions combined with the rivals' mistakes, macroeconomic and political factors, etc. In such conditions, the 1.7+ style is for some time viewed as an ideal and even prophetic leader who can build a harmonic team and, besides that, achieve impressive results. But as soon as the competition is really tough and it is necessary to guarantee maximum output all the time, the lack of a constant and well-displayed orientation for production destroys both the wonderful opportunities promised by the 1.7+ and his charismatic influence. Everyone starts to see that the words and promises of the 1.7+ do not meet the real state of business. Although he makes the team's life positive, although he is polite, pleasing, and nice to deal with, in difficult situations of organizational life his ability to accept responsibility and to lead people turn out to be nothing more than words.

7.6   Cooperation Skills of the 1.7+ Style

Conflict Resolution

Any conflict is a threat to the positive and optimistic mood of the 1.7+ style. His attitude towards conflicts is negative. For him, conflicts are an inevitable evil, and he tries to avoid conflicts or deny them if they take place. When the team is in danger of a conflict, the 1.7+ style does his best to smooth over the arisen disagreement and to protect the harmonic and friendly relationships—as he sees them—which he is eager to create and support. His main means of troubleshooting is to call on team members to calm down and to take things easy, as everything will settle soon.

If the conflict becomes more and more acute and there is no way to avoid it, the 1.7+ has to investigate its roots. Departing from his cultural values, he feels that unsettled conflicts are a serious obstacle for building a harmonic team and have to be somehow overcome. He does not avoid touching the conflict in conversations, he is ready to talk about it, but he never comes to a profound analysis and does not thoroughly seek the best ways of settling the conflict. His general notion of the conflict: a threat to harmonic relationships and cheerful enthusiastic atmosphere. This is what he is ready to discuss with his colleagues. No other measures of handling the conflict are taken. Everything remains at the level of theoretical overview and declarations that conflicts in general are harmful, inadmissible, and groundless.

The 1.7+ style firmly believes that as soon as harmonic relationships have been set up and people are united by optimistic aspirations, there should not be any grounds for controversies and conflicts. That is why, in his opinion, a conflict is a harmful, groundless, and unnatural phenomenon. When a conflict happens, the 1.7+ style tries to distract attention from it. He calms down the colleagues and encourages them. He carefully traces the changes in the team's moods and if he feels that the tension increases, he tries to neutralize it and tries to convince the conflicting sides that their disagreement is trifle and something unreal. He does not try to analyse the disagreement and he does not compare the two standpoints on the basis of facts. Instead, he tries to persuade the arguing sides that there is no real conflict, since there is no place for conflicts in a 1.7+ team, where all people are fine and everything is nice forever.

If there is no chance to avoid a conflict, the 1.7+ tries to calm down his colleagues. He is very convincing and creative when he speaks about the negative and disastrous consequences of the conflict and demonstrates the advantages and positive aspects of friendly and calm relationships. He makes reference to the unlucky circumstances, he underestimates the scale of arisen disagreement, and he imagines a wonderful future where all conflicts are settled by themselves. In the end, if the 1.7+ feels that the arisen conflict might become a real threat to his system of friendly relationships, he can use not only persuasion: "Are your insults and mutual reproaches more important for you than my kind and friendly attitude to you?" Here the conflicting sides start to realize that kind and friendly relationships in the team are so important for the 1.7+ that in order to save them he can appeal to the strictest measures.

The 1.7+ does not see any positive potential in conflicts. He does not see that a conflict might turn out to be a chance of improving the efficiency of the interaction. That is why the profound reasons of the conflict are ignored and are not discussed. Later, such unwillingness to analyse the reasons often leads to even more serious and negative consequences. As a rule, the 1.7+ style does not set clear criteria of efficiency evaluation. Everyone prefers to address themselves to work on the base of pure enthusiasm. They think that planning and clear criteria diminish the employees' eagerness to work hard. The principle is as follows: "If people are gifted and work with enthusiasm, the rest comes without additional efforts." As long as there are no definite criteria, any remark looks like a subjective opinion and nothing more. Meanwhile, a remark should associate real behaviour with an ideal sample and compare them. That is why the evaluation of efficiency is quite difficult as there are no standards of comparison and improvement.

Communicative Competence

The communicative competence of the 1.7+ style is rather high and it lets him establish and support warm and friendly relationships with other people. His typical features are contagious optimism and kind manners; he is empathic, polite, and attentive to the interlocutor, and he can easily set warm and friendly relationships with his colleagues. The 1.7+ style has a subtle understanding of people and their needs and interests, which allows him to profoundly understand their motives and foresee their behaviour.

The 1.7+ style can establish intensive exchange of information in his department. News spreads freely, often through informal talks in a friendly and pleasant atmosphere. The objectives of gathering information and of its analysis by the 1.7+ as a rule have little to do with the task of achieving outstanding organizational results and are not associated with the evaluation of production quality. They are aimed at forming and improving harmonic relationships and the atmosphere of universal enthusiasm and inspiration.

A 1.7+ person actively uses the search and gathering of information to exclude factors that could spark any conflict in the collective and could pose a threat to a calm and optimistic environment. The communication usually does not touch such issues as raising efficiency and lays stress on such things as the quality of interrelationships, positive mood, and cheerful expectations. That is why such questions as "What results do we have to achieve and how?" are replaced by "What shall we do to improve our relationships?" In other words, the attention of the 1.7+ is largely concentrated on questions and things that have no immediate connection with the aims of the organizational activity. Consequently, the 1.7+ style spends much time talking with people about their wishes, feelings, and thoughts and does not contribute to the improvement of their professional activity and even handicaps it because the employees' attention is distracted from the definite tasks.

The 1.7+ uses his charm and impressive eloquence to control where discussions take the team and guides them as he likes to avoid sharp issues that could provoke a conflict and cause unwanted tension.

If anyone makes a mistake or an inaccuracy in his work, the 1.7+ makes no attempts to analyse and uncover the true reasons. The first thing to be done by the 1.7+ is to evaluate how the mistake could affect the atmosphere of the team. If he does not foresee any negative consequences, the 1.7+ only complains a little or completely ignores the mistake. If the mistake might cause critique and conflict, the 1.7+ tries to restore a kind and friendly atmosphere, saying: "I am sure this has happened due to bad circumstances and in general everything is fine. We must not yield to panic and we must not start quarrels because of some trifles. Everything will settle and we can expect a wonderful future!"

The communication of the 1.7+ style is aimed at informational exchanges concerning people's emotions and feelings. Facts and organizational processes are secondary issues. Only in a critical situation which might destroy the harmonic relationships, so important for the 1.7+, can he concentrate on production and resolve the arisen problems.

Active Positioning

The 1.7+ style defends only opinions that help to strengthen warm and friendly relationships and to form optimistic expectations and cannot cause serious objections and conflicts. He defends his opinion quite openly and with conviction, if it does not threaten friendly relationships and influences other people positively. If the 1.7+ foresees objections, he tries to smooth over the appeared disagreements and persuade others that his position is aimed at the interests of the whole team and is beneficial for everyone. If a discussion or collision of different opinions is inevitable, if one has to take sides, the 1.7+ style has enough motivation and energy to articulate and support his standpoint. The values orientation of the 1.7+, which coincides with the team interests, gives him a big advantage in defence of his standpoint. The internal conviction that his standpoint is the standpoint of the team and even of the whole society allows the 1.7+ to significantly influence the opinions and behaviour of other staff members.

The 1.7+ defends his opinion actively and enthusiastically as long as he is sure this is good for the general welfare. If the situation grows acute and may transform into a conflict, which might threaten the relationships in the team, or if the 1.7+ style is accused of personal or sectional motives, then he is ready to give up his opinion. He can return to defending it only if he feels the support of the bigger part of the team.

In order not to compromise good relationships, the 1.7+ style often learns the opinions of other people before he says what he thinks. "I would not like my opinion to influence your standpoints. It is very important for me to know your opinions, each opinion. I am a member of our team, like each of you." Such declarations let others know that the top priority is peace and harmony. When there is evident support and the 1.7+ feels self-confident, he openly expresses his opinion, speaks with confidence, and can even be obtrusive. As a result, colleagues who could express another opinion prefer to keep silent.

When it comes to organizing corporate parties, giving presents, reporting successful achievements, prizes, new appointments, and supply increase, the 1.7+ is among the most active ones. He likes to do all this very much, with pride and inspiration. If he brings this energy into casual business life, his initiatives become "rainbow-chasing". Thus, he can propose to increase the planned performance (which is hard to fulfil even without any increase) or to launch a new project which is objectively unrealistic. These flashes of the 1.7+'s initiative have nothing to do with the orientation for production, as one might think. They reflect an excessive splash of weakly grounded optimism and fantasy. In such cases, colleagues exchange glances that mean "Someone stop him!"

The lack of definite purposes and clear quality criteria does not let the 1.7+ style objectively evaluate his own standpoint and activity, as well as the standpoints and activities of other people. He cannot objectively evaluate the team's work in general. That is why there are so many air castles and illusions of positive development and brilliant future.

Decision-Making

The 1.7+ style makes decisions with great caution. He tries to avoid discontent or threats to the positive psychological climate in the team. Decision-making should not provoke conflicts and spark arguments. It should please everyone. The 1.7+ style avoids making decisions before he discusses the issue with everyone and before he estimates his colleagues' standpoints and their attitude. Usually the decision which is finally made is not the best one. The 1.7+ prefers to choose the variants everyone agrees with. Such decisions help to make the climate more positive and avoid conflicts and contradictions.

The 1.7+ is eager to choose the decisions that guarantee acceptable results and contribute to collective friendship and optimism. He prefers to postpone unpopular decisions or shifts responsibility for the steps that might harm the harmonic relationships and positive organizational climate.

The 1.7+ takes his time to make difficult decisions which can lead to different results. He prefers to wait until all the details are clarified or the conditions are more advantageous. Under any other circumstances the process of decision making is slowed down by lengthy discussions where too many people take part. He does not have any definite decision-making criteria and schemes. Thus, there is no proper control over the discussions and the initial issue is soon forgotten.

In the process of decision-making the 1.7+ style is not independent enough. He tends to correlate his decisions with the opinion of higher executives and with the organizational documents all the time. Thus, his decisions become weightier and allow him not to worry about consequences that might follow in case the decision turns out to be wrong.

For the 1.7+ it is more important to base the decision on consensus. This condition and the very process of decision making are more important for him than the results that this will bring. He tries to make decisions that would, on the one hand, strengthen the system of harmonic organizational relationships and, on the other hand, meet the demands of the front office. Of course, it is very hard to achieve such decisions, and the process is rather stressful and uncomfortable for the 1.7+.

Constructive Critique

The critique and feedback of the 1.7+ usually lack width and constructiveness. He is too positive in his evaluation of the rather mediocre productivity of his colleagues and always wants to encourage and praise them, even if they do not wholly deserve it. The positive value attitudes of the 1.7+ make him find positive aspects in any work and any achievements. He feels uncomfortable when he has to sound negative. Thus, the 1.7+ style is always positive in his critique.

The high concern for people and general concern for organizational values make the 1.7+ style avoid open and objective feedback even for the most careless staff members. He is afraid to harm the general moral and psychological atmosphere of the team. That is why he can try to articulate negative critique only when talking privately. But even in this case such critique resembles compassion and condolence. He tries to be careful with other people's feelings and emotions, his estimations and remarks are very soft, and he always says some words of sympathy and support to sum up his critique. Such an approach makes it possible to support comparatively kind relationships even with the most careless colleagues, but it does not make them change their behaviour and attitude to work at all. Consequently, the more hard-working and efficient employees have to bear more duties.

The 1.7+ usually formulates critique in the form of praise. The differences between evaluations are usually smoothed over in order not to compromise good relationships. The roots of these differences are not deeply analysed for the same reason. At that, the 1.7+ style tries to concentrate on the things that are easy to fulfil and that can help to improve the optimistic mood and support it. Unpleasant and difficult tasks are discussed with reluctance and superficiality.

In his critique and feedback, the 1.7+ shows his special concern for looking at a person without any connection with the quality of his work. In other words, the main subject of essential critique—the quality of the staff member's work—is not touched and remains at the periphery of the 1.7+'s attention.

As for his own work, the 1.7+ gladly accepts positive critique and feedback. Objective and negative remarks and suggestions are accepted with agreement and apologies, if necessary.

The quality of the 1.7+'s critique and its depth are restricted by his own positive notions and feelings. When there are no definite criteria of task completion, critique is often shifted to talking about non-organizational issues and not about the work per se. If someone raises concerns about the quality of the work, the 1.7+ style tries to bring positive emotions and convinces others to concentrate on the positive aspects of the current situation and to think about forthcoming improvements.

The more the problems arise, the more efforts 1.7+ devotes to convincing other people that they should be more self-confident and restore the lost expectations. The main motto of the 1.7+ style is to be optimistic and hopeful under any circumstances. If some people need help in overcoming their failures or obstacles, the 1.7+ style can usually offer only one means: the passive belief that everything will settle after some time. He is not able to organize people and lead them when they have to be active in overcoming troubles in tough conditions. The 1.7+ says lots of words of praise and encouragement; he always finds something positive even in a failure, but he cannot propose any forms of proper troubleshooting.

7.7 Conclusions

While the 7.1− style tries to convert resources (R) into results (O) immediately, ignoring the relationships between people, the 1.7+ style ignores results (O), but tends to use all resources (R) to form harmonic and friendly relationships in the I-ZONE. In short, the primary purpose of the 1.7+ style is a cheerful, harmonic organizational life without any conflicts, full of enthusiasm and positive expectations. This purpose is certainly Utopian and inevitably interferes with the real objectives, tasks, and also conditions in which the organization functions. The 1.7+ style tries to overcome this controversy by building friendly and positive relationships, a nice climate, and enthusiasm in the I-ZONE. Of course, he does not succeed in it. The more his efforts are spent on establishing positive relationships and on getting rid of conflicts and differences, on inspiring people by their future achievements, the more disappointing the end result. As incorrigible dreamers, the employees comfort themselves with unreasonable hopes and constant praise. They do too little to implement their plans and to make dreams come true. Reality disillusions their minds by prioritising production and hence correcting their behaviour. If such corrections do not follow, the team in the end has to face great disappointment in front of the harsh organizational reality as soon as it fully shows itself. Nevertheless, the 1.7+ style has charming influence on his colleagues and orients them towards harmonic relationships and future opportunities (that more often fail than come true, having, however, strong motivating potentiality). The purposeful development of a clear concern for results can bring the 1.7+ style closer to the ideal leadership model.

Style 4.4–: Formalist (Balancing and Compromising)

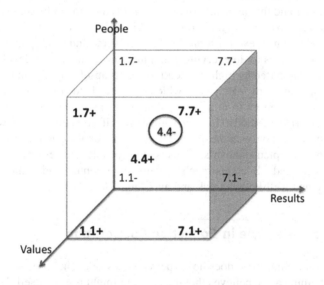

The 4.4– style is characterized by moderate concern for production and people, and by a formal and indifferent attitude towards work and organization. He tends to avoid everything new. He tries to avoid any risk, any conflicts. He likes to do his work in accordance with the rules and instructions. His behaviour and way of thinking are dominated by conservatism. He likes to follow instructions accurately, he is afraid of new and unusual things.

© Springer-Verlag Berlin Heidelberg 2016
A. Zankovsky, C. von der Heiden, *Leadership with Synercube*,
DOI 10.1007/978-3-662-49052-5_8

8.1   Basic Features of the 4.4– Style

The 4.4+ and 4.4– styles are both characterized by a moderate concern for the company's achievements as well as for people. They are alike, but if we compare their concern for values, they are opposite. The 4.4– style is indifferent to the organization and avoids everything new, as well as even the slightest risk and conflicts. To implement and defend this values orientation, the 4.4– style tends to do everything in strict accordance with the rules and instructions and feels very comfortable when he follows the habitual orders and regulations. In a conflict he seeks for compromise, trying to take into account the opinion of the majority, the experience and the habitual state of things. Looking back into the past and calling for order in the company, the 4.4– style likes to say: "We have never done so!", "We have always ridden this road", "These innovations won't bring any good".

The main fear and the main enemy of the 4.4– is the probability of changes and reforms. The 4.4– believes that the only suitable activity pattern is the one proved by time and experience, even if it has evident problems and weak points.

The 4.4– style tries to do everything at a moderate, satisfactory level, which is for some reason admitted by higher executives and is absolutely alright for the 4.4–. He avoids making any decisions which can lead to risky or ambiguous consequences and prefers to aim at decisions that are suitable for everyone and based on well-tried methods. In such cases even if something goes wrong the responsibility lies not only on the 4.4–, but even more on the organizational system and commonly accepted standards. "This is not my fault! This error is an accident. It has always worked." Such approach is politically oriented, and it allows following a reliable and well-known track and avoiding risks.

8.2   The 4.4– Style in Collective Cooperation

When one of the employees does not cope with his work, a 4.4– person waits and undertakes nothing as he believes that the problem might resolve itself. His actions do not have any definite objectives and are not quite clear to his colleagues. For example, the 4.4– chief might arrange a meeting, but he does not tell anyone its topic, he says: "I hear that we are expected to do more and better. I suppose someone might feel like saying something about it." Such approach lets him raise the question without assuming any responsibility for possible conflict. He does not address anyone in particular as well. He hopes that someone will speak to the question and will have to give all the answers. If the circumstances urge the 4.4– to speak, he avoids independent conclusions and, as a rule, makes a reference to the regulations of the company. The 4.4– style can ask the employees what he should do, but if anyone proposes an interesting and challenging idea, the 4.4– will try to ignore or reject it on the base of experience or corporate traditions.

A team of 4.4– stands on rules and formal criteria. "Proper" colleagues are raised and promoted according to their conformity to formal criteria or to their capability of "playing the games". Others just have to wait for a chance.

People's actions are determined by caution and rules. Trust and respect exist, but they are rather reserved and formal. That is why people do not feel self-confident and act very cautiously. Thus, any action decreases that takes more time and personal devotion to work. People feel that they are distant from the working process they take part in. Creative ideas are lost or distorted because of the mechanical comparison to the rules and formal criteria.

8.3   The I-ZONE and the 4.4— Style

Teams 4.4— harbour lots of gossip, as the 4.4— does much to avoid public discussions. He prefers to talk to people privately and only after that does he put forward an issue for open consideration.

Instead of a straight and open discussion, many questions are analysed even without the participation of immediate figures, and such analysis is often based on third-hand comments and private talks. Anyway, for most people this clearly means that no one should hurry to articulate his opinion, which is better to keep. Such cautious manner of the 4.4— style leads to distortions of information because people often make suppositions and conclusions based on gossip or incomplete data. Colleagues become so suspicious that any straight question worries them and they feel uncomfortable and try to elude from giving a substantial answer. All this harms the efficiency of the organizational processes and much effort is required to restore relationships and keep up the efficiency of work at least at a moderate and satisfactory level.

Starting from the moment when such example is given, everyone starts to follow it, and then rumours replace an open and honest bilateral discussion where people could share their disagreements and consider them together. In a 4.4— team, the only acceptable way of discussion is compromise, concession, and following the majority's opinion. This compromise rarely carries essential sense. It is not a means of making the conflict not so acute, but an instrument for ceasing it at any cost.

The internal alienation and lack of loyalty often lead to imitation of discussions instead of considering problems openly and sincerely. People who put forward different points of view to a public discussion are criticized for bringing new problems, slowing down the process and being selfish. However, they compromise with the habitual atmosphere of the team, which is polite, but very formal and devoid of sincerity, and where no one can break the unshakable rules.

Sticking to formal rules lets the 4.4— person feel self-confident and be a full-fledged member of the team. But other people understand that the rules are used as a shield against new arguments. People feel they cannot put forward their opinion: reasonable ideas and creative proposals are rejected for the sake of once established rules. At best, they can propose some ideas, but they cannot influence the majority. Sincere devotion to work and looking for the right decisions are always replaced by formal rules and references to past experience: "In such situations we must act only in accordance with the regulations!" or "This is what we have always done before".

Fig. 8.1 4.4–

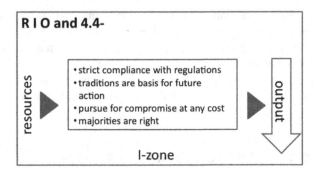

A 4.4– person believes that balance and compromise are a more correct strategy of cooperation than all the risks connected with people's creativity and high level of involvement. It does not matter that production (O) is not as good as it could be. If there is a conflict, the reaction of the 4.4– is not an analysis of evident facts, but quick smoothing over the opposite opinion through compromise and reaching balance between different needs of those involved in the argument (Fig. 8.1).

The 4.4– style considers that a hasty compromise is a victory of both sides, where each of them gets some part of what they have been striving for. But such approach leads to vague and fragile decisions and in the end people feel as if they were tricked. For the 4.4– style it is more important that each of the arguing sides gains whatever. No one should continue to disagree or to be openly discontent. Despite the correctness of the decision made, a 4.4– person avoids extreme separation of the winners from the losers. Although the conflicting sides calm down for a while, the conflict will spark again later or will continue to fester. This will negatively affect colleagues' relationships.

A 4.4– person cannot realize the advantages of genuinely synergistic team cooperation because of his insincere, cautious, and indifferent attitude.

8.4   4.4– Culture and Values

Basic Feature: Formal Rules and Criteria. Fear of Anything New and Any Changes

Trust In the 4.4– culture only formal rules and well-tried methods deserve trust. Excessive trust is also enjoyed by the instructions of higher executives, which are taken in uncritically and without analysis. As for people, the ones who are worth confiding in are those who strictly follow the traditional rules and patterns and also those of high status. "Why should we discuss anything if we have been told to do so?" Change or anything new causes sharp rejection and suspiciousness, even if the disadvantages of the old are evident: "We shall see where all this can take us! You all will regret it." People who generate new and atypical ideas cause mistrust and enmity.

Fairness The 4.4– style considers it fair to support and reward those who behave and act in strict accordance with the formal rules and regulations set. If someone is not able to fulfil the regulations, it is fair to prevent such behaviour and to punish for it. The fairest way of handling conflicts for the 4.4– is a compromise where each side gets at least minimal benefit. If it is necessary to make a decision which does not match the traditional standards, they might be essentially unfair and dishonest. But even unhealthy compromises and unfair decisions, in the 4.4–'s opinion, are fair because they are made for the sake of the majority's welfare and help to protect the current state of things. The top priority is to preserve the status quo.

Commitment The 4.4– style identifies himself not with the company and its employees, mission, and purposes, but with the set of formal regulations and norms which he adopted at the time of organizational socialization. The people of the 4.4– style are in their own way devoted to the company. They identify the company with the unshaken set of rules and categorically deny the chance of any changes in it. They acknowledge only this form of commitment and identity and think that it is shared by most people.

Responsibility According to the 4.4–, reliability is the possibility to understand people's behaviour and to forecast it. In his opinion, it is possible only in case all people strictly observe the set of rules and regulations. In such case, their behaviour becomes legible and predictable: they act according to the rules set and well-tried formalized schemes. They base on the fact that earlier they did the same and were successful. The once established ways and methods make life really understandable and reliable. Changes and new things on the contrary make it unreliable and unpredictable. The necessity of change is not taken into account. The 4.4– style rarely thinks that new times might require changes. The main strategy is to follow the rules, secure the stable function of the system, and move in the direction set without any shifts and risks. The social responsibility of the 4.4– style comes to strict observance of social standards that are considered unshakable truth. Those who shift from them or deny the stable rules are considered by the 4.4– irresponsible and unreliable.

Integrity The 4.4– leader views transparency and integrity as the gradual and strict observance of well-tried habitual methods. If something surpasses the restrictions, it is ignored or estimated negatively. Any innovations are viewed as a breach of the correct course of events and thus rejected. Gathering information and analysing it is restricted by the parameters established by the rules and by the front office. The feedback of the 4.4– is very reserved or acquires the form of complaints to other people. Failures and mistakes of other people are explained as deviations from instructions. If the 4.4– himself has to defy the rules, such deviations are justified by exterior circumstances. Here, the 4.4– tries to rather excuse himself than to find real reasons and arguments.

8.5   4.4– Culture and Power

Focus on Laying Stress on the Formal Aspects of Position and Expert Power

Punishment The top priority for the 4.4– is the meticulous and consistent observance of existing rules and standards. Those who break the rules and afford to shift from their strict observance should be punished no matter the reasons and circumstances. Punishment should be devoid of subjectivity, exactly regulated, and it should also guarantee the system stable and habitual functioning. Punishment is associated with observing the rules, not with the results.

Reward The 4.4– style has a rather cold attitude towards rewards. He firmly believes that everyone must follow the established rules and regulations exactly. That is why those who do so do not fully deserve a reward, because they are doing what they must do. And it goes without saying that those who break the rules or defy them do not deserve any reward at all and are bad employees by default. If there are any rewards, it has no close association with the working process results. The 4.4– style is aimed at results which do not exceed a moderate level. Those who strive for outstanding achievements cause the 4.4–'s distrust and vigilance. He starts to suspect them of wanting to get something special, some privileges.

Position For the 4.4– style, position power is extremely important and is considered a key element of the organizational system, which lies on the basis of the system of organizational rules and regulations. Every level of organizational hierarchy envisages a definite range of official rights within which a manager should act. The 4.4– style is very well informed about his official authority and is eager to use it at full extent so that the employees do not forget about the necessity to observe the organizational rules. In his behaviour, the 4.4– makes the difference between his relationships with his subordinates, colleagues, and bosses clear. The former, in his opinion, should follow the established rules with all exactness and attention. The latter personify the system and thus their instructions and decisions become undeniable rules for the subordinates.

Information The main informational resource of the 4.4– is the organizational documentation which governs the activity of the whole organization and of every employee in particular. The 4.4– style, better than anyone else, knows what each person should be busy with, what rights and duties the colleagues have, and where his own responsibility ends. This information lets the 4.4– style not only protect himself from many current problems and tasks, but also strengthen his own position. Informational exchange goes on in order to preserve the status quo. Communication with subordinates comes to reminding them that it is obligatory to follow the rules and standards. The 4.4– style accepts the instructions of higher officials without specifications and without enthusiasm. He tries to fulfil his tasks formally, at an acceptable level. The most intensive communication of the 4.4–

takes place with colleagues of the same hierarchic level. It is aimed at well-timed preparation for defence from innovations and changes.

Expert The 4.4– style is most of all competent in the sphere of technical legal knowledge: he is very good at organizational instructions, rules, and guidelines; he is an expert of the well-tried traditional approaches and methods. Such people often have quite profound professional knowledge and skills, which are however not enriched or replenished. The dominant thought is that all correct things have been known since long and there is no need to invent the bicycle. The available knowledge and skills are considered sufficient and perfect. He departs from the thought that in his industry there cannot and must not appear anything new. In his opinion, innovative methods are too risky and as a rule they never turn useful, but more often they cause unwanted mistakes and problems.

Referent As a rule, the 4.4– style has a very restricted referent power, as in any situation he acts according to the established rules and regulations. Such strategy is accomplished by the conviction that to know rules means to know the best ways. As a result, other people start to look at the 4.4– as a self-assured and dull person who does the work without sincerity and without emotion. In cases when the 4.4– has to call on colleagues to complete urgent and difficult tasks, his calls do not cause rise in motivation. For many people the 4.4– personifies the formal and faceless rules that many organizations have to bear, especially large ones.

The 4.4– style does not want to differ from others anyhow, that is why he, despite his indifference to the company, does not want to be a bad worker. To be a bad worker means to attract too much attention, receive remarks, conflict with other employees, and in the end be actively involved into organizational life. A 4.4– person will prefer moderate efficiency, normal relationships with colleagues, and exact observance of the established rules—to put it short, all that can guarantee a calm life without conflicts. The lack of mutual trust, respect, and sincerity does not let him build reliable and harmonic relationships. Instead, he builds relationships based on following instructions in accordance with the motto "bad peace is better than good war".

The necessity to be distant from other people and to conceal his indifferent standpoint does not let the 4.4– openly articulate his own views. Instead, his own views are substituted by commonly known facts and established rules. If the 4.4– style has to express his opinion in a case, it is rather hard for him and discouraging for others. He feels self-confident and comfortable only when the interrelationships are based only on formal principles.

8.6　Cooperation Skills of the 4.4– Style

Conflict Resolution

The attitude of the 4.4– style towards conflicts is very negative. A conflict is considered to be one of the most serious threats to a stable and uneventful life. Deep in his heart the 4.4– firmly believes that if people strictly followed the established rules and approaches, there would not be any reasons for opposition and conflicts in the company. Besides that, any conflict carries the danger of getting deeply involved into organizational problems. It requires a creative and not indifferent attitude, which is by all means avoided by the 4.4–. That is why he prefers to keep away from conflicts, behaves neutrally, and waits for the problem to resolve itself. A 4.4– person is aimed at such decisions that do not sharpen the differences. He relies on the formal rules which have been adopted at the organization since long for similar issues. He calls on colleagues to achieve compromise in order to restore calmness and indifference.

If the conflict is inevitable, the 4.4– style can acknowledge it and takes all possible measures to eradicate it. The main way to solve a conflict is to search for a compromise on any conditions. The aim is to get rid of the arisen confrontation with the help of some concessions from both sides. Compromise should be supported by the majority. In the 4.4–'s opinion the support of the majority justifies any compromise: "This is what the majority has decided!"

In case of conflict, the 4.4– style does not go into analysis of evident facts or profound reasons for controversies. He immediately tries to smooth over opposing opinions, looking for balance of interests and the needs of both sides. The 4.4– style tries to reach a compromise as soon as possible and he presents a temporary ceasefire as a significant victory of both sides, as a "win/win": no one loses all, each person gains at least something.

A compromise without a thorough analysis of the internal reasons for the conflict leads to ambiguous solutions: it looks as if the conflict were eliminated and there is some relief, but at the same time there is some dissatisfaction and discontent. In the end, both sides feel as if they were tricked. The 4.4– style feels this, but he does not feel responsible for better and more productive troubleshooting.

For him the most important thing is formal regulation and at least external and fictive stability. He prefers such a variant to a difficult investigation into the roots of the conflict. If both sides of the conflict gain a little, they will restrain their disagreement and discontent for at least a short while. Although the conflicting sides can calm down for a short time, such tactic is devoid of the possibility to use conflict as a resource for organizational development: as a rule, it sparks again later and spoils the interrelationships in the I-ZONE.

A 4.4– person does his best to avoid conflicts and carefully plans any further step. He relies on the rules, regulations, and experience of the company as well as on the opinion of the majority and he will never have to oppose the majority. His main motto is: "It is safer to keep away from a conflict than to regret it later" and "Even if the conflict was not fully eliminated, I have done my best".

Although conflicts are unpleasant, they are rather significant and help to concentrate on development and raise the concern for production. A conflict gives an opportunity to compare the opinions and beliefs of different people and to see whether any of them are useful in terms of the company's productivity. A valuable idea can appear and be beneficial no matter who puts it forward and how it upsets other people. To analyse and cure a conflict at the very beginning means to eliminate problems quite quickly. It would have been much better than wasting time making a conflict chronic through endless compromises. But the 4.4− style does his best to avoid conflicts, considering them definitely destructive.

For the 4.4− any conflict means the victory of one person and the loss of another. That is why a conflict poses a threat to the habitual stability: the loser can oppose the current state of things and demand changes. What is worse, if the conflict escalates, both sides can become opposed to the habitual order. That is why the 4.4− style has to balance between two fires. The general strive of the 4.4− is to eliminate confrontation at all costs. Thus, he is obliged to look for compromise instead of a really constructive solution. And the 4.4− thinks: "If each one gains a little part of what they want, it is better than gaining nothing at all." Under any circumstances the 4.4− prefers to determine "What is acceptable for everyone?" rather than "What is correct?"

If the conflict drags on, the 4.4− style tries to stay as far away from it as possible. The 4.4− style sincerely believes that he tries to handle it in the best way. But in fact he simply departs from past precedents and nothing more. He thinks: "Why can't we stop quarrelling and reach an agreement?" or "We should charge an arbiter with this question". Another possible way of seizing the conflict is to separate the conflicting sides as far as possible. It seems to the 4.4− that the conflict is thus exhausted once and forever and the team is again peaceful. However, the conflict simply becomes latent, at best. At worst, it sparks with new energy because the arguing sides have had no chance to put forward their opinion and to find the right answer.

Communicative Competence

The 4.4− style is characterized by a moderate level of communicative competence and its usage. His eagerness to follow the once established rules and norms considerably affects the communicative competence of the 4.4−, restricting it with formal and procedural hindrances. The 4.4− style actively gathers information to learn about other people's opinions and emotions, which helps him to support normal working relationships with everyone.

The exchange of information allows the 4.4− style to estimate how smooth and stable the working process is. He also watches over the fulfilment of instructions, norms, and regulations. He can speak about such issues profusely and pleasantly, as well as about new procedures and documents. This is the sphere he is great at and he is eager to share his knowledge and experience with everyone, inspiring others to discuss and to ask questions. No one matches him here.

Other subjects are of far less interest for him, though his expertise might be fairly good there as well. However, concerning most issues his opinions are based on the views of his colleagues and on the set of rules. The colleagues' opinions are taken as mere information and not commented anyhow.

If there are differences in opinions, the 4.4– quickly starts to gather information, but he does not share his thoughts with anyone. He acknowledges the presence of other standpoints which are different from his, which has not been articulated yet. Like the 1.7– style, the 4.4– style gathers information rather actively, but the search is superficial. The purpose of gathering information is to detect the majority's standpoint and not to determine the best ways of overcoming the problem. The search of information is carried out in two ways. First come private talks and discussions. Thus, the 4.4– person can discuss the issue with each member of the team individually. He asks such questions as:

1. "What do you feel in this situation?" (to understand the mood of the interlocutor)
2. "What do you think all this will lead to?" (to learn one of the possible variants)
3. "What do you think is going on in our team?" (to estimate the state of the collective relationships)
4. "I suppose that most of us might like such decision. What do you think?" (to estimate the popularity of this or that proposal).

In each of these cases, the 4.4– avoids opening his opinion until he finds out which variant is the most popular one or receives instructions from above.

A 4.4– person often gathers information indirectly to get the necessary data without being involved in the problem and without having to display his opinion. Before that, he tries to analyse the previous experience of handling such problems: he consults the colleagues who can act as experts. But such consultations are not efficient enough. The 4.4– style formulates his questions not straight, he asks them neutrally and impartially: "I know you've had some experience promoting goods to a new region." Or "We do not know which direction to take now". Such questions tell the interlocutor nothing about the genuine purpose of the talk.

The 4.4– style questions are characterized by two peculiarities. Firstly, they are often open questions (i.e. they envisage various answers) and are at the same time rather elusive because the 4.4– does not want to get into a conflict. For example, an employee confidentially tells the 4.4– that another employee criticizes a particular point of the current policy. In such a case, the 4.4– will gather information through elusive questions: "I have heard a lot about the new policy that we should accept. What do you think about it?" or "I have heard you are worried about something in the new policy we should accept". A more efficient and straight question would be something like this: "I hear you disagree with the principles of accountability in the new policy. What exactly raises your concerns?" The 4.4– style supposes that people should give him the necessary information and to get it one should just ask some vague questions and turn the talk into the right direction.

Secondly, the 4.4– does not tell anyone what he thinks until a decision becomes evident. Therefore the 4.4– acquires the role of a mediator. The 4.4– does not discuss the personal opinions of his colleagues about the new policy. His cautious approach protects him from difficult situations and allows him to collect all the information that has to do with the issue. If asked straight about his opinion, he answers "Ok, I can tell you only what I have found out about this question" or makes a reference to the organizational rules: "In our company in such cases we have always done the following. It is not my invention. This practice has been proven right by time and experience". Such words allow the 4.4– to support those who share the majority's opinion.

Active Positioning

The 4.4– style compares his opinion to the expectations of his bosses and to the opinions of the majority of the team. He prefers not to display his opinion before he clearly realizes the possible consequences of his standpoint or it is not fully supported by other people. Thus, he can later put forward the opinion which is supported by the front office as well as by the employees. He can say: "Taking into account these newly arisen circumstances I agree with you."

The 4.4– style tries to be of the safest opinion or of the most widely supported one. If he faces pressure, he concedes. A 4.4– person does not defend his standpoint as long as he is not sure it is popular and widely supported by other people. His beliefs or his certainty about the correctness of his policy are not so important for 4.4–. Political inclinations are of much more importance. According to this cautious strategy, he has to all the time estimate other opinions to see whether they are popular enough and to join the opinion supported by the majority.

The 4.4– style can be convincing in defending his opinion if it is shared by most members of the team. If even this opinion turns out to be disputable, he immediately changes his mind or shifts responsibility for this to other people in order to avoid a conflict. A typical phrase he can say in such a situation: "Why shall we punish the herald who brings bad news? I am telling you the opinion of others" or "Some of us might not like this, but this is what we have always done in similar cases, so now we have no choice". Such words automatically relieve the 4.4– person from the responsibility for the once formulated opinion. If this is followed by critique, the 4.4– hides in the shadow and abstains from any further participation until better times. He says: "Our efforts will come to nothing if we go on arguing. I think we should leave this issue and keep calm." In other words, the 4.4– style prefers to be a mediator and peacemaker between the arguing sides. He tries to smooth over all differences and calls for a compromise. He says: "It looks like we all must think about how to come to an agreement. I think that everyone should make some concession so that we could move forward." Thus, the purpose of the 4.4– style is not to move forward, but to put an end to the argument.

The 4.4– style displays active position which is based on the previous experience and well-tried approaches from the past. He avoids any unexpected things and therefore discusses the various possible scenarios with colleagues. He wants to know how they react to the range of proposals. If he has to adopt unpopular measures, the 4.4– style is sure to justify them by regulations and procedures from past precedents.

A 4.4– person acts quickly and accurately only if he has clear and straight instructions or if he has had to deal with similar cases before and if he has precedents to rely on. The 4.4– style can work fairly well and support working relationships when the direction of the policy is determined by some other person—a charismatic boss or team member. This way, he does not take any risk because the purposes are set by others, by those who initiate the activity. Thus, the 4.4– person can be free from the responsibility for a possible failure. As long as the activity follows a well-predicted route, the efficiency of the 4.4– style is quite high. If a problem arises, the 4.4– stops to wait for further instructions.

The 4.4– style is very cautious in sharing his opinion with anyone. He is afraid to put forward an initiative if he does not have abundant information about the issue: what the majority thinks, what the set traditions are, what happened before in similar cases, etc. If the question might lead to a conflict, he will postpone the decision until he understands the inclination of the majority. The 4.4– style encourages colleagues to compromise for the sake of progress, but at the same time his genuine concern is not an effective and perfect track towards good results, but an elimination of differences in opinions and prevention of conflicts. That is why he does not join any group before he detects the politically correct strategy.

If a conflict takes place, the 4.4– style tries to prevent its destructive consequences and immediately starts to communicate with the arguing sides, but he does not seek for the reasons. In order not to take risks, he assumes the neutral role of a sideliner or mediator in finding compromise. He wants to restore order and he does not want to share any standpoint. But if the conflict grows more acute and there is struggle which might threaten his safe neutrality, he immediately retreats. In comparison to the 1.7– style, the 4.4– style is more eager to put forward an initiative, but only as long as his steps are approved and widely supported by other people. No matter how popular the initiative, amid a conflict the 4.4– does his best to avoid being the target of critique. He says: "I do not approve of this, but I am pinioned" and "I agree with what you say, but I am not the one to decide". Such tactics allow the 4.4– to keep good relationships with both confronting sides. He undermines his own authority as well as the authority of other people. The latent meaning of his words is: "I actually don't care what has been proposed. I wonder why you are interested".

Decision-Making

For the 4.4– the most important factor of decision-making is the opinion of the majority and agreement of the debating sides. For the sake of moving forward, the 4.4– is ready to compromise even if the decision is only partly correct. He prefers to avoid decisions that are unpopular, risky, or non-approved by higher executives or the team. The 4.4– style is very much oriented at the past. His decisions are made on the base of past experience, precedents, and traditions. He does not think about whether such experience is applicable to today's situation or not. He does not care if there are more simple ways or if any facts can be changed.

The 4.4– style decisions are simple and straightforward, as they are based on past experience, generally accepted rules, and instructions from above. If the planned decision does not contain any controversy and if there have been proper precedents, the 4.4– quickly chooses it and effectively works on its implementation. If the decision is not so simple, he turns to lots of devices to ensure further activity after the decision is made.

One of such devices is supporting the majority's opinion. The 4.4– discusses all the peculiarities of the decision and possible options with each member of the team privately to find a variant that would be acceptable for everyone. After that he organizes a public talk to make sure the chosen variant is supported by the majority. Meanwhile, he finds out what the expectations of the higher executives are. During the talks and discussions he conceals his opinion until he learns the inclination of the majority. Only then he exclaims: "That's what I think too!" The 4.4– believes that the strength of his position in this situation is more important than the right decision. The opinion of the minority expressed during the discussion can be very innovative and creative, but this is all rejected: "We have no opportunity to test it" or "That's interesting, but in this situation it won't work".

Another tactical device for decision-making is to find historical grounds. The 4.4– style does not want to risk his head and tries to stick to well-tried procedures. He learns the opinions of those who have had to make similar decisions before. If there have been no similar cases, he looks for other precedents to rely on. The right way towards good result is learning the opinions of other people and investigating before the decision is made. The genuine motive of the 4.4–'s investigation is not being eager to make the most suitable and reasonable decision, but his unwillingness to take risks, to discover, to argue.

The third typical feature of the 4.4– style in decision-making is being sure that people should be treated with fairness. But, the 4.4– has his own notion of fairness, which is rather peculiar. He believes that prizes, bonuses, and other goods should be given equally, without any connection with the real contribution of an employee or a department. It can happen that some employee is better qualified for some particular project, but the 4.4– gives the task to another, less qualified person, just in order to redistribute tasks equally. Of course, it makes the efficiency worse, as the tasks are distributed without taking into account the skills of these or those employees, their strong and weak points. The employees' motivation goes down. The 4.4– style prefers to treat everybody equally, but in fact this is a mask of his indifference and fears.

Constructive Critique

The 4.4– style does not use the large potentiality of constructive critique by giving or receiving open and objective feedback in a constructive form. He prefers informal and indirect feedback, the content of which is rather vague. If he has to say something unpleasant, he tries to do it indirectly through hints, in order not to insult the criticized one and to preserve moderate relationships.

A 4.4– person presents critique in a vague form. The really weak points and mistakes are described in hints and vague phrases even if they are serious. The 4.4– very much generalizes critique and as a rule he is not exact in formulating particular things. The degree of the 4.4– openness is not high.

The 4.4– style turns to critique only if he really has to. He can start criticizing someone when the work is being totally neglected or when he has to react to remarks from above. Usually he criticizes informally, in a private talk. He makes references to past precedents and the experience of the organization all the time, as well as to the norms of average efficiency. During such a talk he touches only the questions that might break the normal operation of the team. New creative ideas that could lead to better results and synergetic effect are not welcome or completely neglected. Any alternative ideas that surpass the restrictions of schedules and regulations carry the threat to the habitual operation, according to the 4.4–. In such cases he says politely but firmly: "Yes, it is very interesting, but the idea is premature. Let's return to it next time."

The level of 4.4–'s critique is under the level of necessary efficiency because the 4.4– style does not give particular information and does not request it. Instead, his vague and "open" questions are aimed to make the interlocutor give all the necessary information. Such elusiveness is especially clear when the topic of the talk contains a controversy and might lead to a conflict. For instance, when someone is late for meetings all the time, the 4.4– leader gathers all the participants of the meeting and puts forward an elusive critical remark: "Have we got any problems with meeting attendance?" or "Shall we postpone our meeting until afternoon so that everyone can arrive in time?" An employee often takes a sick leave or compensatory leaves without sufficient grounds for that. The 4.4– could tell him straight what he thinks about such behaviour. He starts a long talk about the advantages of the organizational rules concerning sick leaves and holidays. The employees know all this well, they have heard this from their boss many times, but they have to listen to him again. These examples demonstrate that the whole team will have certain troubles because of the boss's unwillingness to openly discuss the behaviour of some employees who are to blame for these troubles. His feedback consists only of a few vague and rather dull remarks.

The approach of the 4.4– to critique is characterized by three main nuances. Firstly, as long as there is no compromise, all personal opinions are concealed or presented in a very covert form. Such approach allows the 4.4– style to take active part in the discussion and to conduct it without having to display his own stand-point. The 4.4– has the possibility to conceal his own point of view and he does so as long as the team is coming to an agreement. Then the chief joins the collective opinion: "I wholly support your opinion."

Secondly, the 4.4– minimizes the risk of conflict through learning other members' opinions in order to pass them to the other interested sides. Thus, the 4.4– can present information positively. For example, a 4.4– person has learned from one of the employees (let it be Julia) that another employee (let it be Andrew) has repeatedly made use of her ideas presenting them like his own. The 4.4− transmits this news to Andrew as follows: "I would like to tell you that Julia is a little disappointed with the way you've presented those ideas, but I've talked to her and we've settled everything." This phrase is too soft and it does not wholly correspond to the reality of the arisen conflict. Besides, it is rather vague. Instead, a critical remark—an unpleasant, but an honest and exact one—is the best means of dealing with controversies.

In the end, the members of the team get accustomed to looking for compromise between them and to resolving problems for the sake of moving forward, instead of relying on open and honest critique. Progress seems evident, but it is greatly restricted and does not work for prospective. Ironically, such relationships lead to even worse conflict in the future. The 4.4− style welcomes compromise and calls on colleagues to abstain from critical speeches. He hopes that discontentment and differences can eliminate themselves or that they can be handled later, when there is enough time. Meanwhile, unsolved conflicts as a rule become latent and continue waiting for resolutions. And solutions can be found only amid open and honest critique.

8.7 Conclusions

The 4.4− style has a high potentiality for improving the output of his team. However, this style implements at best half of his potentiality for the welfare of the organization and the team. One of the main reasons lies in his formal and indifferent attitude towards his work, his fear of everything new and unusual, and his wish to do everything in strict accordance with the rules and regulations, as well as to avoid any conflicts at all costs. The 4.4− feels quite comfortable when he strictly and exactly follows the habitual instructions.

This strategy allows the 4.4− style to achieve moderate results and to support normal, calm relationships with the colleagues. In the end, he cannot strike outstanding results and has mixed results in taking proper care of people as well.

In a conflict situation, the 4.4− is always aimed at looking for compromise, he follows the majority's opinion and acts in the scope of organizational experience and habitual course of events. His biggest fear and his main enemy is the possibility of changes and reforms. The well-tried methods, even if they are not devoid of evident disadvantages, are considered ideal by the 4.4− style. Changes are considered something negative, a breach of order. "It's against the order"—this is the reaction of the 4.4− to any deviations from once accepted rules.

The 4.4− style tries, if possible, to make decisions. If the circumstances urge him to make decisions, he rejects the alternatives which may cause ambiguous or risky consequences and prefers only the variants that are acceptable for everyone and are based on well-tried methods and past experience. Such decisions allow the 4.4− style to shift responsibility as soon as anything goes wrong. At such an approach, the 4.4− style is able to achieve only moderate results. Such results comfort him quite well because they allow him to stay inside his protective capsule.

On the one hand he does not overwork and feels good, on the other hand the higher executives might not be always content, but they do not criticize him much and have to accept the outcome as it is: "He is not the best employee, but definitely not the worst one."

Style 4.4+: Patriot (Pride and Persistence)

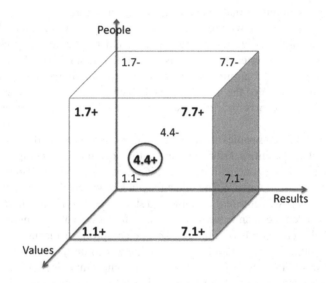

This style is characterized by an average concern for results and people combined with a clear orientation towards organizational values. A person of this style cares for his work and organization and takes pride in its success. The 4.4+ genuinely wants to contribute to the preservation of the company's traditions and do every-thing possible to ensure its normal and stable operation. The 4.4+ is a sincere patriot of the organization. They are loyal, committed, and proud of their own involvement in the organization's history and achievements. At the same time, the person displays traditionalism of thought and behaviour, prefers proven, well-tried approaches and decisions, and seeks to create an atmosphere of stability, reliability, and healthy conservatism.

© Springer-Verlag Berlin Heidelberg 2016
A. Zankovsky, C. von der Heiden, *Leadership with Synercube*,
DOI 10.1007/978-3-662-49052-5_9

9.1   Basic Features of the 4.4+ Style

4.4– and 4.4+ both exhibit medium levels of concern for the company's success and its staff. Despite a certain similarity, however, he differs in his values orientation. The 4.4+ has a clear concern for the company's values, is interested in his work, and is willing to do all it takes to ensure the company's reliable and stable operation.

His motto is "no good deed goes unpunished". The 4.4+ sincerely cannot understand the need for constant changes and reforms being brought up so often, regardless of the actual state of affairs. Change, according to the 4.4+, is called for only when something has gone wrong or no longer works properly. Something that works well does not need changing; what it needs is continuous effort to keep it operational.

The 4.4+ is convinced that everything new is just forgotten past, which has worked well before. Those who founded or were employed by companies before us were not naïve or primitive; otherwise there would not be so many companies around whose uninterrupted operation is essential for our lives. Therefore, the needed evolution is, according to the 4.4+, a product of the company's own traditions, while people of the 4.4+ style have been and will be the main strength and mainstay of any organization ensuring its reliable, stable, and continuous operation.

Indeed, in many companies there are managers and other staff members who have long held his positions, know all there is to know about the company's issues and affairs after having gone with it through it all, and remain loyal and proud to be an integral part of his company. The management knows that they will never let the company down and will ensure its reliable and stable operation in all circumstances.

The pronounced focus on value helps the 4.4+ find a workable compromise even in the most difficult conflicts. For the 4.4– a compromise means escaping the problem, smoothing it over at all costs, or finding a seemingly win–win solution to satisfy all parties. For the 4.4+, by contrast, a compromise is something totally different, consisting in a search for constructive solutions which not only alleviate confrontation, but also ensure a reliable attainment of the company's goals. At the same time, the 4.4+ is not after maximum results. A priority for them is not to allow conflicts and contradictions to disrupt the normal work process. A 4.4+ person looks for a reliable balance between the focus on results and on people. It is this balance, according to the 4.4+, that gives organizations stability and reliability.

The 4.4+'s preferred rule is that of the "golden mean". They are convinced that going after results alone may lead one to achieving them, but it always comes at the expense and to the detriment of personal relationships. Conversely, bonding too closely with one's co-workers and staff damages the performance. It is the golden mean—maintaining normal personal relationships with co-workers and medium, but constant results—that helps the organization to move forward step by step, without failures and breakthroughs.

The 4.4+ is democratic in his organizational approach, demanding equal conditions and rights for all staff members, regardless of his position.

At the same time, the 4.4+ always stays distant from all his co-workers, especially subordinates. Thus, the proper way that has been there before us is preserved, with everyone getting his desserts. Proper management excludes having informal relationships, fraternizing with one's subordinates. The 4.4+ is very well aware of all the company's issues, which allows him to find compromises that are acceptable both for the organization and for all parties involved.

The 4.4+ tends to follow the procedures and rules, while the usual routine helps them feel at ease. They prefer tried-and-true practices that ensure compliance with corporate standards. The work is to be regulated by clear rules and done at a measured pace. However, if a familiar, time-tested method has obvious drawbacks and causes problems, the 4.4+ will readily abandon or change it.

The 4.4+ always seeks to draw on from past experience. He works in a reliable, stable way and motivates others to achieve good results. This kind of person creates a favourable working environment, which is propitious for reliable performance. The 4.4+ is characterized by acting in a well-weighed, deliberate, and conservative way.

In making decisions, the 4.4+ is influenced primarily by the majority opinion, the company's interests and past experience. They are convinced that significant changes and reforms may bring real benefits to the company only in exceptional cases.

9.2 The 4.4+ Style in Collective Cooperation

The 4.4+ always seeks to act with certainty and make decisions that are acceptable to all and based on proven methods. This approach, according to the 4.4+, allows organizations to avoid risks by following tried-and-tested procedures which conform to the general accepted opinions and standards.

If a staff member fails to properly do his job, the 4.4+ will readily give him a hand, suggesting proven approaches and solutions that the 4.4+ has repeatedly and successfully employed himself. His actions are always clear, goal-oriented, and understandable to co-workers. The 4.4+ will not seek to make the goal or the result seem insignificant. It is, however, sometimes an outcome of his actions, as a consequence of the 4.4+'s very worldview that consists in the belief that everything—work, relationships, achievements, and life in general—should be normal.

Within the team, the 4.4+ is friendly and willing to meet others halfway, often acting as a facilitator in his colleagues' social interactions. This role allows them to treat colleagues equally, while at the same time keeping a certain distance. They often talk with people, especially privately, to get and provide insight into the current situation and move forward. As a facilitator, the 4.4+ can interfere with the work of others if he perceives a deviation from the "standard" which, in his opinion, can harm the team work. This, on the one hand, helps others learn and avoid mistakes, but on the other hand robs co-workers of the freedom to experiment and take initiative, which sometimes leads to inactivity and indifference. The 4.4+ tries to draw people back to mainstream approaches, standards, and rules.

The team enjoys working under the 4.4+. As in a team led or joined by a 1.7+ person, the members bond together and spend a lot of time talking about work and personal matters. It is a case where employees may become so relaxed at work that the company's business and performance is no longer his priority. However, as with the 1.7+, these relationships are generally not deep, as the expression of trust, respect, and sincerity is restrained to following the norms. Despite all his friendliness and attention to each other, co-workers are reluctant to engage in an open, candid discussion of the company's issues, take the initiative, set themselves higher goals, or look for constructive solutions to conflicts.

For the 4.4+ personal requirements are oriented at an average person who embodies a kind of corporate majority. The ideal worker, according to the 4.4+, should work like everyone else, without standing out or lagging behind; they should have normal, smooth team relationships, observe the rules and traditions, and be loyal and committed to his organization.

There is trust and respect in a 4.4+ team, but these are very discreet and somewhat formal. This results in a discreet and prudent behaviour, which increases the time of social interaction and reduces personal commitment. On the one hand, people will have greater potential and will be ready to work more for the benefit of the company and its development, but on the other following the customary rules and tradition will make them complacent and satisfied with the stable routine life. Creative ideas and initiatives will thus peter out finding no support or real prospects.

9.3   The I-ZONE and the 4.4+ Style

The relationships between staff members in a 4.4+ team are stable and lasting, as they are cemented by the total focus on the company's values. People care about his work and organization, and they are loyal and committed. However, attempts at open and direct discussions often stumble on regulations and formalities, as they will cause concern and anxiety for the 4.4+ to violate them. Thus, most workers are clearly aware that his initiative and activities should be limited by the usual rules and aimed primarily at ensuring the usual, traditional working routine. This atmosphere leads to the concealment or underestimation of important new information, because staff members get used to patterned thinking based on precedents and traditions. They become very cautious, and when faced with a direct question, they experience anxiety and discomfort, trying to recall a similar past situation. All this reduces the operational efficiency and results in the need of a great amount of effort to maintain the operational efficiency at least at average levels in a changing environment (Fig. 9.1).

Unanimity and cohesion are very much appreciated in a 4.4+ team. For that reason, a compromise is the most popular and accepted way to deal with contentions. But, unlike the 4.4– style, which seeks to compromise at all costs even to the detriment of the company's objectives, the 4.4+ is aimed more at finding a constructive solution. For them, the compromise is not so much a means to reduce

Fig. 9.1 4.4+

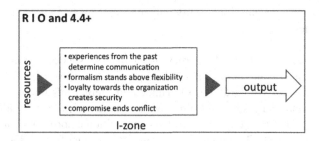

tensions as a way to ensure a stable, reliable operation and compliance with corporate or institutional rules and traditions.

People who bring up critique and innovations in a group discussion are criticized for having failed to sufficiently develop their proposals and draw from the company's wealth of positive experience, as well as for disrupting the normal course of work. In fact, they challenge the 4.4+'s firm belief that everything is fine as it is. Following rules and traditions gives the 4.4+ confidence and makes him feel fulfilled and successful. Others, however, realize that rules are used as a protection against the uncertainty and risks posed by innovations and reforms that cause discomfort and alarm for a 4.4+ person.

The desire to do what is familiar and correct is constantly at odds with the ever-changing corporate environment. Attempts to use the established norms and previous experience in a new environment often puts the 4.4+ in a difficult position, but he will not change his views. At times he complains: "Look what a mess this is! The rules are changing every day! How can we work like that?" However, a sincere feeling of commitment forces the 4.4+ towards compromises and solutions to ensure the company's reliable and continuous operation in all circumstances.

The 4.4+ style believes that a unanimous, working compromise, which takes into account the interests of the company and its staff members, is the best form of social interaction, with no true alternative. Because of his traditionalism and fear of subjecting his past experience and well-established standards to critical analysis, the 4.4+ cannot experience the benefits of synergic team work for real.

9.4   4.4+ Culture and Values

Basic Feature: Stability, Traditionalism, and Trust in the Organization, Fear of Change

Trust The 4.4+ culture is based on confidence in the organization, its rules and regulations, past experience and history, decisions, and practices that have proved his reliability and efficiency. Accordingly, only those who strictly follow the company's rules and regulations, and are loyal and committed, can be worthy of trust. New approaches and solutions cause fear and anxiety, while people exhibiting unusual behaviour or generating original ideas are met with distrust and suspicion.

The new gains credibility only after the new knowledge is acquired and sufficiently tested.

Fairness The 4.4+ fairness is egalitarian; success is rarely mentioned, the golden mean is the main rule in place providing for the same, averaged performance and reward standards for all. This culture represents mainly a majority justice, rather than real justice and objective assessment of each individual's contribution to the overall result. Decisions based on traditional norms and past experience are considered just. The fairest way to resolve a conflict for the 4.4+ is to find a compromise which, above all, takes into account the interests of the company and creates the conditions for further work done on the normal, average level.

Commitment The 4.4+ displays very high identification with his company, its employees, mission, and goals. The company's norms, traditions, and tried-and-true practices are of special importance for the 4.4+. This style's commitment and identity are all the more pronounced if the established norms, traditions, and proven approaches, of which he is an ardent champion, are shared by a majority of staff members and supported by the management. The 4.4+ is loyal and devoted to the company and perceives himself as its mainstay. He values his contribution to the organization and the duration of his employment.

Responsibility For the 4.4+ responsibility means following well-tried practices and complying with the company's established standards. The 4.4+ believes that in this case each and every staff member will work in a reliable, stable, and correct way. The established traditions and values, loyalty, and commitment to the company are, according to the 4.4+, the main foundations of the social system.

Being focused on the majority the 4.4+ feels deeply responsible both for the staff members and for the company as a whole. In addition, he feels reliable for the company's role and image in society. He supports socially acceptable solutions and feels for his own actions. Reliability and social responsibility for the 4.4+ mean following the good traditions and accepted organizational and social norms, which ensure life's stability and continuity. The need for change is associated with reduced reliability and social instability.

Integrity In the 4.4+ culture, honesty and transparency are understood as adherence to traditional methods and proper social norms. Information on well-established standards is provided and exchanged accurately and objectively. Changing standards cause rejection and distrust, which can lead to the information getting distorted or partially withheld. Relationships are characterized by a fairly high level of integrity. Loyalty and commitment to the organization, pride in its history, and success may result in the real situation being shown favourably and optimistically. Innovations are perceived warily and require convincing and justification of his necessity and effectiveness, as well as quite a long period of adaptation and adoption. Feedback is given in an accessible, albeit somewhat polished way, with negative issues given a positive cover and presented without specifics. It slightly reduces the level of transparency and honesty, making these qualities seem embellished.

9.5   4.4+ Culture and Power

Focus on Laying Stress on the Position-Based and Charismatic Authority

Punishment The 4.4+ believes punishment to be a forced measure to influence those who will not understand, even after repeated explanations, that certain behaviours are unacceptable, because they harm the organization, its traditions, and the work as a whole. The 4.4+ tends to see ineffective or unconstructive behaviour as resulting from errors of judgement rather than foul intent, and he believes it can be rectified by explaining what the right behaviour should be like. If punishment is still inevitable, it should be devoid of subjectivity, well-regulated, and ensure the keeping of traditions and reliable operation of the system. Punishment has more to do with a failure to comply with traditions and a threat to disrupt the company's work than the outcome.

Reward The 4.4+ believes that everyone who follows the established traditions, norms, and rules does his job at an acceptable level, and shows loyalty to the organization, deserves a reward. The 4.4+ is aimed at achieving results that do not exceed average levels and allow the organization to function properly. Outstanding successes are rewarded in the same way as the average, moderate ones. The 4.4+ does not consider it necessary to specifically reward and motivate those who have set themselves a high achievement goal. Thus, reward is egalitarian and only distantly related to actual performance.

Position For the 4.4+ style, authority is very important because it is the foundation of a company's traditions, rules, and regulations. The person of this type is convinced that the organization will only be efficient and reliable, if each employee at each level does his job properly. The 4.4+ knows his required amount of work very well and often reminds others of the need to do his job in full. They are reluctant to delegate his responsibilities to subordinates, and lose confidence and become indecisive when innovative solutions are required that go beyond his authority and the routine.

Information The basic information resources for the 4.4+ are the established institutional traditions, rules, and regulations, which are reflected in corporate documents, or passed on informally as part of the existing corporate culture. The 4.4+ style is well aware of who should do what and knows the staff's rights and duties very well, as well as the beginning and the end of his own area of responsibility. The exchange of information is carried out in order to ensure the company's reliable operation and to strengthen one's own position.

In dealing with subordinates, the 4.4+ tends to emphasize, as a rule, the need for loyalty and adherence to the rules and standards. The 4.4+ receives the managers' orders with enthusiasm and tries to carry them out on time and at an acceptable level. The most intensive debates the 4.4+ ever starts happen within his team and focus on finding new solutions when changes and innovations are needed.

Expert The 4.4+ has greatest competence in the field of tried-and-true approaches. People of this type are well equipped to deal with situations that require worked-out and standard solutions and decisions. The 4.4+ is highly competent, deriving his skills from the company's traditions, and knows the proper way of conducting business and the mood at the top well. Often, however, the 4.4+ fails to realize that something could have been done better, as he does not question the current standards. Such specialists often have rather solid professional skills, but see his available knowledge and skills as quite sufficient and requiring no constant training. The 4.4+ believes that "perfect is the enemy of good" and that strict adherence to proven approaches and technologies will inevitably ensure the company's steady and reliable operation.

Referent The 4.4+ style usually enjoys quite a strong referent power, as he does not lose his presence of mind under any circumstances, knows and can keenly feel the needs and interests of staff members, and always tries to act in the company's interest. This behaviour is complemented by his conviction that even the most serious problems are not new and have repeatedly popped up before. Therefore, by following the company's traditions, using proven approaches and following the majority, one can cope with any difficulties and crises. As a result, others perceive the 4.4+ as reliable and strong people embodying the organization and its traditions. For that reason, when the 4.4+ is forced to call on his co-workers to perform urgent or difficult work, his call may be motivational. At the same time, wariness of novelty and changes, as well as insufficient focus on results do not allow the 4.4+ to fully develop robust, harmonious relationships based on mutual trust, respect, and sincerity.

9.6   Cooperation Skills of the 4.4+ Style

Conflict Resolution

The 4.4+ has a negative attitude towards conflicts, considering them a major threat to the company's reliable, stable performance. The 4.4+ is convinced that if all staff members followed the company's traditions and norms, were loyal and did their job at a level not below the average, then there would be no reason to give rise to confrontation and conflict within the company. In addition, the conflict is a threat to established traditions and norms that the 4.4+ cares to protect and support.

If a conflict still happens, the 4.4+ appeals to all parties to find a workable compromise that will primarily allow for the work to continue in a normal, stable way. Even in the worst conflict situations, the 4.4+ can find feasible compromises profiting on his manifest focus on the company's values. Compromise has a completely different meaning for the 4.4+ than for the 4.4–. If for the latter compromise means avoiding the problem, relieving the conflict at any price and finding half-working solutions which give something to every party, the 4.4+ looks for constructive solutions, which not only lower tensions but also ensure a reliable achievement of the company's goals and strengthen employees' loyalty.

In case of conflict, the 4.4+ seeks to avoid a fall in performance rather than to maximize it. His priority is to prevent conflicts and contradictions from disrupting the normal course of work; the 4.4+ looks for a reliable, sustainable balance between the focus on performance and concern for other people. It is this balance, according to the 4.4+, that gives the company stability and allows it to overcome any problems and difficulties.

Understanding that ignoring conflicts is a serious threat to the normal working process, the 4.4+ never attempts to withdraw from conflict situations and take a neutral position, waiting for the problem to resolve itself. However, the 4.4+ is focused on solutions which are based on traditions and precedents which often prevent him from uncovering the root causes of the conflict and using its positive potential to increase efficiency.

It is very important for the 4.4+ to ensure that the compromise receives the vast majority support. For this, the 4.4+ is prepared to spend a lot of time and make every possible effort to persuade the conflicting parties to seek a compromise solution, which will provide for the company's stable and reliable operation.

A compromise for the benefit of the organization, but without a deep analysis of the conflict's internal causes, produces solutions that strengthen traditional practices, but often miss new opportunities and prospects. Although most staff members are relieved that the conflict has been resolved, the creative people and those seeking new approaches are left with inner frustration and disappointment. The 4.4+, as a rule, pays little attention to it, believing that a slight dissatisfaction of several people can be exchanged for the reliable status quo, supported by the majority. This tactic prevents the use of conflict as the most important resource for the company's development, slowing progress and cultivating passivity in those who might help generate it.

Although conflict is associated with a confrontation and rising tension in the I-ZONE relationships, it plays an important role in moving the team forward, opening up the possibility for an in-depth consideration of the issue, as well as for the evaluation and gathering of different opinions and beliefs. A useful idea can emerge to the company's benefit regardless of whether it meets or contradicts the established rules and regulations. Analysing and identifying the conflict's root causes means solving issues in a systemic way, rather than seeking a reasonable and constructive compromise that ignores fresh thoughts.

For the 4.4+ style conflict means a deviation from or even a threat to the established, functional order. Therefore, if the conflict lasts too long, the 4.4+ can go all the way down to suppressing it. However, he will not do that like the 7.1— by using his power, but by appealing to the commonly shared views and opinions of the majority. The pressure from the majority and the 4.4+'s personal authority usually directs conflict into a more spirited search for compromise, which they quickly find realizing the error of stubborn confrontation. In sincere attempts to resolve conflicts for the company's benefit, the 4.4+ is convinced that his conflict resolution model resolution is optimal.

Communicative Competence

The 4.4+ exhibits a high level of development and use of communicative competence. He actively communicates with all staff members, discusses ideas and suggestions. He is characterized by careful attention to the information received from managers and the most knowledgeable of colleagues. If decision-making requires detailed information, the 4.4+ gathers it in advance, asking around if necessary. The 4.4+ is willing to answer direct questions and is prepared to accept other viewpoints.

Still, the drive to follow the established traditions and order limits the 4.4+'s communicative competence. The 4.4+ style actively gathers information to find out the opinions and attitudes of the majority of staff. He constantly monitors the majority's mood and feels relaxed and confident when it is in line with the company's standards and oriented towards work in the usual style and at the usual pace.

The information exchange lets the 4.4+ see how steadily and smoothly the company is running, as well as ensure that its traditions and standards are respected, and the motivation and loyalty of staff members is maintained at a high level. Similarly to style 4.4—, the 4.4+ can talk pleasantly and profusely, mostly about topics related to the company's rules, procedures, and regulations. It is his favourite area and he is ready to share his knowledge and experience with all those who are sincerely loyal to the organization and share its values. No one matches the 4.4+ in this sphere. However, while the 4.4— uses organizational rules, procedures, and regulations to prop up his positions and protect his overt or concealed indifference to the company's activities, these are not just pure formalities for the 4.4+.

For him following traditions and rules is filled with deep personal meaning: they believe traditions and rules to be time-tested behavioural patterns, which they earnestly follow and which the organizations and the vast majority of its employees need. Drawing on this value orientation, the 4.4+ follows rules and encourages others to do so, not because he is forced to (the law is harsh, but it is the law), but because it is right. Employees understand this view, which helps the 4.4+ to ensure compliance with formal requirements without internal resistance from his colleagues.

The 4.4+ has extensive knowledge in many other professional fields. However, he never emphasizes his own role and opinion, trying to reconcile them with the established traditions, and the majority's opinion. The 4.4+ listens to the opinion of colleagues and subordinates with interest and gratitude, especially if it is in line with traditional customary practices and solutions. If the view is new or unusual, the 4.4+ will not immediately reject it. He will suggest that his colleague should substantiate it and prove that the new practice is better than the time-tested one. To the 4.4+'s great satisfaction, such discussions usually end up with the old practices proven true once again.

If the argument takes longer than usual and opinions remain divided, the 4.4+ invokes successful precedents and tries to enlist the support of the majority. He admits the existence of different opinions, but only if they cannot damage the organization or its system. The 4.4+ eagerly collects information, but passes it through the filter of tradition, often ignoring the new and promising data. Information often serves to validate traditional practices and the majority's opinion, not to find the best solutions.

The 4.4+ style often goes directly to his sources for information: documents and specific individuals. The 4.4+ does not hide his partial attitude towards the issue and the important role information plays in the organization. This style is usually well informed about the company's past experience in dealing with similar issues but is always ready to consult with the staff, who is expert on the subject. Such consultations are quite effective, as the 4.4+ does not hide his goals and ask questions directly, framing them to be specific and objective, "I know you have had experience promoting goods in a new region. We now have a similar task. What difficulties have you faced during the first stage of the project?"

The 4.4+ does not conceal his sincere commitment to the company and is openly proud of it. For that reason, those who are familiar with the company's traditions and rules can easily predict what turns his dialog with the 4.4+ will take. In the same vein, the genuine acceptance of and loyalty to the organization will inevitably win the 4.4+'s trust, bringing opportunities to influence and manipulate him.

Active Positioning

The 4.4+ has active social standpoint in a sincere belief that he and the organization as a whole have a very important and essential job to do. This person cares for his work and is proud of its affiliation with the organization and its achievements. The 4.4+ seeks to contribute to preserving the organization's traditions and ensure its normal and stable operation. He will actively defend his standpoint both by leading by example and providing convincing arguments.

Despite the fact that the 4.4+ has concerns for the management's expectations, the company's tradition and the majority's opinion, he will speak his mind openly, honestly believing that it reflects the interests of the entire organization. This helps the person of this type to be extremely convincing and receive support from his subordinates, even if the latter do not fully agree with him.

The 4.4+ person prefers sticking to time-tested methods, and stands his ground when pressured, trying to convince his opponent that he is right. The 4.4+'s characteristic traditionalism of thought and behaviour makes him especially compelling when there is a need to defend proven, time-tested approaches. If faced with an unfamiliar, new situation, which requires non-standard, creative solutions, the 4.4+ either sticks to the standard approach or is forced to agree with the new opinion, feeling the pressure of the management and the majority of staff. This outcome is extremely uncomfortable for the 4.4+, compromising his values orientation towards stability and reliability, and shattering his usual world view.

To make the 4.4+ adopt a new approach, it is important to convince him of the benefits of the innovation for the company's normal operation. It is vital for the person to realize that the new practice, for all its strangeness, will not damage the organization. This attitude forces the 4.4+ to constantly and critically evaluate new practices in terms of their usefulness and popularity.

The 4.4+ will convincingly defend his opinion if it is in line with that of the management or the majority of employees. But if this opinion is questioned, the 4.4+ can resentfully withdraw into self-isolation. This may be accompanied by the following typical cry: "Well, if our glorious traditions mean nothing, while nobody needs my knowledge and experience, then I wash my hands! Let's see what benefit all these new practices will bring!"

However, even saying so does not absolve the 4.4+ from his responsibility for the organization and its future. The person will never sit on his hands or avoid work and will continue to perform his duties, even under the most unfavourable circumstances. According to the 4.4+, work must continue, no matter what. His motto is "The show must go on!", and the 4.4+ will defend this creed to the end. The 4.4+ takes an active standpoint, which is based on the person's loyalty to the organization, past experience, and time-tested approaches. If an unpopular decision must be taken, the 4.4+ will necessarily stress that it is a necessary step to preserve and maintain the usual corporate activity. The person seeks to create an atmosphere of stability, reliability, and a robust conservatism, and as long as the activities are routine, the 4.4+ will show high efficiency.

When problems that require non-standard solutions arise, the 4.4+ style does not feel at ease. However, even in this situation, his values orientation and commitment to the organization provide a strong basis to search for constructive solutions and compromises.

Decision-Making

The most important factor for the 4.4+ style when making decisions is to ensure it benefits the organization and is supported by the management and the majority of staff members. To make such a decision, the 4.4+ is willing to compromise a lot and even sacrifice a part of his own interests. The 4.4+ style is very much focused on the past, preferring well-tried approaches. The person of this type treats innovation and reform with great scepticism. Decision-making is part of the routine course of action, traditions, and precedents. The 4.4+ has no doubts that past experience is not only relevant today but will be so in the future.

The 4.4+'s solutions usually receive praise from the management and the majority of staff members because of their simplicity and clarity, since they are based on past experience and common rules that are familiar to everyone. If a similar decision has already been taken in the past and it will, according to the 4.4+, ensure the stable running of the organization, the decision is adopted and implemented quite quickly and efficiently. If a difficult approach is required, the 4.4+ often prefers sizing the expectations of the higher officials and the majority's opinion, while holding detailed discussions with all interested sides concerning all aspects of the decision and its possible alternatives.

The 4.4+ is very hostile towards decisions whose consequences may be dangerous to the organization and even cause it serious damage. In such cases, convincing the 4.4+ of the correctness and validity of a risky decision will be extremely difficult, if not impossible.

Left without a precedent to follow, the 4.4+ tries to find a past decision which was even remotely similar to the one needed today, to make it this time again. Even if the decision is quite trivial, the 4.4+ will find out his co-workers' opinions believing this to be good for the company.

Another important feature of the 4.4+'s decision-making is his conviction that a loyal, committed employee is always a valuable and efficient specialist. For that reason, the 4.4+ at times appreciates ostensible, paraded loyalty and commitment more than actual performance. This, of course, reduces labour motivation and gives rise to internal conflicts.

Thinking about possible solution, the 4.4+ considers exclusively those that have repeatedly proved successful, almost always ignoring unusual, innovative alternatives. If someone insists on trying new approaches and solutions, the 4.4+ will find convincing arguments to reject them, deploying as the most forceful argument the risks of irreversible damage which, according to the 4.4+, will inevitably accompany the new practices. To minimize these risks, the 4.4+ style suggests using proven, conventional approaches.

Nevertheless, in crisis situations when there is no avoiding a new solution, the 4.4+, for all his conservatism, is prepared to make changes which, in his opinion, will serve the good of the organization. Once the decision is made, the 4.4+ usually ensures a clear and rigorous follow-up on its implementation until it is wholly carried out.

Constructive Critique

For the 4.4+, constructive critique is an opportunity to give feedback to others about the extent to which his behaviour and actions correspond to the traditions and norms prevailing in the organization. Considering the established, well-tried system as the only true system of benchmarks, the 4.4+ considers deviation to be a violation that needs to be rectified. He displays his critique openly and objectively, in an honest belief that this is a good thing to do for the benefit of all.

If the 4.4+ has to say something unpleasant, he tries to do it in a tactful, friendly way, explaining to the target of his admonishing how one should behave in such situation in an organization, and how the person's improper behaviour may harm the company. At the moment the 4.4+ person levels his critique, he believes to be representing the company himself and acting on its behalf. The 4.4+ style knows what proper behaviour is and has no intention to discuss the reasons or motives of the conduct he finds wrong. However, he is not inclined to think that improper behaviour is the result of deliberate malicious intent. The 4.4+ believes improper conduct is caused by ignorance or a lack of understanding of how a normal employee who is grateful to his company for its care should behave. The 4.4+ is absolutely convinced that all employees must be as loyal and committed as the 4.4+ himself. His constructive critique is thus a form of training and education of his co-workers.

If the company is on the rise and safely positioned in the market, the 4.4+'s constructive critique style focused on maintaining the status quo is justified and effective. However, if the company affairs are far from ideal, such critique can only worsen the situation, impeding improvement. A similar pattern is observed in cases where the 4.4+'s critique model applied to both laggards and the most efficient staff member. If someone lagging behind receives his censure, the effort to pull the person to normal efficiency levels has quite a positive effect on the company. If the most effective staff members are admonished for his excessive "zeal", lack of innovation, and respect for tradition, his work motivation and commitment will inevitably suffer.

The 4.4+'s critique is guided by average-employee requirements. On the one hand, this kind of critique is well received by the majority of employees for being clear, concrete, and ensuring the normal working routine. On the other hand, this style of critique often blocks any attempt to introduce non-standard thinking and quests for new solution into the company's activities.

If everything goes according to the established routine, the 4.4+ is rarely critical. Then, the 4.4+ is too keen to praise and can hardly conceal his satisfaction when everything goes as it should. In a discussion, the 4.4+ will not talk about long-term prospects or possible threats, often saying, "Do not trouble it until it troubles you". The 4.4+ will only bring up issues that can disrupt the normal course of work. New creative ideas that could really lead to synergies are not welcomed and met with strong scepticism. Alternatives that subvert the existing paradigms constitute, according to the 4.4+, a misguided risk and may threaten the company's proper functioning. In such cases, the 4.4+ will politely but firmly and confidently say, "Yes, it could be an interesting idea, but it is only an idea, which may come and go, while our organization has functioned and will function, maintaining its time and life-tested rules, principles, and traditions. It is necessary, first of all, to avoid losing our achievements, rather than engaging in project-mongering and fantasizing."

The 4.4+'s critique never reaches the required efficiency level, as representatives of this style impede the development of new ideas and approaches, trying to fit them into the Procrustean bed of traditional approaches and standards. In the end, the most efficient and creative team members get used to working like everyone else and compromising, instead of using open and honest critique to identify new opportunities and prospects. Such an approach to critique has limitations and fails to generate good prospects, hamstringing the most promising employees. The employees who cannot realize their potential are increasingly eager to find employment somewhere else, where there is a possibility of open and honest constructive critique.

9.7 Conclusions

The 4.4+ style has great potential to strengthen the capabilities of his team, drawing primarily based on his loyalty, commitment, and an honest focus on the company's values. In addition, the 4.4+ can ensure the company's normal operation at a good moderate level in all circumstances. This is what makes the 4.4+ a "corporate person"; the 4.4+ people are the mainstays of many organizations, since even in difficult circumstances, they will never let their company down and will ensure its system's reliable, stable operation. These people are honest patriots of their organization and are proud of being involved in its history and achievements.

However, the 4.4+ does not fully use his potential for the benefit of the organization and its staff. This happens mainly because of the traditionalism of thought and behaviour, the preference for proven, tried-and-true methods and solutions, as well as the mistrust, scepticism, and fear of everything new and unusual. The 4.4+ style is eager to create an atmosphere of stability, reliability, and good conservatism, trying to follow through the settled traditions and norms, and doing everything to comply with well-established procedures and rules.

This helps the 4.4+ to achieve reliable, stable results at a good average level, while maintaining cordial working relationships with colleagues. However, ultimately, the 4.4+ approach fails to produce high results or team synergy.

In a conflict situation, the 4.4+ always focuses on finding compromising solutions that take into account the interests of the company and the majority of its staff and that are based on past experience and the usual routine. The 4.4+ regards every opportunity to change and reform with distrust and anxiety. The 4.4+ considers the familiar, time-tested method of action an ideal to be preserved and cherished.

The 4.4+'s decision-making style rejects options which seem risky or vague, and prefers only decisions which are acceptable to everyone and are based on past experience and already tested methods. If the organization as a whole is stable and secure, the 4.4+ is acceptable, ensuring normal, average performance. However, in dynamic market conditions and volatility, the traditionalism of thought and behaviour can only worsen the situation, impeding the search for optimal changes and reform.

The 4.4+'s constructive critique has its advantages and limitations. On the one side, it helps push those lagging behind to the average performance levels; on the other, it inhibits the most effective and creative staff members, depriving them of high achievement motivation. In his work, the 4.4+' is guided by average-employee requirements, which also hinders the implementation of innovations. In the end, the most valuable employees with high creative potential and motivation get used to working like the majority and making compromises, rather than fully contributing to the company and its development.

Style 1.1−: Indifferent (To Avoid and to Evade)

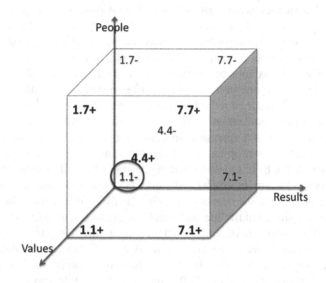

Low concern for production, low concern for people, indifferent attitude towards work and organization. Strong conviction that people's lives cannot have any higher meaning and that life cannot and must not be changed for the better. The desire to dissociate oneself from the whole, hide, avoid everything, to be imperceptible. The slogan is: "I wish no one bothered me!" The 1.1− style avoids articulating his position and point of view, trying not to ask questions; errors are hushed up and concealed. Decisions are postponed until someone else makes them or the problem resolves by itself. Almost no interest in work and other people. Being a leader, evades responsibility, letting things take their course. No desire to show up, evading all problems, always ready to be fired. Avoids meetings and discussions, as well as conflicts with other team members. Other staff members feel that the 1.1− style does not need anything in work, nor in life. The main motivation

© Springer-Verlag Berlin Heidelberg 2016
A. Zankovsky, C. von der Heiden, *Leadership with Synercube*,
DOI 10.1007/978-3-662-49052-5_10

is to avoid any form of involvement. Actual interests lie beyond organizational life. Always distances himself from responsibility for the results, tries to avoid personal problems. When under pressure, he takes a passive or supportive standpoint.

10.1   Basic Features of the 1.1− Style

The 1.1− style has the lowest levels of focus on all three factors: production, people, and organizational values. The keywords to characterize this type of behaviour are indifference and cynicism. He is profoundly indifferent towards the results to be achieved; he does not care about the people with whom he works and is indifferent to the organization as a whole. He has a cynical attitude towards everything that surrounds him. He believes that all people just pretend that they are deeply passionate about something or that they are willing to sacrifice themselves for work, He regards any behaviour as manipulative and false. The 1.1− style always suspects others of insincerity and desire to do him some harm. The 1.1− style believes nobody and trusts no one, feeling comfortable when being well hidden from everyone in his shell of indifference and self-distancing.

The 1.1− style is the least remarkable person in the team. He seeks to avoid real involvement in the organization affairs at any cost, carefully doing his job (only what is necessary and under pressure, straining from doing a little more). The 1.1− style tries to create an atmosphere of predictability, making it clear that no one can count on the fact that he has to do something beyond what had been planned. Based on this behaviour pattern, he emphatically does not see any advantage in getting out of his shell and trying to see new opportunities. He firmly believes that involvement in work brings nothing but trouble, and should be avoided at all costs. If one tries to engage the 1.1− style in organizational life, as a rule, his answer will be the following: "Maybe", "We'll see", or "I'll think it over". However, colleagues and subordinates are well aware that this will be followed by nothing, and these excuses are another form of withdrawal. Left alone, the 1.1− style stays the same: by himself and in no way encumbered.

In order to dissociate himself from work, people and the organization in general, the 1.1− style tries to do everything formally, so that he can always shirk responsibility, hiding behind the instructions: "And in the instruction it isn't stated that I'm in charge of it." If there are problems, but formally he is not responsible for them, the 1.1− style does not pay any attention to them, ignoring them completely. He, however, may pass the problem to someone else, but he never tries to make his own decision. When there are no rigid guidelines or instructions, the 1.1− style thinks: "This is not my problem." However, he would never say it out loud for fear of being involved in a discussion that would be useless and can be dangerous. When the 1.1− style makes a decision, he is afraid to be appointed to perform it himself. Therefore, the 1.1− style thinks it would be safer and better to wait for somebody else to notice the problem and solve it.

10.2   The 1.1— Style in Collective Cooperation

Being in self-imposed isolation, the 1.1— style is the least involved in the common collective work. Therefore, he does not feel like a staff member who does not carry out his tasks, reducing the overall efficiency of the group. Even if an inefficient member of the team has a negative effect on the results, the 1.1— style does not try to do or change anything, saying: "It's not my fault, so I do not have to bear responsibility for it."

The 1.1— style will never makes any suggestions about how to improve efficiency. He will do that only when persistently asked to. If others express their disagreement about his suggestion, he immediately retreats, thankful that he does not have to be responsible for the result. Not sharing organizational values, as well as not having the desire to achieve good results and maintain effective relationships, the 1.1— style represents the weakest link in the team. His attitude is expressed by the following rule: "Whatever you say or think about me, I don't care." Other team members, knowing that the 1.1— style makes the least efforts, get used to not relying on him. They leave to him only clear and simple tasks that do not require taking the initiative.

The 1.1— leader shows the body of work to his subordinates and expects that they will take the responsibility for it. If the minimum amount of work is completed, he is willing to obediently follow others. In such circumstances, even the most committed employees feel tired and irritable. Enthusiasm for work considerably reduces, as the 1.1— leader seeks only minimal results. Feeling that their commitment to the organization is not shared by their leader, the highly motivated employees who set high goals lose motivation and satisfaction.

The 1.1— style sees no connection between the orientation for organizational values, concern for people, and concern for production. There is minimal interest in all that prevents him from experiencing all the advantages of harmonious relationship and teamwork for the organization. The motivational basis of such behaviour is a reluctance to be deeply involved in relationships and work, being afraid of difficult situations and having a profound neglect of organizational values. Therefore, the 1.1— style tries to create a predictable environment around him, communicating with others very rarely and resisting any change. Creating a shell of formal procedures and rules, he studiously ignores both challenges and opportunities. The established rules and regulations become a justification for his indifference, protecting him from participation and complications: "You cannot pin that on me. It is not the responsibility of my department." The 1.1— style can deny the need for change, giving a pessimistic outlook: "If we begin to change something, it will do more harm than good".

10.3   The I-ZONE and the 1.1− Style

Usually, relations between those focused on organizational values and the indifferent 1.1− style leader become polarized. Staff members feel resentment, as they have to take responsibility not only for their work, but also for the work of their boss. The 1.1− leader never feels as a part of the team, he keeps distance and protects himself from taking initiative. The longer it lasts, the more polarized the relations are, because the team is doing more and more, and the 1.1− leader is doing less and less. The response to the 1.1− leader's behaviour can vary from mild disappointment: "I hoped that he's at least a little worried about what is going on," to outright condemnation: "He pulls back the whole team."

Over time, the 1.1− leader becomes an object of permanent indignation. Depending on the organization's corporate culture, critique can be soft, indirect, or include direct accusations. The 1.1− style takes such critique with indifference, as if he had nothing to do with all unresolved problems. When responding to particularly sharp critique, he uses the same formula: "This is not written in my job description" or "No one told me it should be done".

The 1.1− style is pessimistic about the relations in the team and their potential. He perceives them as unpleasant stress and burden, which in turn reduces the level of trust and respect to him from the part of colleagues and subordinates. All this causes a feeling of uncertainty and fear of difficulties. Seeing a deeper involvement in work, the 1.1− style suspects a test, check-up, or revision, assuming the worst: "They are looking for a reason to remove me from office. They're just waiting for me to make a mistake." The 1.1− style leader tries to do enough to keep his position, often with a hidden subtext that employees should be grateful to him for that. The 1.1− style fears that even his minimal involvement may bring his opponents some solid arguments, which they will use against him. Therefore, the nature of his relationship with the staff is always cautious and restrained. He will never express his opinion until he is told to do so. If it happens, it is usually very neutral, as the 1.1− style is doing his best not to cause disputes and not to draw attention to himself (Fig. 10.1).

As a rule, 1.1− leaders keep their principles, even if the conditions which led to them have changed. They still prefer to hide in a shell of self-alienation, putting

Fig. 10.1 1.1−

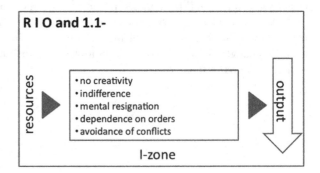

R I O and 1.1-

resources

• no creativity
• indifference
• mental resignation
• dependence on orders
• avoidance of conflicts

output

I-zone

calmness and indifference before all the joy and meaning that can be gained in common collective work based on trust, honesty, and full involvement.

10.4   1.1– Culture and Values

Culture of Mistrust, Indifference, and Alienation

Trust The 1.1– style trusts no one. He believes that all people just pretend that they are deeply passionate about something, that something is important for them, that they are willing to work for wear, to worry, and to sacrifice themselves. So in any manifestation of commitment and interest he sees something sham and false. Therefore, he always suspects everyone of insincerity and fears that others' behaviour can cause him harm. The 1.1– style does not trust himself, and so he feels comfortable only when he is hidden in his shell of indifference and self-distancing.

Fairness Like many other values, fairness and justice are understood by the 1.1– style very specifically. The highest expression of justice for him is the principle: "I don't touch anybody, and they mustn't touch me." In his conception of fairness there is no place for real human efforts and merits in a promotion. If the 1.1– style fulfilled the minimum requirements, he perceives any additional requirements and attempts to engage in a more active organizational activity as a violation of justice. He also considers it unfair when he cannot satisfy his interests in the context of a serious problem. "I ask anything so rarely, and they still don't want to help me," thinks the 1.1– style indignantly, not associating this refusal with his poor contribution to the common cause. Faced with cases of real injustices, e.g. the apparent underestimation of a staff member's contribution, the 1.1– style prefers not to pay attention to it, thinking: "Naive people! Who needs their enthusiasm and diligence? It is better to do your work so that there are no claims, and live peacefully and happily, as I do!"

Commitment The 1.1– style is indifferent and cynical by nature. So he does not even try to demonstrate his commitment to the organization, nor his identification with the company. That can be changed very quickly, however, if he is to explain or defend his indifferent attitude publicly. In order not to be involved and take responsibility, he is ready to verbally declare his commitment and identity. However, the declared commitment and identity instantly disappear if his indifference is not expected to be punished. The 1.1– style continues to work in the company not because of his commitment and identity, but because it is safer to stay and work here than go to another company. Changing jobs means uncertainty and fear, and one does not know where all this may lead.

Responsibility The lack of organizational commitment and identity is directly related to a lack of responsibility. The 1.1– style cannot be relied upon in difficult organizational situations, as they require working for the team with a full neglect of personal interests and grievances. In such situations, the 1.1 – style is not even able to discard his indifference and cynicism: "Why cast pearls before swine?" If the 1.1 – style sees someone's error or mistake, which does not directly affect the work adversely, he will prefer not to notice it to avoid the threat of greater involvement in organizational activities.

Integrity The 1.1 – style treats transparency and integrity in the organization with contempt and indifference. He simply does not believe that people and organizations can truly be committed to these values. The 1.1 – style is convinced that managers who encourage others to work transparently and honestly are never fully honest themselves. At the same time he has the opportunity to receive valuable information that further allows him to provide manipulative impact on team members. Those who are in close interaction with the 1.1 – style begin to understand the real motives of his behaviour fairly quickly and respond to it with explicit or hidden disbelief, trying to keep eluding him.

10.5   1.1 – Culture and Power

Focus on Reward and Position Power that Are Used to Avoid Commitment and Involvement

Punishment The 1.1 – leader considers punishment a non grata measure, as he fears that punishment must be verbally justified and can cause discontent. If the punishment is inevitable, it must be justified according to organizational regulations. Punishment is more associated with the threat of unwanted involvement in organizational problems than with the objective results of staff members' performance.

Reward The 1.1 – style uses reward as a form of protection against involvement and responsibility. The 1.1 – leader encourages only those who do the work at an acceptable level, ignoring those who make "unacceptable" requests and demands to do something, to do better, to show goodwill, and so on. The 1.1 – style is not aimed at the achievement of results, so he does not see the link between performance and rewards. Thus, outstanding achievements are rewarded in the same way as average, moderate, and even insufficient. Reward is used as a means of self-imposed isolation and is not related to performance.

Position Position power is important for the 1.1 – style leader, as he sees it as an effective means of protection of employees, their initiative, and critique. The 1.1 – style appeals to his position in the organization in order to justify the appropriateness of his indifferent attitude. Answering to reasonable arguments and calls to do something useful for the organization, he refers to his position power. The 1.1 –

leader knows his powers well and uses them to do as little as possible. The 1.1— style leader willingly delegates his responsibilities to subordinates, if it does not require personal involvement and responsibility. He completely loses control when circumstances require innovative solutions that go beyond mundane practice.

Information Key sources for the 1.1— style leader are formal organizational instructions, which are reflected in the organizational documents. They allow him to do minimal work, protecting him from accusations of inefficiency and low motivation. The 1.1— style knows his rights and duties very well, he is pretty aware of where his area of responsibility begins and ends. But he hardly knows what the duties of his subordinates are. In fact, he is not interested. The exchange of information is carried out in order to protect one's own position in the case of critique. Senior management's guidelines are perceived as a necessary evil. It is better to perform them formally to avoid possible problems.

Expert The 1.1— style may have quite a high competence in his professional sphere. However, his knowledge and skills are not used to achieve the best results, to create an effective and synergetic team, but to strengthen one's position, avoiding key organization challenges. This alienated and indifferent attitude deprives the 1.1— leader of the expert authority. If, in exceptional circumstances, he tries to use his expertise for the benefit of the team, the team does not take it seriously, reasonably believing that the man, who had never tried to contribute to the common cause, cannot do it in this case either. The 1.1— style assumes that it is better not to do anything, because all efforts and plans are ultimately futile and doomed to failure. His slogan is: "Sit quietly, and soon you'll see the corpse of your enemy by you, being carried past you".

Referent The 1.1— style usually completely lacks reference power, as in difficult situations he tries to be invisible and absolve of any responsibility. Such demeanour is accompanied by the conviction that even the most talented and motivated people are most likely doomed to failure, and the most ambitious projects under their declaratory purposes hide simple human greed. In such circumstances, the most correct and decent is the behaviour of disengagement and indifference. This standpoint leads to the fact that others are beginning to perceive the 1.1— style as an unreliable individual with the lack of initiative who does not care about results, people, or the organization as a whole. Therefore, in cases when the 1.1— style is a manager and is forced to call on employees to perform urgent or difficult work, his calls are confusing and are not taken seriously. All this prevents him from building solid, harmonious relations, based on mutual trust, respect, and sincerity.

10.6   Cooperation Skills of the 1.1− Style

Conflict Resolution

The 1.1− style's typical strategy for resolving conflict is avoidance. "Conflict? I don't understand", says the 1.1− style, carefully turning away from any conflicts that arise in the organization. He avoids the situation of conflict as much as possible, hoping that it will resolve by itself. The 1.1− style struggles to occupy the position of an outside observer in order to remain neutral: "This is your quarrel. I won't be involved in it", or "Do what you want, but leave me alone". The 1.1− style avoids direct conflicts, giving indirect signals in the form of complaints or silence. He never raises controversial issues himself, but quickly agrees with others when the general mood becomes evident.

Reluctance to pay attention to conflicts often causes team's outrage. Team members quickly learn that if problems arise, they cannot rely on their leader. This does not bother the 1.1− leader, as he does not want involvement in the work. However, this begins to affect relationships, bringing in hostility between the leader and the group. The more the 1.1− style declines team work principles, the more trust and respect in the team suffer. Employees begin to express thoughts like: "Do not even try to ask him. The answer is known in advance."

The 1.1− style uses various techniques to avoid being caught up in the conflict. To do this, he can pretend to be concerned about the organizational rules, having too much work, or just appeals to the standards of convenience. This gives him the opportunity to stay out of attention. For example, the 1.1− style can be on time for meetings, prepare reports that meet appropriate requirements, attend social events, "check in", and so on. However, if problems arise, he retreats, offering only vague remarks: "Yes, I will consider it carefully" or "This looks like a problem to be addressed".

Another way is to try to show his uselessness to resolve the conflict. In this case, the easiest way is to play the role of a very busy man. People are less inclined to turn to someone else for help when he looks totally immersed in other problems. The 1.1− style can also use a more sophisticated way and respond to questions by e-mail or voice, in cases where direct communication would be preferable. The 1.1− style may intentionally answer at the time when he knows that the recipient is not in place. For example, he calls during lunch and leaves a message: "I have called you, but you were not there" or "I tried to call you, but you were not at the workplace". Another way can be the voluntary adoption of any duties that would protect him from active interaction with colleagues. The 1.1− style can respond to the conflict by going on vacation, leaving on a business trip, or doing something else that will allow him to withdraw from participation in the conflict physically.

Another way the 1.1− style resolves conflict is by transferring the information to the people who are likely to take action. The 1.1− style depends on those who are committed to achieving the highest results. He knows that, after learning the problem, these people will take responsibility for constructive conflict resolution. By submitting information, the 1.1− style does not bother to somehow interpret or edit it. He prefers to simply repeat what he heard and do it literally. Being questioned, he says: "I know as much as you do. I can only tell you what I heard."

Information is distributed in such a way that it will be completely safe if a problem occurs. This approach is particularly useful when the distribution of information creates a conflict. The 1.1− style once again confirms his neutrality and shifts all responsibility to others: "I only convey what I was told. If you have doubts, you can ask them yourself."

If the conflict is prolonged, the 1.1− style tries to get out of the discussion as soon as possible: "Well, if you like, do what you want." He can also make a statement that would divert attention: "Why are we losing time in the debate? Do as you choose, and let's move forward!"

In those rare cases when the 1.1− leader still takes part in the conflict, it often does more harm than good. Because he is poorly informed, the action he takes usually indicates that events are perceived wrong, and his myopic strategy serves only to stop the current conflict. The 1.1− style rarely makes serious effort to understand the real causes of the conflict and resolve it constructively.

Communicative Competence

The 1.1− style's communicative competence is rather low due to the fact that he tries to minimize his communication with colleagues and subordinates as much as possible. He perceives open communication as a threat to his detachment and non-involvement in the organizational life. The basis of this position is the 1.1− style's profound conviction that work in the organization is a labour service that people are forced to do to survive in this cruel and wicked world. Only the naive or manipulative ones show their passion to the organization. The former do it as they are so misguided, the latter do it for the sake of their personal benefit. The 1.1− style does not want to play this, in his opinion, uninteresting and empty game in which, ultimately, everyone is doomed to lose. Therefore, the 1.1− style follows the principle: "Less communication—less problems."

When the 1.1− style needs information, he uses a third party, and does not address the source directly. He does not like to directly ask or answer questions on controversial issues because he does not want extra responsibility or trouble. If the 1.1− style hopes to stay on the sidelines and do no wrong, he is ready to support any point of view, even if internally he does not agree with it. In conversation, he usually touches upon issues that affect only the surface of the problem. Since knowledge assumes certain responsibilities, his credo is expressed by the formula: "The less you know, the better you sleep." So he communicates to get as less information as possible. For example, when discussing a new project the 1.1− style is interested only in those points that are related exclusively to his duties. Even if the 1.1− style does not quite understand what is discussed at the meeting, he will still remain silent to keep communication to a minimum and not be drawn into the debate.

If the 1.1− style is afraid of being involved in any extra work, he will gather information indirectly through unofficial sources and conversations. This gives him the opportunity to obtain information and to set possible ways of "defence" of the new tasks without being involved in the discussion. The 1.1− style avoids asking questions, as he is afraid to hear: "You have raised a very important issue! Would you like to make a decision and take the lead?" When a new project starts, the 1.1− style is willing to join him only after someone else takes the initiative, works out the program, and starts the work. If the project fails, the 1.1− style will always have something to say to justify himself. His constant position is: "This is not my project, and I do not bear any responsibility for it. I just do what I'm told."

In conversation the 1.1− style is usually very cautious, he tries to speak vaguely and evasively, avoiding any promises and commitments. This saves him from bearing personal responsibility. He often uses the phrase: "It is difficult to say something. We have much more experienced experts in this field" and "It is possible, but I'm not sure. You'd better ask someone else." This passive attitude depresses other team members, as they have to make a huge effort to get any information. As a result, all ends up exactly as the 1.1− style wanted: people prefer not to ask him any questions or count on him!

Active Positioning

In defending his views, the 1.1− style is evasive and reticent. He rarely expresses his attitude towards work and does it in a neutral way, which makes it impossible to understand what he really thinks: "This is probably the right thing" or "I would probably agree with this opinion". The 1.1− style believes that the best approach is to withhold information until he is forced to speak; and even in this case he reveals only the information that cannot cause interest and give rise to any liability. This attitude leads to the fact that, even if the 1.1− style has a particular opinion, it is still vague and uncertain, which inevitably leads to critique. The 1.1− style says: "I would prefer not to say what I think about this," or "Now I find it difficult to give preference to anything".

In defending his position, the 1.1− style follows the most common opinion, reflecting the popular view: "Whatever we decide, the results that we get are the most important thing!" or "If you think that this is what we must do, then I agree". This cautiousness allows the 1.1− style to criticize the actions of others when difficulties arise: "I had doubts about it from the very beginning."

The 1.1− style defends his views only when he is asked directly to do so, and when he feels certain support. In other cases, he tries not to express his opinion, and before agreeing with someone else's position, he prefers to wait as much as possible. If the 1.1− style feels that his opinion is not popular, he is ready to immediately give it up. Another feature of the 1.1− style when he is defending his opinion is a special restrained understatement manner, which often sounds like a grim prophecy of inevitable difficulties and obstacles. When the result is difficult to predict, the 1.1− style expresses his fears and doubts. This position is a protective mechanism, so if difficulties do arise, he says: "I knew it was going to happen." Thus, the 1.1— style reduces the possibility of being accused of anything.

The 1.1— style leader does not like to clearly identify his position, especially on controversial issues, and takes initiative very reservedly and passively. The 1.1— style does his job just at the expected level. He rarely goes beyond these limits and rather prefers to see everything running its course than taking any steps to influence the course of events. This low level of initiative is more efficient when working in accordance with the instructions and guidelines. If someone addresses the 1.1— style directly, he replies enigmatically: "It's not a bad idea," or "This is probably going to work". The 1.1— style typically uses such phrases as "possible", "probable", or "I do not know", because they can protect him in case of a problem. The 1.1— style would say: "I never said that I liked this idea," or "I never said that we should make this decision".

The 1.1— style shows the minimum acceptable level of initiative, focusing on the expected results. He rarely takes initiative beyond the framework of the expected and does so only under the pressure of circumstances or management. He avoids any initiatives that may cause conflict.

The 1.1— style leader usually delegates his powers to others without a particular reason. As soon as he sees a problem, he tries to approach it in a specific way, entrusting its solution to someone else: "Anna has problems with drawing up a new work schedule. Will you help her?" Being a senior manager, the 1.1— leader delegates too many of his responsibilities to others, leaving almost no work for himself.

As a rule, the 1.1— style responds to problems delayed, when only the blind cannot see them. But he is in no hurry to do something, looking for those who can help. Even if the 1.1— style knows what is to be done, he still waits for instructions from above. If he sees a problem in the work of other employees, he prefers to remain silent, believing that it is not his business. If he sees that one of the team members is facing difficulties in the implementation of the project, he will pretend not to notice, thinking: "If I get involved, I will have very hard times, bearing responsibility for everything." If a staff member needs to leave work prematurely, the 1.1— style does not feel obliged to help him by taking care of his duties. If he is asked in person, or it is predetermined by the rules, the 1.1— leader can take on additional responsibilities, but he never does it voluntarily.

Another form of avoiding initiatives is: "I'm too busy to be disturbed." This is a false manoeuvre to prevent the possibility of engaging in other people's problems. The 1.1— style leader uses his pretended business to stay out of problems. He creates an impression of a manager wrapped up in work; and others begin to be afraid to bother him. For example, the 1.1— style may close his office door, spend more time than necessary outside the office, or simply immerse in paperwork. All these are ways to say: "Do not disturb me."

Decision-Making

The 1.1— style always tries his best to get away from making decisions or to delay them, especially if it might cause controversy or displeasure. If circumstances force him to make a decision, he will usually find a compromise, and it will be in strict accordance with the precedents that had already occurred in this situation. The 1.1— style is focused on short-term results and, as mentioned earlier, he prefers to wait until life itself leads to a solution. He is waiting for suitable conditions for a decision; however, what may seem like tenacity and perseverance, in fact, is a banal indifference. To map out a plan of action, the 1.1— leader will use precedents and traditions (just like the 4.4— style). If the 4.4— style will surely make a decision where there had already been a precedent, the 1.1— style will still prefer the situation in which this decision is made by someone else.

The leading motivation in the decision-making of the 1.1— style advocates fear of personal responsibility and involvement. This fear completely cuts him off from organizational and group goals and from the people he works with. He only thinks about how not to get in trouble if something happens. Therefore, he often says in his heart of hearts: "I am not so naive to put my head on the block!" or "They are trying to persuade me and promise me the moon, but if I accept this decision, it will be me who's going to have troubles!"

The 1.1— style leader likes to convince everyone that delegating responsibilities is the best leadership model for every situation: "You have to trust your subordinates and delegate even the most important decision-making to them. We must rely on those who will make our organization succeed, and give them the opportunity to get valuable experience in leadership and decision-making." These words are true, but the problem here is that he delegates his authority even to those who are utterly unprepared. As he tries to minimize his contacts with colleagues and subordinates, he usually is not informed about who is really able to take this or that decision. Someone may have a desire, but not have sufficient expertise; someone can be fully loaded with work on another project, not having time to be fully engaged in anything else, but the 1.1— leader will hardly notice these details, and will give the following instructions: "Well, if you want responsibility, go ahead! This is your chance, and I won't deprive you of this!"

Another approach is to delay or postpone the decision, hoping that the need itself will disappear, or that someone else will take the responsibility: "Let's think about it later", or "The problem requires further elaboration and discussion", or "Let's wait and see, what happens". The 1.1— style likes it when the responsibility for decision-making is on others. In this case, he is largely indifferent about how decisions are made and what the consequences are. Usually, he agrees with all suggestions coming from others and tries not to take part in a controversial decision, if he is not forced to.

Thus, decision-making is one of the 1.1— style's weak points. He does not want to make decisions that will attract attention to him or lead to additional obligations. In addition, the 1.1— style usually has scarce information about problems and people, and he avoids greater involvement in organizational processes. Without all this, it is impossible to critically assess the problem, to see the alternatives, and to assess the risks. This makes the 1.1– leader poorly prepared to make effective decisions. Without the desire to go deeply into the work, he is left with only one possibility: to postpone the decision, to delegate it, or to support someone else's opinion.

Constructive Critique

The 1.1– style treats constructive critique with great distrust and fear, as it could seriously undermine or even destroy his aloofness and indifference. He avoids giving people feedback, rarely criticizes their work, and is not ready to listen to critique from others. If the 1.1– style is forced to criticize, it looks like an appeal to the arbitrator without the desire to find a concrete solution.

The idea of using constructive critique as a tool to improve personal and team efficiency will never occur to the 1.1– style. His level of interest in work is so low that he does not see any sense in increasing its efficiency. If circumstances force him to use critique, it looks like an unprepared improvisation that was provoked by someone else's requirements and organizational circumstances. If someone asks the 1.1– style to give critical comments on any occasion, he usually gives vague answers like: "Well, of course, we can talk about it at any other time"; "I thought that all went well"; "I wouldn't worry too much about it, next time it will be much more successful". So, the main purpose of the 1.1– style's critique is to put an end to it as soon as possible.

One of the reasons why the 1.1– style does not feel at ease and his critique is inefficient is that he does not have sufficient information for analysis. Effective critique is based on observation and communication with the people, on comparing their behaviour with the objectives and performance standards. The leader, using effective critique, gives particular examples and articulates his observations in an objective and constructive manner. The 1.1– style is involved in critique in the safest way, including critical remarks in the context of discussions on other issues, and acts as an observer, without active participation.

The weakness of the 1.1– style's critique is that it creates an organizational environment in which the process of acquiring more effective behaviour is random. There are no critical comments before, during, or after any work. And consequences are described simply as an accomplished fact: "It has already happened. Wear sackcloth and ashes, or not, it won't change anything." The 1.1– style feels comfortable being a subordinate and doing what is expected from him. He avoids risks, because he does not want to stand out and be sorry in the case of any problems. Faced with failure, he tries to avoid critique and steps aside.

Trying his best to avoid trouble, the 1.1– style is not ready to realize the reason for the failure. In addition, he is does not use the potential of effective relationships, and so he cannot rely on trust, respect, and support from the staff. The 1.1– leader thinks: "They think that I have let things take their course" or "They'll probably accuse me of all the deadly sins". The correctness of this view remains unclear, as the 1.1− leader does not try to explain the situation or refute these assumptions.

The difficulty in the use of constructive critique also stems from the fact that the 1.1− style does not feel comfortable talking to people and, therefore, he primarily sees the flaws and disadvantages of cooperation with others. This is particularly evident when dealing with feedback and the need to express things that can cause emotional reactions. He is so isolated from other people that when it comes to a deeper approach to the problem, the 1.1− style is in complete disarray. This manifests itself in inappropriate jokes or comments that are often not understood and can even be offensive. Not trying to find the real causes of his failures, the 1.1− leader concentrates his attention on the shortcomings of his own, which further increases his isolation. The low concern for production leads to the fact that the 1.1− leader is completely unprepared to deal with complex organizational issues. The lack of concern for people does not allow the 1.1− style to open up and share feelings with colleagues and build a relationship with them that will help to find the strength and the means to overcome setbacks. The rejection of organizational values does not allow the 1.1− style to see and feel the profound social and personal meaning of professional activities.

10.7   Conclusions

The 1.1− style is characterized by a complete absence of eagerness to be involved in joint activities and relationships in the I-ZONE. The 1.1− style leader does not believe in the mission of the organization, nor in his efforts and the potential of effective relationship. He does not see any benefits in actions that lead to positive change, or allows improving the usual course of affairs. The 1.1− style demonstrates what can happen when people have no commitment to the business in which they are engaged. He devotes little of himself to work and gets that little in terms of personal development. The only goal that he follows is to survive until the end of the day, week, month, or entire career with minimum effort and difficulties.

The 1.1− style makes minimum contribution to the organization's commitment and effective relationships. He would like to establish a constructive relationship but, in fact, acts as a third party, a stranger. In order to survive, the 1.1− style does much to create the appearance of a part in the general affairs but, in reality, never truly feels involved in the organizational processes. The 1.1− style maintains discipline and comes to work on time every morning, but he always strives to be detached and aloof from the institutional activities and tasks. He regularly comes to meetings, but is usually silent and adheres to a neutral position. He almost always delivers reports on time, but never risks to offer something new, or to criticize the shortcomings. The 1.1− style is a diligent staff member, but without real commitment to the objectives of the organization or intention to take any risks.

The 1.1− style does not encourage the establishment of a relationship of mutual trust and respect in the team. There are no conditions for the emergence of synergy. If one member of the group is of the 1.1− style, while others show different behaviour styles, it often leads to conflict over unequal individual contributions to the overall work. This further enhances the feeling of isolation for the 1.1−individual. If all members of the group follow the 1.1− style they are, in fact, just in the same room, working individually and not feeling involvement in the common cause. Their only real goal is to wait until the end of the day, and in the long term until retirement.

Style 1.1+: Inhibited, Unfulfilled (To Wait and Hope)

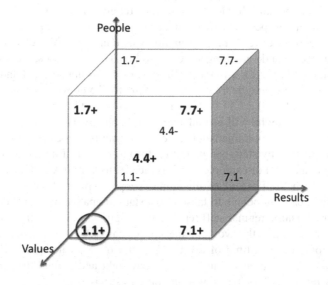

Low concern for production; low concern for people; high, but often hidden and unrealized commitment to the organization; not indifferent, but passive attitude to work. The desire to contribute and show initiative usually occurs only in dreams and fantasies. The internal slogan is: "If circumstances were different, if they understood me, I could move mountains." Interest in work is often manifested in efforts to approach actual problems and tasks of the team, without attracting anyone. However, these plans often remain unknown to others in the desktop. In real activity he avoids articulating his position and point of view, does not ask questions, and shows minimal initiative. Decisions are postponed until someone else makes a decision or the problem resolves by itself. Being a leader, he shies away from the leadership group, letting things take their course. This mismatch between internal desires and real activity can be explained by a negative experience

A. Zankovsky, C. von der Heiden, *Leadership with Synercube*,
DOI 10.1007/978-3-662-49052-5_11

under the guidance of a 7.1— style, rigid job structuring in which the boundaries of effort are strictly formalized, and minimal dialogue, as well as personal characteristics. Colleagues often treat him with compassion, seeing the duality of the 1.1+ style's aspirations. With the support of the management and the team, the 1.1+ style is capable of much more and is able to realize his potential, and make a significant contribution to the achievement of organizational results.

11.1   Basic Features of the 1.1+ Style

The 1.1+ style is a behaviour type with low levels of concern for production and people that paradoxically combines with high commitment to the values of the organization. The key word for this type of behaviour is restraint, freezing aspirations, and potential. In fact, he is not indifferent to the results to be achieved, and he cares about the people with whom he works. But the objective circumstances and subjective experiences lead to a situation where in reality his behaviour is very passive and he cannot do anything as he would like. His is cautious, sceptical, but at the same time he hopes for a miracle: "If the world was not so cruel and unfair to people like me, we would be treated very differently." Yet even though people are often cruel and unfair, the 1.1+ style remains optimistic at heart, without losing the last hope that one day he will be understood and objectively estimated.

Usually people do not immediately take on the quality of the 1.1+ style, but form such behaviour step by step, compensating for the impact of an inefficient and/or dominating manager. For example, the 7.1— leader usually forces 1.1+ individuals to hide in their shells. The lack of attention to people, typical of the 7.1— style, can be destructive, causing people to lapse into a state of apathy and dependency. The 7.1— leader who hosts regular staff reprimands or ignores their creative suggestions eventually discourages the work of the entire team. As a result, the following attitude is formed: "I'm tired of all this. Let him do what he wants! I'll just do my job and keep my mouth shut." People may fight and defend themselves, but finally they retreat as 1.1+ types, wanting only to survive.

The 1.1+ style can also be formed in the context of resource R shortage. This can happen with the manager who was promoted, but is not ready to take on new responsibilities. Perhaps in the past he was kept under tight control of the management, and now he is expected to show more independence and act as a true leader. But without the necessary resources in the form of training, experience, or qualifications, the person may lose confidence under the pressure of new demands and without the support of leadership, gradually transforming into a 1.1+ type. The 1.1+ style can also be formed when leaders, like the 1.7— or the 4.4–, discourage people to work on solving complex problems and take risks. After some time, without sufficient consideration for increasing participation, people become passive: "Apparently, this organization is more concerned about compliance with the rules than results."

The formation of the 1.1+ style in the organization may be explained by rigid job structuring in which the boundaries of effort are strictly formalized, and communication is minimal. Over time, the whole culture of the company can develop 1.1+ style staff members, because of excessive regulation that blocks independence and creativity. A typical example of this transformation is a state institution, where each employee is considered as a screw of a common mechanism.

An important role in shaping the 1.1+ style behaviour is played by individual personality features. Even simple organizational situations and conflicts can be perceived by people with increased anxiety, vulnerability, and self-doubt as traumatic and very painful situations. These people perceive a mismatch of desires and capacities in an especially acute manner. In such cases, frustration is inevitable, which is a mental state that accompanies the actual or perceived inability to meet different needs. In order to dissociate himself from frustrating experiences, the 1.1+ style tries to do things formally, at the minimum acceptable level, and can always shirk responsibility, hiding behind formal rules and regulations. He tries to delegate the solution of problems to someone else, not attempting to suggest or support a decision. At the same time, he can do a great job within himself, trying to find optimal solutions. However, he never tells anyone about his efforts because of the fear of being involved in the actual work, which carries a potential hazard and may result in an even greater disappointment. When the 1.1+ style needs to take any action, he is afraid of the risks that it bears in itself and, therefore, he feels safer to withdraw and wait for somebody else to notice the problem and offer the solution.

11.2   The 1.1+ Style in Collective Cooperation

Because of fear and uncertainty, the 1.1+ style behaviour appears as extremely passive to onlookers, and he is involved in the joint venture only nominally. He is deeply and excessively focused on his feelings and fantasies, so the joint team work, its real problems and difficulties, often remain on the periphery of his attention. Hence, the 1.1+ style often does not notice the decisive contribution made by the joint activity of employees' performance. He also does not try to do anything with staff members, whose inefficient work has a negative impact on the team results and even his own performance.

The 1.1+ style will never make suggestions about how to improve work efficiency. At the same time he cares about efficiency, and within himself he could think over very effective steps to optimize synergies, but prefers not to say anything to anyone. He will articulate his opinion only if the organizational climate is fair and he is asked about it with respect and tact. Then the 1.1+ style may suddenly surprise everyone with his competence, analytical thinking, and enthusiasm. But if others do not show any attention to his opinion or express their disagreement, the 1.1+ style will immediately close and hide in his protective shell. This protective response can be provoked even by such a trifle as a bad joke or a misunderstood word. Sharing the organizational values, but not having the objective or subjective possibilities to contribute to the common cause, the 1.1+ style is a valuable, but often underestimated team resource. His attitude is expressed by the following rule: "If the organization really valued and used the resources of each and every employee, I could bring real benefits, and I would be much more pleased with myself."

Team members with sufficient empathy treat the 1.1+ style with sympathy, trying to support him and give confidence. However, the dynamics of organizational life does not imply much free time for that. Team members believe that the 1.1+ style is indifferent to results, avoidant, lazy, and generally very passive. So they get used to not relying on him. They leave him only plain and simple tasks that do not require taking the initiative, as they know that he cannot be counted on if there are real problems. In response to this attitude, the 1.1+ style withdraws into himself even more, not trusting his colleagues and subordinates.

The 1.1+ style always has the fear of making a mistake. He is rarely ready to acknowledge and correct mistakes, as in the past he had negative experiences associated with this. He does not have the courage and confidence to put forward any demands, to defend his opinion and position. So he hides under the mask of an observing outsider. However, the representative of the 1.1+ style is constantly working all personal situations through and trying to act constructively in conflict situations in which he is involved. He avoids political conflicts, tries not to attract other people's attention, and, as a rule, never expresses his opinion, or a critical point of view, doing this only under very strong pressure of circumstances. At the same time, he transmits information to employees and is ready to answer questions. His contribution is not enough, even though he knows he can do more. He is dissatisfied with his role in the organization and is internally ready for change.

11.3   The I-ZONE and the 1.1+ Style

In contrast to the 1.1− style, the 1.1+ leader usually does not have polarized relationships with those who are focused on results and effective relationships. People rather feel sympathy and pity, because they see the problems of their boss; they see that he is unable to independently overcome external and internal barriers and to become what he would have wanted to be in reality. Therefore, they have to take responsibility not only for his work but also for their boss's work. From time to time they try to help and support him and give him a chance to prove himself, but he does not always correctly perceive this initiative, for his fears and concerns are so great that he simply does not notice these signs of good will. Furthermore, under strict pressure of organizational plans and demands, team members do not have the time and motivation for the emotional support of the 1.1+ style leader.

As a result, the 1.1+ style does not feel part of the team; he keeps distance and protects himself from taking initiative that can bring new disappointments. The longer it lasts, the more the 1.1+ style is convinced that the safest and most reliable is a detached and passive behaviour. Over time, the 1.1+ style and the team get used to this form of interaction and fail to see any alternatives to the current situation. Depending on the culture of the organization, the 1.1+ style behaviour can be criticized in a mild, indirect, or direct form, including even accusations of problems or mistakes. Facing this critique, the 1.1+ style seems calm and even indifferent, but

Fig. 11.1 1.1+

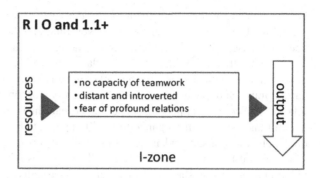

inwardly he is very deeply concerned about it. Responding to particularly sharp critique, he can say: "But I can't do anything in these conditions!"

Without realizing it, team members often drive a 1.1+ leader even further in his behaviour style, accusing and condemning him for the lack of involvement in the overall work. Thus, the increasing intolerance makes the 1.1+ style distance more and more, and he gradually loses control of the situation, not feeling as a member of the group. All efforts to make the 1.1+ style take more initiative only force him to hide deeper in his shell, because they are perceived as hard pressure, and that was once the starting point for the formation of this behaviour style. Without encouraging support which can only be provided by team members, the 1.1+ leader is left alone, and in order to survive, he uses the only way he knows, which is to step back from it all and stay away unnoticed (Fig. 11.1).

The isolated attitude of the 1.1+ style is a result of past attempts to show his worth which were destructively criticized. If you try to draw the 1.1+ style to a more active participation in organizational life, you will get the typical cautious answer: "It's possible", "Let's see", or "I will think it over". However, if colleagues and subordinates show tact, respect, and patience, the 1.1+ style can dramatically change his performance. As a rule, 1.1+ individuals adhere to the values of this style even if the conditions have changed. Thus, a sociable and creative person can become 1.1+ because of a 7.1− manager, who demoted him. And even five years later, when this manager already resigned, the 1.1+ style will still remain aloof and indifferent. Left alone, the 1.1+ style sticks to his fantasies, where his role and contribution are recognized by all members of the organization.

11.4   1.1+ Culture and Values

Basic Feature: Internal Duality. Big Hopes and Imposed Passive Behaviour

Trust Internally the 1.1+ style sincerely and deeply recognizes the value of trust as the basis of harmonious interpersonal relationships. He sincerely wants to trust others and at the same time fears that trust will cause new troubles and frustrations. He believes that in reality all people are inherently kind, honest, and trustworthy, but circumstances often force them to act otherwise. Therefore, he holds a cautious, sceptical attitude towards everyone and everything. At the same time the 1.1+ style does not cease to hope for a harmonious relationship, full of trust and sincerity, as he is committed to it internally and lacks it. He still believes that one day circumstances will change and his relationships with others will become more harmonious and effective. Even repeatedly becoming disillusioned with relationships with other people, deeper in his heart, he is still optimistic and remains hopeful that one day the organization will appreciate his potential. The 1.1+ style does not trust himself and is sure that in many respects he is to blame for the situation that has formed around him. All this leaves no other alternatives than to hide in his protective shell of detachment and passivity.

Fairness The 1.1+ style's duality of external and internal behaviour directly relates to his notion of fairness and how it manifests in his behaviour. Fairness, according to the 1.1+ style, is the match between a staff member's contributions to the organizational welfare and the benefits received by him. In other words, his sense of justice is very close to his interpretation of the organization. However, the 1.1+ style leaves his understanding of justice for himself. In fact, in behaviour patterns, this sense of justice takes a completely different form: "If the organizational conditions are unfavourable for me, no one understands or appreciates me. Then I have the right to completely distance myself, thus expressing my inner protest." The 1.1+ style does not link justice to the real merits and contribution. Therefore, the 1.1+ style's fulfilling minimal requirements is not a violation of justice for him, as in fact people themselves forced him to hold such a position. Faced with cases of real injustices, e.g. apparent underestimation of the real contribution of a staff member to achieve the common goal, the 1.1+ style prefers not to say anything publicly and just thinks: "They treated him the same way they treated me! Objective and fair estimation of a person can be so rarely found. I am right protecting myself from these disappointments, distancing from everyone and everything." At the same time, when there are sincere attempts to create favourable conditions for the 1.1+ style to strengthen his faith in justice and his powers, involving more active organizational activity, the 1.1+ style is able to open up and show a completely different attitude.

Commitment The 1.1+ style is inwardly a committed and passionate person. But all this is concealed from others, as his commitment and identification with the organization is manifested only in exceptional cases, e.g. a force majeure situation, when the failure to meet time constraints could threaten (even leading to bankruptcy) the entire organization. In such circumstances, the 1.1+ style can discard his personal fears and, to the surprise of others, show remarkable activity, creativity, and total dedication: for the real or imagined threat, which is his constant fear, ceases to be only personal and becomes a common problem. Feeling free from his internal constraints and fears, the 1.1+ style can show passion for his work and commitment to the organization, and is willing and able to make a significant contribution to its work. In fact, the main reason for keeping the job, although not being satisfied with it, is the 1.1+ style's deeply concealed and sincere commitment to the organization and its staff members.

Responsibility Like the 1.1− style, the 1.1+ is not focused on results and people. However, the 1.1+ style is much more focused on organizational values, which makes him a more reliable and socially responsible member of the organization. As noted above, despite his apparent disengagement and passivity, he can be relied on in difficult organizational situations. In cases of general threats and general enthusiasm, the 1.1+ style is able to express his inner, true face. When staff is required to work for the team discarding personal fears, interests, and grievances, the 1.1+ style is able to put aside his passivity and detachment and make a significant contribution to achieving organizational results. Noticing a mistake which could reduce the quality of the overall work, the 1.1+ style will not remain indifferent: he will tell a person about it in a private conversation, what to do or who can help to prevent more serious consequences.

Integrity The 1.1+ style appreciates the transparency of organizational processes and honesty in relations. He believes that people and organizations are for the most part truly committed to their values, but within his own behavioural pattern he rarely fully follows these values. The 1.1+ style fears that people may use his honesty against him. This is the negative legacy of his past experience. Here, the 1.1+ style manifests a particularly acute sense of inner duality: he appreciates honesty, convinced of its importance in the organizational environment, and at the same time he is afraid of his own honesty, which can carry with it new challenges and disappointments. Those employees, who are in close interaction with the 1.1+ style, fairly quickly understand his real motives for being aloof and treat him sincerely and honestly, regardless of his passive behaviour.

11.5   1.1+ Culture and Power

Focus on Reward and Expert Power that Are Used to Reduce Anxiety and to Defend from Real and Imagined Threats and Injustices

Punishment The 1.1+ style leader considers punishment a measure of unwanted effects, as he himself usually has a negative personal experience associated with the 7.1− style, which uses punishment as the main method of obtaining influence. In addition, punishment is contrary to the 1.1+ leader's internal notion of harmonious interaction with subordinates. If punishment is still inevitable, it must be justified by organizational instructions and be legitimate in terms of organizational values. The penalty is more concerned with violations of organizational norms and values, and not with the objective results of this or that staff member.

Reward The 1.1+ style leader uses reward as the main form of influence on subordinates. The 1.1+ style himself, due to external or internal causes, is not focused on achieving results, so he does not associate performance and rewards. Therefore, often the reward is not granted to those who do the work at a high level, but to those who work at an acceptable level and at the same time are focused on organizational culture and values. Thus, outstanding achievements are rewarded in the same way as the average, moderate, and even insufficient efforts. The reward is used as a means of maintaining the organizational norms and values, and has little to do with the work results.

Position For the 1.1+ style leader position power does not play a significant role, as he is against any kind of emphasis on status distinctions and authority. The 1.1+ leader never appeals to his status position in the organization in order to back his decision or plan. The 1.1+ style often quite poorly knows the scope of his formal powers, as he actively delegates his functions to highly active and professional subordinates. He gladly answers their questions and shares knowledge, abilities, and skills, helping to cope with difficult tasks. In force majeure, the 1.1+ leader transforms completely, taking control and finding innovative solutions that go beyond his powers and routines.

Information Informal communication with employees is the key informational resource for the 1.1+ style leader, which helps him not to exert direct pressure and engage in active cooperation. At the same time, this kind of communication fosters the inner motivation of employees, orienting them on organizational norms and values. This allows the 1.1+ style to perform his own work at an acceptable level, as well as to expect fairly high efficiency and motivation from the part of subordinates. The 1.1+ style does not have sufficient knowledge, he does not know his rights and obligations, at what point his area of responsibility begins and ends. However, he is well aware of what his subordinates have to deal with. He is highly concerned with his team's spirit. The exchange of information is carried out in order to encourage his initiatives and focus on organizational values. The 1.1+ leader takes senior management's instructions with attention, trying to keep them under control, as he is afraid of possible problems.

Expert The 1.1+ style leader is usually highly competent in his professional field. However, his knowledge, skills, and abilities are very rarely used to solve current problems. His professional skills are rarely aimed at achieving the best results, as he has no desire to create an efficient, synergistic team, but nevertheless the staff knows that in difficult situations which are dramatic for the team, the 1.1+ style can always provide them with his expert support. Therefore, if in exceptional circumstances he begins to actively use his expertise for the benefit of the team, the team takes it very seriously, realizing that the situation is really critical. Therefore, even the normally aloof and passive 1.1+ style leader is not deprived of expert power.

Referent   The 1.1+ style usually has little reference power, which, however, can be manifested in difficult situations when the 1.1+ style is able to discard his fears and concerns and largely realize his positive organizational-orientated potential. Therefore, despite his detachment and passivity in normal operating situations, the 1.1+ style leader is treated by his subordinates with compassion, as they all feel his unspent and desired capacity to help the organization. Therefore, in cases when the 1.1+ style holds a managerial position and is forced to call on employees to perform any urgent or difficult work, his appeals strike a chord and are taken seriously. All this allows the 1.1+ leader to maintain normal working relationships, which hold out hope for even more effective and harmonious cooperation.

11.6   Cooperation Skills of the 1.1+ Style

Conflict Resolution

The 1.1+ style dislikes fears and avoids conflicts. In the history of his organizational life it was a very painful situation when even minimal conflict solving activity ended in fierce aggression and negative consequences (most often in collaboration with the 7.1– style). Thus, the 1.1+ style reached a radical conclusion: conflict is evil which should be avoided at all costs. So the 1.1+ style tries to avoid conflict situations.

The 1.1+ style's main strategy for conflict resolution is a denial of the possibility of conflict. "There cannot be a conflict here, as conflict is impossible", he calms himself down when facing a controversy or confrontation. It may seem that the 1.1+ style does not notice or is completely indifferent to the emerging tensions and confrontation. However, this is not quite true. As a rule, the 1.1+ style, although apparently not trying to resolve the conflict situation, is very often well aware of its nature and causes. He tries to find the best options for the resolution, based on the common interests of the organization. But he does this within himself. In reality he seeks to live without conflicts and continues to work further to completely eliminate them. Reluctance to pay attention to conflicts often causes negative responses from the part of colleagues and subordinates. Employees see that when problems arise, they cannot rely on their leader. This reaction worries the 1.1+ style leader, as it begins to affect relationships, bringing hostility between the leader and the group.

The 1.1+ leader ignores a conflict as long as possible. If it is no longer possible, he tries to find a compromise to avoid an open confrontation. For this purpose he most often applies to external rules or instructions. Such compromises do not address the real causes of the conflict, but allow the work to be continued at an acceptable level without open opposition. The 1.1+ style fully understands the consequences that repressed conflicts can bring, but does nothing. In fact, conflicts are not resolved, and the 1.1+ style seeks for a way to somehow continue. This inevitably affects the quality of team work, making it difficult to build relationships of trust and respect.

If the conflict still flares up and could seriously damage the future work, the 1.1+ style can all of a sudden, in a convincing manner, urge emotionally blinded opposition parties to cooperate constructively: "Well, if a victory over your enemy is so important, continue in the same vein. But we are not at all opponents! We are in the same boat, and if you do not stop rocking it, it will inevitably sink to the bottom. Let's try to pull ahead together!" In such rare cases when the 1.1+ leader takes part in the conflict, he can prove to be very helpful due to his focus on organizational values: "Well, even if the forever and ever silent 1.1+ leader decided to speak out, we really need to change something in our endless disputes and conflicts!" These actions the 1.1+ style takes in this case usually indicate that the situation is perceived by him properly and constructively. It becomes obvious that the 1.1+ leader's dismissal had nothing to do with the indifference of the 1.1− style, as his desire to avoid conflicts is due to uncertainty and increased anxiety, but not fear of involvement and inner emptiness.

Communicative Competence

The 1.1+ style's communicative competence is rather high due to the fact that, by not communicating too much with colleagues and subordinates, he is in constant internal dialogue with himself. Open, full communion for the 1.1+ style is hindered by self-doubt and fear that involvement in organizational life will bring threat and frustration. At the basis of such a position lies the 1.1+ style's bad experience in assuming a more active role in organizational life.

When the 1.1+ style needs information, he makes a detour by asking a third party, e.g., and never addresses to the source directly. He is afraid to ask or comment on controversial issues directly, as he is afraid of misunderstanding and unwarranted aggression. If the 1.1+ style feels certain of the protection and support from others, he is capable of constructive discussion, and openly expresses his own opinion. However, examples of behaviour like that are quite rare, because the 1.1+ style often sees a threat even in quite innocuous questions and comments. In normal conversation, he usually touches upon issues that do not involve personal interests, as he is afraid of tension and conflict escalation.

The 1.1+ leader diligently builds communication to obtain information, without hurting the interests and emotions of others. If this is not possible, he will prefer to avoid the general discussion of the problem, even if the latter is extremely important. For example, when discussing a new project, the 1.1+ leader will be interested only in general formal aspects which have something to do with his duties. Even if the 1.1+ style leader does not quite understand the idea of his participation in the project, he will still remain silent if, e.g., he sees that his colleagues are in a hurry and do not want to delay the discussion.

If the 1.1+ style fears that his questions could be misunderstood or perceived unfriendly, he will gather information indirectly through unofficial sources and conversations. This gives him the opportunity to receive information and to identify different ways for his participation, avoiding possible differences and conflicts.

In communication, the 1.1+ style is usually pretty cautious, he tries to speak briefly, avoids any liberties, jokes, or associations that could hurt or anger his interlocutor. He rarely critically comments on the work progress, activity planning, or work quality at the end of the project. Sometimes you can hear suggestions to verify the course of action. Together with the focus on organizational values, such form of communication allows the 1.1+ style to support quite a constructive exchange of information with a number of colleagues and subordinates. However, a bad joke or a hint of possible trouble could have a sudden and strong influence on his desire to continue the dialogue, which significantly reduces the efficiency of this communication.

When the 1.1+ style feels a real or virtual threat to his position in the organization, he begins to rely solely on the opinions of others, and tries not to express his opinion, even under pressure. Questions become rare, and even the standpoint on important issues is not expressed. The 1.1+ style leader usually provides his staff with the minimum necessary, but insufficient information. The information is not specified, but simply fixed. This collection of information is not focused on results and objectives, while conflicts are is almost completely ignored.

Active Positioning

Active standpoint is not typical for the 1.1+ style. Initiative appears only when there is clear guidance and expectations from management. In daily work the 1.1+ leader is characterized by "watchful waiting" behaviour. He expresses his opinion only upon specific request. If the 1.1+ leader is sure that he will be supported by other members, he speaks openly.

In defending his views the 1.1+ style is reticent and not always consistent. He rarely directly expresses his attitude towards this or that decision, or does it in an indirect way, which makes it impossible to understand what he really thinks about. Even if the 1.1+ style becomes determined about his opinion, it still remains blurry, vague, and tends to follow the majority's opinion. However, if the overall thrust of the discussion is beginning to acquire non-constructive forms, contrary to organizational values, the 1.1+ style is able to overcome his fears and insecurities and clearly define his standpoint.

In everyday work the 1.1+ style dislikes stating his standpoint clearly, especially on controversial issues; and he takes initiative very reservedly and passively. He defends his views only when he is asked directly to do so, and when there is a strong belief in support. In other cases, he tries not to express his opinion; and before agreeing with someone else's position, he prefers to wait as much as possible. The 1.1+ leader prefers to do the job just at the expected level. If the 1.1+ style feels that his opinion may provoke resistance or critique, he can easily give it up.

The 1.1+ leader likes it when everything runs its course. He is far from attempting to take any steps in order to influence the course of events. He rarely takes the initiative beyond the expected framework, and does so only under the pressure of circumstances or management. He never takes initiatives that may cause conflict.

The 1.1+ leader is willing to delegate his powers. Knowing people quite well, the 1.1+ style finds capable and active employees, who are enthusiastic and ready to perform new functions. At the same time, without experiencing the usual concerns and uncertainties, the 1.1+ style provides them with active and effective support. Even if the 1.1+ style knows what is to be done, he is still waiting for instructions from above. When he sees problems in the work of other employees, he comments and tips in a soft, veiled manner, so staff members usually cannot understand whether they are praised or criticized.

The 1.1+ leader develops and sets goals, but without involvement, without trying to change or improve anything. He works only during set hours, in accordance with the instructions, without showing particular willingness to take responsibility. He is afraid of making a mistake and of correcting it, as he had a negative experience in the past. He does not have the courage and confidence to put forward any demands. However, within himself the 1.1+ style constantly examines emerging situations and tries to act constructively and professionally. His results are not enough, although he knows that he can do more. He is dissatisfied with his role in the organization and internally is always ready to change.

Decision-Making

The 1.1+ style struggles to get away from or delay making a decision, because it is in such moments that he is especially stung by uncertainty and concerns about the risks that are always associated with solutions. Therefore, if he is forced to make a decision, it is usually a compromise, in strict accordance with the precedents that have already been used in similar situations. The 1.1+ leader is focused on short-term results and, as we noted earlier, he prefers to wait until life itself leads to a solution. He seems to analyse all possible alternatives; however, what may seem to be diligence and perseverance is, in fact, mere fear.

Decision-making is probably the most difficult skill for the 1.1+ style. He tries to delay it as much as possible, until it is unavoidable. The 1.1+ style's solution is rarely straightforward and often requires different options. All this makes it difficult to assess the quality of the solution. Objectives are agreed upon in such manner that they can be achieved without much effort from the part of managers and employees. Objectives are set en passant, with no adequate matching between the leader's and team members' understanding. The 1.1+ leader's approach is based on the idea that employees "will somehow cope by themselves".

The motivation behind the 1.1+ leader's decision is contradictory: on the one hand, the fear of personal responsibility requires the adoption of the most familiar and proven solutions, on the other hand, focus on organizational values urges to find effective and socially responsible solutions.

The 1.1+ style leader likes to bring forward arguments in favour of delegation as the optimal model for training new leaders. The 1.1+ style finds capable and active employees, who are enthusiastic and ready to perform new functions. Delegating allows the 1.1+ leader to get rid of his usual fears and uncertainty, and to provide active and effective support.

However, decision-making is the 1.1+ leader's weakness. He does not want to make decisions that could cause future troubles. The 1.1+ style leader is always afraid of making a mistake. He lacks courage, support, and faith in himself. Nevertheless, he keeps internally working on a variety of situations and tries to model solutions that can bring optimal results. This allows him to critically assess the problem, to see the alternatives and to assess the risks. This inner work with the support of management and staff members makes the 1.1+ style leader potentially valuable, but not an eagerly sought source of effective decision-making.

Constructive Critique

The 1.1+ style regards constructive critique with apprehension and anxiety, as in his view, it can bring trouble and frustration. He avoids giving people feedback, rarely criticizes their work, fearing a negative reaction and aggression. In turn, the 1.1+ style is quite willing to listen and accept constructive critique from others. This prevents the 1.1+ style from using constructive critique as a tool to improve personal and group effectiveness.

Although the 1.1+ style can make any suggestions for improvements very rarely, he cares about the problem of efficiency, and he can invent very effective steps to optimize synergies, but prefers to do it exclusively within himself. He is willing to share his opinion only in a favourable environment. Then suddenly, the 1.1+ style may surprise everyone with his competence, analytical thinking, and enthusiasm. However, disregard or neglect can further block his further efforts, forcing him to retreat and hide in his shell. If circumstances force him to use critique, the 1.1+ leader's words have the character of an unprepared improvisation that was provoked by someone else's requirements or organizational circumstances. If someone asks the 1.1+ leader to critically comment on any occasion, his remarks will be very uncertain. The 1.1+ leader uses constructive critique in the safest way, including critical remarks in the context of discussions on other issues, or acting as a passive observer.

The weakness of the 1.1+ style's critique is that it is one-sided and irregular. He does not take any specific steps towards finding objective criteria for critique. Faced with failure, the 1.1+ leader tries to avoid critique and steps aside. Trying his best to avoid trouble, the 1.1+ style is not ready to see the reason for the failure. In addition, he does not use the resources of constructive relationships, and so he cannot rely on the staff's trust, respect, and support.

The difficulty in the use of constructive critique also stems from the fact that the 1.1+ style is very painfully aware of his own shortcomings and, therefore, first of all responds emotionally when in cooperation with others. The 1.1+ leader excessively concentrates on his own shortcomings, while detachment denies the possibility of sharing feelings and concerns with colleagues. Nevertheless, the pronounced focus on organizational values allows the 1.1+ style to see and feel a profound social and personal meaning in his activities, opening great opportunities for professional and personal growth.

11.7   Conclusions

The 1.1+ style paradoxically combines high commitment to the values of the organization and low levels of concern for results and people. At the same time, he cares about the results to be achieved and about the people he works with. Objective facts and subjective experiences lead to a situation in which the behaviour of the 1.1+ style is actually very passive and not implemented as he would like. The 1.1+ leader is characterized by barriers that prevent him from showing his potential. The formation of a standpoint in the organization may be influenced by personal and organizational factors, such as the behaviour of the 7.1− style senior manager. Among the individual and personal features that may contribute to the formation of the 1.1+ style are increased anxiety, vulnerability, and self-doubt, which turn even neutral organizational situations into traumatic experiences.

Because of the externally observable fear and uncertainty, the 1.1+ style behaviour looks extremely passive; he is only formally involved in the common work, concentrating deeply on his negative feelings and fantasies. However, in contrast to the 1.1− style, the 1.1+ style usually does not have polarized relationships with those who are focused on results and effective relationships. People rather feel sympathy and pity, because they see the problems of their leader, who is unable to independently overcome external and internal barriers that do not allow him to be what he would want to be. Therefore, they have to take responsibility not only for their work, but also for the work of their leader. From time to time they try to help and support him and give him a chance to show himself, but he does not always correctly assess these initiatives, or his fears and concerns are so great that he simply does not notice these signs of goodwill. Furthermore, under strict pressure of organizational plans and demands team members cannot always find the time and motivation for providing emotional support to the 1.1+ style leader.

Team members with sufficient empathy treat the 1.1+ style with sympathy, trying to support him and boost his confidence. However, the dynamics of organizational life does not give many of them enough time to delve into the causes of the 1.1+ leader's specific behaviour. In their opinion, the 1.1+ style does not seek to achieve results, does not want to communicate, is doing the minimum possible efforts, and is generally very passive. So they get used to not relying on him. They leave him plain and simple tasks that do not require taking the initiative, knowing that he cannot be counted on if a problem emerges. In response to this attitude, the 1.1+ style withdraws into himself even more, not trusting his colleagues and subordinates. Sharing organizational values, but not having objective or subjective opportunities to contribute to the achievement of high results and maintain effective relationships, the 1.1+ style is a valuable, but often not an eagerly sought resource of the team.

Style 7.7−: Opportunist (To Use and to Manipulate)

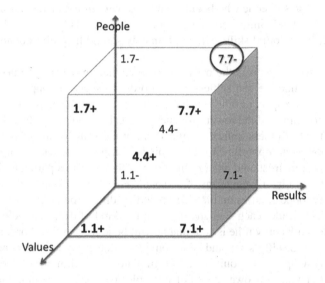

High concern for production, high concern for people, indifferent pragmatic attitude towards work and organization. The high focus on results is not used for boosting the organization's progress, but for personal ends. This overt or covert focus on self-interest leads to mistrust from the part of colleagues and subordinates. In the focus on people, selfishness and the desire to manipulate are manifested to an even greater extent. People soon recognize the real motives of the 7.7− and begin to distrust and even fear the 7.7− style's charm and his ability to build relationships, because they are afraid of being cheated and used. The 7.7− style relies only on the approaches that preserve and enhance his benefits.

© Springer-Verlag Berlin Heidelberg 2016
A. Zankovsky, C. von der Heiden, *Leadership with Synercube*,
DOI 10.1007/978-3-662-49052-5_12

12.1   Basic Features of the 7.7− Style

The life philosophy of the 7.7− style is reduced to the formula: "The fish seeks the deep, and the man seeks the best." The 7.7− style is convinced that nothing in this world is done without a reason. Everyone is looking for benefits and gain, while speaking of spirituality, commitment, and other matters. And if any organization works for profit, any employee has the right to think about his own benefit; the thing is, not everyone is successful. So the 7.7− style's job in any organization begins with the following reflections: "Can I draw any benefits here?" If the answer is yes, then an opportunist tries to do his best to create the impression of a man with business acumen, sincere interest, and commitment. Showing a high focus on results and concern for people, and loudly proclaiming his commitment to organizational values, the 7.7− style is often very convincing. Sometimes not only an observer, but also someone who begins to interact with him on a regular basis, falls under the 7.7− style's influence, accepting everything at its face value. He has the full range of behavioural skills, which ultimately should help him obtain personal benefits.

The 7.7− style perceives the organization as a theatre, where you need to play the role of an attractive and selfless hero in order to succeed. Opportunists never gain the trust and respect of others by hard work and enthusiasm, as this approach is too lengthy for him, and the reward for such efforts is not entirely clear. He prefers to gain the trust of others immediately and enjoy the fruits of his labour immediately. As soon as an opportunist reaches his selfish goals, he easily forgets about loyalty, friendship, trust, and other obligations. If the work in a particular organization ceases to be attractive in terms of personal benefit, the 7.7− style immediately considers new opportunities on the side, including direct competitors.

For the 7.7− leader each step and decision is a kind of deal: you help me and I help you. He works only if he is sure that he will benefit from this. For him there is no such thing as a selfless act, and he is convinced that everyone thinks and acts in the same way. Opportunists quite clearly formulate their willingness to act: "I'll do it for you, but you will owe me." For example, he may not communicate with someone, unless there is a need to get some information from this person. Then he reminds: "You know, somehow I helped you, and now you owe me something." Most often, a reminder of the obligation is put in a completely harmless form: "Do you remember that I helped you last week? Now I need your help." If someone asks an opportunist for help, he first weighs the request in terms of how this person helped him in the past: "Since you helped me last week, I'll help you now."

The 7.7− style behaviour is difficult to recognize, as it can take completely different forms and be inconsistent. For example, an opportunist can express great interest in a project in which he is involved, but little interest in the very course of the project. His relationships with colleagues are superficial. And the 7.7− style maintains these relationships only if he wants something for himself now or in the future. If the 7.7− leader's colleagues face any problems, he offers his help and support only if he sees personal interest. Opportunistic behaviour can be recognized by unmotivated activity in establishing relations. The more relevant a person is for his selfish goals, the closer the 7.7— style gets. However, he is not interested in long-term, mutually beneficial relations, which are usually built on trust and respect.

12.2   The 7.7— Style in Collective Cooperation

The 7.7— style analyses any instance of collective interaction in terms of personal benefit. If a staff member cannot do his work in time, the opportunist estimates how he looks in comparison to this employee. If he wins the comparison, then he will try to emphasize it and "comfort" the unsuccessful employee with the words: "They are really expecting too much from you, Andrew." At the same time, the opportunist will say to a senior manager: "It is too bad that we cannot rely on Andrew, but maybe I could be useful in this case?"

The 7.7— style's reaction to critique will depend on whether he wants to maintain a good relationship with the critic. If the opportunist needs his support, he will take it positively. If the opportunist does not need his support, he might just verbally take critique into account and promise to correct his mistake, but will never do this in the future. The 7.7— leaders prefer individual relationships to collective ones, for collective interaction immediately reveals the inconsistencies of the opportunists' behaviour. A classic example of an opportunist's behaviour is the following: a sales agent offering goods at home, who will tell clients all kinds of lies in an effort to sell a product, and then will quickly disappear.

Once the egotistic opportunist nature is unmasked, colleagues and subordinates become vigilant, expecting all kinds of deception from him. In this case the opportunist usually moves to another department or even leaves the company.

As a rule, the 7.7— style belongs to those who frequently change jobs, rarely staying long in the same company. Only the most flexible ones can survive in the organization for a long time, provided that the opportunist is able to reduce his selfish needs and behave in a more sincere and friendly manner. Therefore, the 7.7— style feels much freer in a company with high personnel turnover.

Successful opportunists behave very cleverly and convincingly in the collective interaction. The only way to succeed in the company is to maintain a good and trusting relationship with your colleagues. Opportunists make every individual feel special and privileged: "I want to tell you a secret, but please do not tell anyone else", or "I do not want him to know about it now, it might upset him". This approach allows the opportunist to set specific relationships of trust with each of the team members and thus minimize the chance of exposing his true aspirations and desires.

Opportunists find different approaches to each and every team member, depending on what he wants. The 7.7— style can go on to change his behaviour style without any apparent reason, which often leads to other employees' confusion: "Why didn't he just come up and say what he had in mind?"

In any competition opportunists tend to stay on top, and this can harm the collective work. Regardless of whether this is an inner struggle of individual members of the group for a small bonus or a serious investment project, opportunists will make every effort to win. They can even use deceptive tactics, undermining the authority of other team members, or even splitting the team. Such destructive competition within the team will draw strength from all the people who will be forced to find excuses for their actions, while the outcome of the struggle— the desired result—can become ultimately uninteresting.

The 7.7— style always considers the relationship as an opportunity to achieve his own goals. Any meeting, discussion, or suggestion should be, according to the opportunist, used to bring him even closer to victory. However, there will be no personal insults or undermining of the common team goals. If by chance an opportunist provides an opportunity to another team member to gain an advantage, no one will suspect him of being selfish, and the opportunist will benefit from it. The opportunist gains advantages and gets benefits by skilfully performed "relationship games". A convincing impression on other members of the team is achieved through hard work in building friendly relations: recognition of other members' personal qualities, expression of common interests. This can be expressed in a helping hand in an emergency situation, taking the blame for the mistakes of others, or hard work. At the same time, the opportunist expects such actions from others in response to his service.

12.3   The I-ZONE and the 7.7— Style

Since the 7.7— style leader's main priority is to achieve his own goals at the expense of others, he cannot get in relationships of mutual trust and respect. From the perspective of the opportunist, a relationship always means the beginning of the end. Interaction with other people is always superficial and often random in nature, it is necessary only to the extent that it helps to achieve one's own goal. The opportunist is unreliable, as he maintains relations only when he needs something, but is not set to maintaining closer contact after he receives his benefits. Relationships with people and team work are perceived as unattractive, but unfortunately necessary.

The opportunist considers himself the most intelligent and well-educated member of the team, and he is proud of it. His participation in the process is just part of a game in which he does not seek to use all his knowledge and skills, contributing to the overall success (Fig. 12.1). The feeling of superiority simplifies his task of using people for his own purposes: when he feels contempt and disregard for a person, it is much easier to deceive him: "If he is not smart enough to understand what is really going on, then he is doomed to failure. One can't be so trustful!"

The opportunist does not bring any benefit to others, as he also refrains from taking on any obligations. "I am a free man and owe nothing in this life", these are the opportunistic principles. However, the 7.7— style tries to never burn bridges completely, as a person may still be useful to him. Due to the fact that the opportunist is afraid of finding himself in a difficult situation, when he supports a stupid or poor idea, he refrains from showing any feelings towards other people.

Fig. 12.1 7.7–

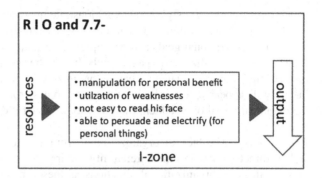

Therefore, it is impossible to establish strong relationships with colleagues, as the opportunist does neither have the necessary motivation, nor the adequate level of confidence.

12.4 7.7– Culture and Values

Culture of Mistrust, Manipulation, and Alienation

Trust The 7.7– leader likes to talk about the importance of trust, but he does not confide in anyone, considering that the main motive of human behaviour is personal gain. The 7.7– leader shows quite a high level of performance. However, his focus on results is not used for work in the organization but above all for personal results and interests. This overt or concealed focus on self-interest creates distrust from the part of colleagues and subordinates. But even more selfishness and the desire for manipulation is manifested in the focus on people. People will soon begin to distrust and even fear the 7.7– style leader and his ability to build relationships, because they will become afraid of being cheated and used.

Fairness In words, the 7.7– leader is actively fighting for justice, creating a favourable impression on others. However, in close co-operation it quickly becomes clear that the 7.7– leader's real ideas of fairness are reduced to the formula: "Justice is an opportunity to get what I need, regardless of my real effort and merit." And if someone can keep his own benefit, without interfering with me, that is also fair. The main thing is not to interfere with each other. If the circumstances do not let the 7.7– style satisfy his own interests at least partially, he perceives such a situation as an obvious injustice. Faced with cases of real injustices, e.g. the apparent underestimation of a staff member's real contribution to the common goal, the 7.7– style verbally expresses his outrage and support, but then grins to himself: "Serves you right! Everyone has to fight for his interests, for no one will do this for you!"

Commitment The 7.7− style tries to demonstrate his commitment to the organization by all means and often makes an impression of a very high level of identification with organizational goals and principles. This changes very quickly, however, if he is unable to realize his personal goals. In fact, he considers the organization as his personal property. The deliberate organizational commitment and identity instantly disappear if a more attractive offer comes from the side. Thus, leaving the organization all of a sudden, the 7.7− style can let it down.

Responsibility The lack of organizational commitment and identity of the 7.7− style is directly related to the unreliability and irresponsibility. He cannot be relied upon in difficult organizational situations as these situations require team work and complete detachment from personal interests and grievances. Even in such situations, the 7.7− style is not able to abandon his habit of assessing everything in terms of personal gain: "And what is my interest here?" If the 7.7− style leader sees someone's error or mistake that does not directly impact his work, then he will prefer not to notice it in order not to spoil personal relationships. The 7.7− style would talk about social responsibility, but in fact, for him it is a very abstract concept that cannot compete with his desire of personal gain and personal success.

Integrity Like other organizational values, the 7.7− style uses transparency and honesty for manipulation: he declares his commitment to these values, but in reality he is pursuing the completely different objective of becoming closer to his personal gain. Calling on others to make their behaviour and activities transparent and honest, the 7.7− leader remains never fully honest himself. At the same time, he has possibilities which subsequently allow him to gain personal benefit or to provide manipulative influence. Those employees, who are in close interaction with the 7.7− leader, soon begin to understand his real motives and to show explicit or hidden disbelief, trying to keep distance.

12.5   7.7− Culture and Power

Focus on Reward, Information, and Referent Power that Are Used for Personal Benefit

Punishment The 7.7− leader considers punishment an emergency measure for those who do not want to understand that certain types of behaviour are unacceptable, as they prevent the 7.7− style from achieving his personal goals. In this behavioural pattern, he is inclined to see the intent of defending personal interests. The 7.7− style is very reluctant to use punishment, fearing a negative reaction. If punishment is still inevitable, it must be justified by high organizational principles, to ensure the maintenance of traditions, reliable work of the system, and so on. The punishment is more concerned with the threat to achieve the 7.7− style's personal goals, and not with the staff members' objective results.

Reward The 7.7— leader uses reward actively, but he believes that only those who know how to live, who follow the motto "Self comes first" are worthy of rewards. The 7.7— style is confident that he knows how to live better than anyone else. Of course, those who interfere with the 7.7— leader's achievement of his personal goals never deserve any reward, even if they have made a significant contribution to the work of the organization. But those, who knowingly or unwittingly helped the 7.7— style to achieve his personal goals and benefits are worthy of reward. At the same time, the 7.7— leader does not mind if someone, without disturbing him, also acts solely for his own benefit. If they do not compete with the 7.7— style, these people are accepted by him. Thus, the reward is also used for his own purposes and personal gain and is related to performance only indirectly.

Position For the 7.7— style position power is the only important one because it opens up more opportunities to realize his personal goals. If it does not affect his position in the organization, he is indifferent to the efficiency of organizational performance. The 7.7— style knows the amount of his official powers, but, first of all, he tries to perform the functions that can bring personal benefit. He never delegates these functions to his subordinates.

Information The 7.7— style owns valuable resources in the form of gained knowledge, skills, and experience. He wants others to depend on the necessary information that he has. Thus, it is enough to let the team know about the latest developments in technology, to talk about the key aspects of competitors, to be aware of the latest news and events, as well as internal company information. Key sources of information for the 7.7— style are formal and informal communication channels that are primarily used in order to understand where he can most likely obtain personal advantages and benefits. The 7.7— style is well aware of his subordinates' duties, as well as of their rights and obligations and area of responsibility, and where the gold mine is. The exchange of information is carried out with the purpose of personal gain and strengthening of one's positions. The interests of the organization are on the periphery of the 7.7— leader's attention. In dealing with subordinates he typically declares very beautiful slogans that often mislead people. The senior management's instructions are accepted by the 7.7— leader with enthusiasm. He tries to fulfil them on time and at a high level. The 7.7— style's most intensive communication is limited to a narrow circle of people and is based on the principle: "I help you, you help me".

Expert The 7.7— style has a fairly high professional competence. He can professionally implement projects that can bring significant profits. In such cases, relying on personal gain, the 7.7— style can be at the same time extremely useful to the organization. However, if self-interest is lower than expected, the 7.7— style's motivation decreases sharply. He is good in situations that require calculations, non-standard actions, and decisions. The 7.7— style has high competence in those areas that promise to give him the greatest benefit and personal gain. However, the 7.7— leader has no desire to use his expertise for the benefit of the organization. If the available knowledge and skills are insufficient to achieve his own goals, the 7.7− style takes active steps to improve his professional level.

Referent The 7.7− style usually has a pretty powerful reference power, as in any situation, he does not lose his presence of mind, he knows the needs and interests of employees, but always tries to act according to his own interests. On the one hand, such behaviour is accompanied by declarations of sincere commitment to the organization, and on the other hand, the desire to manipulate the consciousness and behaviour of other people. This leads to the fact that others begin to perceive the 7.7− style leader as an unreliable person, who cannot be counted on both in the daily work and force majeure situations. Therefore, in cases where the 7.7− style is forced by circumstances to urge employees to fulfil any urgent or difficult work, his calls are not capable of arising enthusiasm. The opportunist's motivation reflects his desire to obtain advantage and personal benefit on the one hand, while on the other hand the fear of exposure does not allow the 7.7− style leader to fully build solid, harmonious relationships based on mutual trust, respect, and sincerity.

12.6   Cooperation Skills of the 7.7− Style

Conflict Resolution

The 7.7− style refers to any conflict with caution: in a situation of confrontation he risks showing his real face, and the opportunist does not want it under any circumstances. If the 7.7− style can gain benefit from the conflict, he tries to control it, in accordance with his personal interests and without revealing his true intentions and goals. His conflict resolution tactic is to get the support of others and, at the same time, to express his sympathy to the conflicting parties. If the 7.7− leader has no personal interest in the resolution of the conflict, he tries to avoid it by all means.

Conflict creates a situation in which it is difficult to flexibly change the behaviour, and that is a problem for the opportunist. Conflict makes people decide whose side they are on, and this leads to a polarization of opinions. If the boss is not prepared for the conflict, the 7.7− style may try to influence his behaviour. He prefers to resolve the conflict alone and does not like collective confrontation. The method of individual conflict resolution helps him garner universal support, as the opportunist can simultaneously hold two conflicting positions. The 7.7− style carefully tries to never stick to a certain position in an open conflict.

The 7.7− leader avoids conflicts, keeping a safe distance. When the conflict is underway, the opportunist is usually keeping out of it. Such avoidance of conflict apparently can take many forms. If the opportunist has power, he can stop the discussion and divert attention from the potential conflict problems: "It can be discussed later!" If the opportunist has a lower level position, he avoids involvement more evasively: "I do not know what happened there. Now it is more important to concentrate on work!" This allows him to maintain good relationships with each of the conflicting parties, while portraying innocence.

Another 7.7– style's way to participate in the conflict is to support the opinion that, most likely, would be preferred by other team members. If an employee is involved in a conflict with the boss, an opportunist may try to please the boss and make a good impression: "I hear you have a problem with Peter. I also heard only brickbats about him." The 7.7– style is very inventive in finding ways to stay away from conflict. If he feels that the risk of being involved in the conflict is too great, he may even take on the role of the martyr, not allowing the conflicting parties to win. In fact, the opportunist allows others to win, only to look better himself. Such an approach is cynical in a sense, as the opportunist unmasks other egoists, while acting like a victim: "I could not do anything, because then it would hit the entire organization. I know that was wrong, but at least my conscience is clear." In fact, in this situation, the 7.7– leader acts as a selfish one, while his opponents turn out to be victims.

Another 7.7– style's approach to resolving conflict is to convince both sides, urging them to cooperate. To prevent conflict, the opportunist forces each side to come to any decision. Such actions, of course, bring some benefit to the opportunist, but it is unlikely that such an approach can be useful. The 7.7– style motto is: "I just wish that things went well." The purpose of the opportunist in negotiations to resolve conflicts is to reduce tensions and ensure a comfortable atmosphere. This approach is similar to the 4.4– style's search for a compromise, but the opportunist is interested in a truce because he is still pursuing his personal interests. An effective way to resolve the conflict can be considered as an alternative, but only if it yields dividends to the 7.7– style.

Another 7.7– style's approach to resolving conflict is to find a compromise with the enemy. With his fairly high professional and communicative competence, the opportunist understands what the situation requires and what people are afraid of. Such tactics may be veiled or overt but, as a rule, the opportunist uses them when he feels a threat to his personal interests. The 7.7– style can be tough with the opponent if drawn into the conflict against his interests: "Don't get me involved in this, if you do not want your failure with the same project 3 years ago to be known." Manipulation can be put in a more subtle way: "Remember how I helped you during the inspection of the headquarters at the end of last year. Yes, no one can survive without mutual help, so thank you in advance for a small service I expect from you right now." Of course, the service in question is usually not that small.

Regardless of the method chosen, the opportunist uses the conflict to achieve his selfish goals and never uses his positive energy to achieve organizational goals.

Communicative Competence

The 7.7– style has a powerful and multifaceted communicative competence. Taking part in the discussion and debate, the 7.7– style constantly assesses the level of support that other people are ready to provide to his decisions and actions.

He needs this support to achieve his personal goals and benefits. He persuades others to rely on him, while keeping the opinion and assessment of what is happening to himself.

The 7.7− style is actively involved in the exchange of information, using it to get advantages. Any problems and shortcomings which do not affect his personal interests are ignored or presented in such a way that frees him of any liability. In case of making a wrong decision, the 7.7− style will immediately make others pay attention to beyond-control circumstances that prevented the adoption of a decision.

Full ownership of information helps the 7.7− style work with a sense of superiority over others, because he knows exactly when and how to strike. The opportunist knows when and where he needs to involve a particular topic, which will then be used as a basis. And by the time these comments acquire a variety of rumours, the source of the information is already forgotten.

The 7.7− style should always be aware of all the events for two reasons: firstly, he wants to be the most informed person in the company, and secondly, he wants to know what other team members think about what is happening. Professional knowledge such as modern technologies, competition methods, and techniques allows the opportunist to be one step ahead of others, and much more prepared to fight for victory. Such a need for information requires certain skills.

First of all, the 7.7− style establishes close contacts with individuals who are key to the realization of his personal goals. To obtain the necessary information about the past, present, and future strategy of the company, he offers information exchange and imposes his services. The right information usually comes from external sources through his own channels. For example, the 7.7− leader befriends an employee of the department of personnel in order to obtain information about who will soon be promoted. He is usually the first to know about who is hired and who is fired. The 7.7− style is always a step ahead of everyone else, thanks to being kept informed.

The 7.7− style has the talent to draw information from others. He knows what is needed and how to influence others to have them share information, even when they are not interested in it. This ability is a part of the opportunist's gift of persuasion. He firstly analyses the behaviour and actions of others, and only then begins to ask the right questions. The 7.7− style draws information from others in the form of questions that reinforce his credibility and strengthen the faith in his powers. Using the information received makes it easier for the opportunist to achieve his goals. He blocks other opinions if they do not suit him.

Any information received is constantly checked and rechecked. The 7.7− leader does not want to risk his position and therefore, as a rule, he trusts no one; first he gathers all the necessary information, and only then begins to arrange cross-checks. Thus, he can immediately respond to any conflict so that it does not hurt his personal interests.

Active Positioning

The 7.7− style expresses his views and arguments actively only when he is convinced of the possibility to benefit from the results. If there is no such certainty, he is likely to support the ideas of others in order to still ultimately achieve his goals. The 7.7− leader uses information in order to transform it to his own benefit. To avoid exposing his true intentions, the opportunist packs the information in an attractive organizational wrapping. He takes the different circumstances into account: background, prospects, and the views of other members of the organization. The 7.7− style always calculates how to behave better in this or that situation in advance. Despite the fact that the level of being informed allows him to participate in the discussion of strategic issues, he tries to avoid such discussions.

The 7.7− leader considers his position an opportunity to lobby his interests and eliminate the opposition. First, the opportunist identifies his allies and enemies, and then makes them work for his personal goals. Usually he unmasks his enemies in a hidden manner, so that his own true motives are not exposed. The Style 7.7− can start spreading rumours and doubts in order to undermine the credibility of a particular team member. In all this backstage fight the opportunist will always protect and defend his positions.

The views and principles articulated by the opportunist depend on the people around him and on his personal goals. If the 7.7− style sees no possibility to benefit from the situation, he will express his views in order to gain others' trust for future use. He sincerely believes that such situations are not dangerous and are beneficial to him. In the absence of sufficient information, the 7.7− leader delays the expression of his views as long as possible. If the opportunist is surrounded by more informed people, the fear of being unmasked keeps him from expressing his views. Here he prefers to play the role of a listener, sometimes asking questions and offering assistance.

The 7.7− leader exhibits his standpoint only if it promises personal benefit. He aims to gain support by any means: using intimidation, flattery, negotiation, encouragement, or effort to win the trust of others. If the 7.7− style feels that there is no benefit for him, he will no longer show any activity. In a conflict situation, he will look for another way to achieve his own goals.

When interested, the 7.7− style takes a very active standpoint, but always manipulative. The opportunist's standpoint must always prevail over other views. He can attain this in various ways. If other people involved are less active than him, the 7.7− style will act decisively and energetically. At the same time, if necessary, he will take advantage of the team members' support. In this case, he will demonstrate interest in people à la 4.4+ style: "This project is just what we need to be proud of our company. I promise that each of you will have a smile on your face, and our traditions will be inspiration for us again."

If others involved are more active and decisive than the 7.7− leader, he will undertake a sophisticated approach to each of them. He will probably present his idea so cleverly that the paternalist boss will take it as his own. Interacting with a paternalist, the opportunist will emphasize respect and admiration: "I will be very grateful for your advice. I know you will help me put my ideas into practice." With the 7.1— style, the opportunist will stress his interest in final results: "With the implementation of this project it will be possible to increase the pace of our performance. As a result, we can increase productivity by 15 %." Such statements will, of course, caress the boss's ear!

Whichever approach is chosen by the 7.7— style, it will persistently move him towards achieving his intended purpose. If the support of other team members weakens, the opportunist will find a way to increase the enthusiasm of the team as soon as possible. At a time when others would simply stand idly, the opportunist will be the first to assess the situation and, if necessary, prepare a convincing response. As a means of persuasion the opportunist can use subtle comments and suggestions in order to create fear and doubt or, conversely, confidence. In case the opportunist does not see any possibility to gain benefit, his enthusiasm for taking initiative weakens. However, he continues to look for opportunities that will strengthen his position and bring personal benefit.

Decision-Making

The 7.7— leader makes decisions based on his personal interests. When the solutions are put forward in a brainstorming, the opportunist will try to find their strengths and weaknesses, not forgetting the personal benefit. The key success of this approach is that opportunists will always escape safe. The 7.7— style tries to keep everything under control and uses his decisions since his solutions were ready, and the disputed issues were not addressed. Similar manipulations can take any shape depending on the situation. When issues beneficial to the opportunist are discussed, he will say: "That's a good question. Let's work it through."

When he sees the discussion shifting to a direction, he will try to distract attention by saying: "This is an interesting alternative, but it leads us away from the key issues. I remember a good suggestion that was put forward..." If the 7.7— style cannot divert attention away, he will try to postpone a decision. The opportunist understands that decisions made alone require less effort than collective ones, especially if the opportunist holds a high position in the company and should not be accountable to anyone.

He makes decisions that will contribute to the achievement of his personal goals, but they are presented as the general solution of employees. As long as an opportunist cleverly disguises his true intentions and goals, people will put up with his decisions based on self-interest. The opportunist helps others only if he can expect some help in return. If he holds a high position in the company, he does not care about what others might think about his decisions.

Regardless of the overall organizational objectives, the 7.7— leader lobbies the decisions that may bring him benefits. He encourages others to rely on him and trust his decisions. Thus, the purpose of the 7.7— leader's decision-making is also his personal gain.

Constructive Critique

The 7.7− style uses critique to strengthen the existing support from other people and generate a new one. As he is always aware of the latest developments in the field, the innovative ways of developing and perfecting the organization, he always has some advantage over other team members.

The 7.7− style uses the information received from the critique in order to dress himself up. Any problems and shortcomings are presented in such a way that frees the opportunist from any liability. In case of making a wrong decision, the 7.7− style immediately draws attention of others to circumstances beyond his control. If the result of the 7.7− style's team is worse than that of other teams, the critique received will be redirected in order to completely shift the responsibility for the poor results to specific employees. The opportunist uses critique to pay attention to other competitors' weaknesses and shortcomings and thus undermine their reputation.

For example, the 7.7− style may provoke critique in a meeting, drawing attention to others' minor errors and shortcomings in order to divert attention from the overall picture of what is happening. The opportunist may bring forward critique using biased or incomplete data in order to accuse someone. If a person who has been criticized by an opportunist tries to present an alternative point of view, the opportunist will accuse him of unscrupulousness and self-justification. Since all the cards are in the hands of the 7.7− style leader, the accused is unlikely to be given the opportunity to defend his reputation.

The 7.7− style focuses all his efforts on achieving his own success. Full ownership of information helps the opportunist to work, being aware of his superiority over others, because he knows when and how to strike. The opportunist knows when he needs to touch a particular topic, which will then be used as a basis. Later, when his comments are "overgrown" by rumours, the source of the information will be forgotten.

The opportunist's solid position fails if the critic is able to expose his true intentions and goals. In this situation, the entire structure, built by the 7.7− style is ruined, and he is left with no choice but to leave the organization. Being well prepared professionally, the opportunist can often predict the organization's activity, and he always finds a way to avoid the consequences. He can foresee the troubles and deftly put another person at risk. If the opportunist is not able to avoid confrontation, he suggests all kinds of justification for his actions in order to reduce the degree of guilt. For this he is ready to blame other people, especially the absent ones. The 7.7− style may even tar someone's reputation, but he never finds the courage to take responsibility for it.

12.7   Conclusions

The 7.7− leader never relies on teamwork. He prefers to work alone, and believes that the only way towards personal gains is hiding true intentions and belittling the merits of other team members. Team work, which implies shared responsibility and joint management of resources, for the 7.7− style is only a temporary compromise necessary for pursuing his personal interests. The opportunist never comes close enough to people to understand that shared responsibility can lead to completely new developments. His anxieties and fears, caused by the constant need to wear a mask, never weaken, as he cannot have sincere feelings and share his success with others.

The 7.7− style is characterized by increased resentment and lack of understanding of the benefits of teamwork. Therefore, eventually, he does harm to himself, while his efficiency is very low. However, proper team support can cause the opportunist to still consider the need for and the benefits of working in a team. The opportunist, as a rule, has solid knowledge and skills, so his contribution to the common cause can be considerable.

It is known that the organizational world is cruel and wicked. The laws of competition often enact in their primitive form: either you crush a competitor, or he will crush you. Nevertheless, life progress is determined by harmony. Thus, competition will inevitably interact with cooperation. And in real life the 7.7− leader, who is incapable of real cooperation, will inevitably feel lonely: no one wants to work with him. People want to trust their colleagues, because they are fed up with feelings of mistrust from their competitors, clients, and other third parties.

Nobody wants to be close to a person who can use you for his own purposes at any moment. Trust is the core value of teamwork. Opportunism undermines trust. Opportunism is the behaviour style which is less likely to be changed. People do not rush to help opportunists to change, as they recall having been used by him earlier. The 7.7− style needs to work hard in order to prove his sincere intentions and motives to everyone, but it is difficult to regain the lost trust.

Style 7.7+: Ideal, Visionary (Devotion and Contribution)

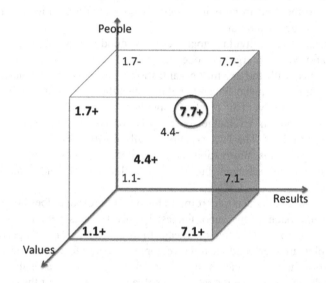

High concern for production, high concern for people, high concern for the organization work, and desire to create an atmosphere of commitment and involvement. The 7.7+ style knows the worth of each employee, constantly demonstrates his commitment to achieving the highest standards of activities aimed at finding and adopting optimal solutions that will be supported and shared by everyone. He is characterized by the desire to develop and improve his own abilities and to help employees realize their potential, while respecting the organizational traditions and values. The 7.7+ style tries to ensure the greatest involvement in work and sincere commitment of all team members. He analyses all the facts and listens to all points of view in order to reach an understanding and ensure synergies.

© Springer-Verlag Berlin Heidelberg 2016
A. Zankovsky, C. von der Heiden, *Leadership with Synercube*,
DOI 10.1007/978-3-662-49052-5_13

13.1   Basic Features of the 7.7+ Style

The 7.7+ style is characterized by the highest commitment to the values and mission of the organization, as well as the highest level of focus on people and results. The difference between the 7.7+ leader and other Synercube-model styles is that the 7.7+ can seamlessly overcome contradictions that arise in the process of achieving a high level of all three factors of effective leadership. This allows the 7.7+ style to build a more effective joint action based on synergy.

7.7+ leaders can direct all their energy to the good of the organization. This interaction combined with the achievement of the organizational goals gives managers a sense of self-worth, because they know that their personal contribution changes the organization for the better, and these changes lead to the best results. The 7.7+ leader can resolve any conflicts arising in the organization. This is possible due to the gain in permanent centripetal forces that unite all employees around common goals and values.

Organizational and individual goals begin to sound in unison, concern for both production and people merge into one stream, and focus on profits is realized in strict compliance with the existing organizational ethics. The 7.7+ leader has an authentic, trusting style, who sincerely believes that the best results can be achieved only through the involvement of all the available resources of the organization. Therefore, information exchange is broadly based on the knowledge and achievements of others. The 7.7+ style is initially positive, he wants to contribute and do his best. This motivation is associated not only with the leader's achievements and commitment, but also with achievements and commitment of all employees.

The 7.7+ leader never acts according to his own interest and does not encourage this kind of approach in his subordinates. He always acts very thoroughly and accurately, trying to use all available means to improve relations and performance.

The complete merger of all the three vectors is a unique feature of the 7.7+ style. The strength of the 7.7+ leader is in the correct, logical, and reasonable notion: if there is a problem, undertake it openly and solve it for the good of the organization and the people. The 7.7+ leader is really objective, he is not afraid of open and honest efforts to solve complex problems.

The 7.7+ leader tends to act in compliance with organizational values. This means that he takes his overriding priority the success and growth of the entire organization. Such a desire can lead to what his subordinates and colleagues might perceive as a problem, showing indifference, protest, or superficiality. It depends on their style of behaviour and specific aspirations. However, it should be noted that regardless of differences in behaviours and worldviews, the 7.7+ leader can change everyone, capturing them with his ideas and strong convictions.

The 7.7+ leader has high ethical demands towards himself and his colleagues. For him the fundamental human values are justice, honesty, trust, and responsibility. These are the values that are shared, appreciated, and supported by everyone. In summary, the 7.7+ leader is objective and honest, humble and very self-critical, and he supports others, thinking about the future. He does not seek changes just for the sake of changes, but considers them the engine of progress. This means that the 7.7+ style is an effective leader in a corporate culture that encourages teamwork and universal organizational cooperation.

13.2   The 7.7+ Style in Collective Cooperation

When one of the staff members cannot cope with his work, the 7.7+ leader critiques his colleague only if he has facts. He is not afraid of conflict and can be firm if necessary. He discusses the progress of the work to develop a mutual understanding of the purpose that they are facing, and to reach agreement on the improvement of the activity. If a team member does not want to work in this direction and is not doing anything to improve his performance, the 7.7+ leader clearly shows him all the consequences of this for him and for the organization as a whole.

The 7.7+ style listens carefully to critique and asks questions to reveal its real significance. If the critique is proper and valid, the 7.7+ leader immediately adjusts his way of action, taking into account what was said. If observations are not justified, the 7.7+ leader is ready to reveal the contradictions and achieve better mutual understanding.

The 7.7+ style is convinced that good results O can be achieved only when everyone has the really necessary and relevant information that enables to carry out duties as best as possible. Communication must not only be accurate, clear, and concise but also express sincere commitment to the organization and its values. Only thus can team members put an end to political games, favouritism, and intrigues, and be able to openly and honestly express ideas and make suggestions.

Groups with 7.7+ leaders have enthusiasm, confidence, and cohesion. They are characterized by the constant improvement of the quality of interactions among team members. Employees can discuss ideas without fear of making a mistake or being accused of anything. People know that they always have a chance to speak and that their views will be heard, even if the ideas expressed are not accepted. The 7.7+ leader helps everyone to overcome communication barriers, allowing employees to feel secure and confident, ready to express even those ideas that seem unrealistic today. Such an approach, by actively involving people in the activity, allows a deep commitment to the organization and a heightened sense of personal responsibility. If the employee's creative idea becomes part of the company's strategy, he will feel even more committed to the implementation of this strategy. People are always keen to feel part of the project in which they are directly involved.

People feel enthusiasm and commitment to the 7.7+ leader's team, as they are more informed. The information is not hidden and is not distorted. The high involvement of the 7.7+ style in achieving the goals requires an open and frank exchange of information, so that it is possible to consider all possible alternatives. This means that problems are discussed openly and honestly with constructive critique, and staff members support each other on the way to perfection. If people are well informed, problems are resolved at the outset, and some problems may never arise. If employees have all the information, it is much less likely that facts will get out of control because of rumours and speculative activities. Awareness helps to overcome misunderstandings and remove resentment as it is possible to discuss and solve conflicts.

The 7.7+ leader's high involvement in activities creates an atmosphere of confidence in the team. Mutual trust and respect increase as people feel free to express their feelings and opinions and are not afraid to take a risk with extraordinary and creative solutions. The contribution of each and every team member is assessed according to real merits, and not according to the chatter or the ability to play politics. Therefore, the fears that are inherent to all the other styles are replaced by a sincere desire of employees to help each other. If someone's idea leads to unpleasant consequences, the whole team shares the responsibility for this effort and tries to correct the error.

But despite the heightened team spirit and mutual support, the 7.7+ leader's approach does not reduce the sense of personal responsibility and personal contribution to the common cause. The increasing support within the group means that individual employees have more opportunities to express creative ideas without fear. And since the contribution of each and every team member is assessed according to real merits, some people are even more proud if their personal suggestions lead the team to success. As a result, the team holds the bar high, while healthy competition makes people constantly learn and improve their efficiency.

13.3   The I-ZONE and the 7.7+ Style

The high level of openness and sincerity reduces the level of stress in relationships, because people feel free and able to express their feelings. People trust each other and offer their support. Team members help each other to overcome the circumstances and achieve both their personal goals and those of the organization. Relationships of this kind help to overcome all obstacles and failures, as collective resources are now being used with maximum efficiency. But this does not mean that the political behaviour, detachment, fear, and unhealthy rivalry disappear for good. They occasionally appear as an integral part of any group interaction. But the difference is that the probability of the impact of these symptoms on efficiency is reduced because discussions are based on the principle of fairness, consistency, and validity. If the interaction takes place in the team openly and honestly, then all manifestations of improper behaviour become immediately traced and corrected, so that work can be continued at maximum efficiency. Openness and sincerity give the team a chance to detect the problem and quickly resolve it, rather than to deny or hide the problem, to embellish the information "until the bomb explodes", damaging and pushing the desired result further.

Relationships based on mutual trust, respect, and sincerity contribute to achieving synergies. It is difficult to achieve synergies if the atmosphere in the team is not good for open expression of opinions and convictions, and creation of new ideas. If

Fig. 13.1 7.7+

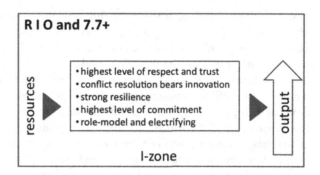

this really open working atmosphere can be achieved, then the information that usually floats on the surface or becomes concealed and glossed over is now discussed in an atmosphere of objectivity. On achieving synergies, the information discussed makes it possible to put forward completely new, great ideas and discover opportunities that each member of staff individually could never achieve.

The 7.7+ style shows commitment on individual, collective, and organizational levels. He wants to know that his efforts lead to positive changes. The 7.7+ leader works with enthusiasm, commitment, and respect for colleagues. If the 7.7+ leader still sees untapped potential, he and his colleagues begin to work on the unlocking of this potential. Only in the context of the 7.7+ leadership can everyone actively develop and expand his skills and gain experience—valuable for the team and for the person himself. If the 7.7+ leader feels that the desired result will justify the risk and sacrifice in the way of achieving it, then he will be able to put forward illustrative examples to explain it to others and reach understanding and commitment (Fig. 13.1).

The 7.7+ style sincerely wants to contribute to the common cause, but without sacrificing human beings or results. He does not accept personal or collective goals that are contrary to the organization's goals because they conflict with his focus on the values of the organization. The same is right for the company's objectives, which are contrary to the collective or personal goals. The 7.7+ leader is never afraid of constructively identifying these differences and working them out by finding a mutually beneficial solution.

The "What is right?" motivation allows the 7.7+ leader and his subordinates to feel that they have tried very hard and did their best. And it helps to take all the consequences—both positive and negative—without any regrets.

13.4   7.7+ Culture and Values

Culture of Trust, Fairness, Commitment, Responsibility, and Integrity

Trust For the 7.7+ leader trust is the natural type of interaction with other people. He is convinced that every person is endowed with many talents, and nature has bestowed many good qualities upon him, though circumstances may not always allow people to realize it. By acting openly and honestly, and trusting each other, people help each other to disclose their talents. The 7.7+ style operates openly and honestly, and he is confident that others will come and do the same. The 7.7+ leader is sincere in all that he does and never tries to manipulate others. He shows respect and attention both to managers and subordinates, always observing courtesy and never allowing humiliating or insulting the interlocutor. He believes that everyone has great potential, which because of certain circumstances or personal characteristics cannot always be revealed. By showing greater confidence in others, their abilities, and thoughts, people help each other and enrich themselves. The 7.7+ leader's attitude generates confidence in the organization and the sense of a sustainable management of the situation in which you want to work. Trust permeates the present and future of the organization. People believe in the success of their company. The company welcomes the success of its employees.

Fairness The 7.7+ style is convinced that his behaviour proves that promotion and achievements are interrelated things. The 7.7+ leader establishes all the criteria for rewards and punishments and discusses them in detail with the staff. The 7.7+ style believes that any improvement in work, skills, or motivation should be encouraged. The reasons for any deterioration in work, skills, or motivation should be identified and analysed. This promotion is in no way limited exclusively to financial rewards, and includes a wide range of non-material rewards: the attention and support of the boss, public recognition, additional features of the personal and vocational development, and so on. Decisions concerning career development and shape and size of material rewards are conveyed to employees with reasons and explanations. All this creates a situation in which people strive to maximize their performance and success. This tendency corresponds to a company's culture that encourages initiative and achieving outstanding results.

Commitment The 7.7+ leader, in compliance with his individual values system totally identifies himself with the organization. Occupying even the smallest position, he feels not just a part of the organization but a staff member who is responsible for the fate of the entire company. And it is not an instance of inflated self, but a result of deep identification with the company. All activities are performed by the 7.7+ style with the highest responsibility, as well as with respect to the people and the company. The 7.7+ leader shows innovative thinking and willingness to take risks, he is ready to bear full responsibility for this. The protection of the company's interests, of its intellectual and physical property, is perceived as the protection of his own interests and property.

Responsibility The 7.7+ style is convinced that reliability and responsibility are the most important values of the organization, which can be ensured only with constant observance of the requirements of the highest corporate culture in all aspects of organizational performance. At the same time, the best achievements of science, technology, and management are to be used as paradigm. The 7.7+ culture provides management with reliability and, at the same time, creates a space where people can work independently and reliably. The 7.7+ leader feels responsible not only for his own mistakes, but for his self-improvement and development. This standpoint allows him to fully share the policy of corporate social responsibility and contribute to it in every possible way. The 7.7+ style believes that the company and all its employees are and feel responsible for the life of society and mankind as a whole, for the preservation of the environment for future generations and the future of the company. The 7.7+ style is a supporter of permanent, active, and responsible reforms aimed at the future. Feedback is used to plan and organize the process in such a way that they are secure and they can be corrected if something goes wrong. Feedback processes necessarily include objective feedback. The 7.7+ leader uses feedback as an important management and training tool.

Integrity For the 7.7+ leader, openness, honesty, and transparency of organizational life is the basis for efficient cooperation and synergies. Without openness and honesty partners and colleagues cannot trust each other, as there is no assurance that we can predict their future decisions and actions. In the absence of openness, honesty, and transparency management planning is carried out at random, introducing significant uncertainty in the rest of the work. Thus, it becomes impossible to use feedback to adjust and optimize operations. This makes it very difficult and even unrealistic to achieve higher goals. Only in conditions of transparency and fairness is it possible to plan the processes precisely and accurately, organize work and measure results, and, respectively, adjust future activities.

13.5   7.7+ Culture and Power

Focus on Information, Expert, and Referent Powers

Punishment The 7.7+ leader believes in positivity and talent of human nature and, therefore, is a staunch opponent of the use of punishment as a means of influence. The punishment is applied only in exceptional cases, when all other means of influence have proved useless. At the same time punishment for 7.7+ leader is a reasonable, logical consequence of actions, which are contrary to commonly agreed standards and to some extent detrimental to the organization. This causal link and the inevitability of punishment are emphasized, as the punishment itself is legitimate or carried out correctly.

Reward The 7.7+ leader regards reward as an encouragement for timely and well-done job. Encouraging is always specifically linked to the criteria formulated down in advance. Unlike other styles, 7.7+ leader uses the entire range of rewards, including a large set of intangible assets. His arsenal includes personal gratitude and praise, public recognition, greater responsibility, more challenges, and greater freedom of action. Recognition is always associated with concrete results, it can be of different sizes and individualized based on the needs and the personal characteristics of employees.

Position The 7.7+ style never tries to emphasize his authority, stressing the importance of partnership in which the key role is played by professionalism, dedication, and commitment. Most commonly the 7.7+ leader uses his status to represent the interests of the organization or department, explaining and defending them.

Information The 7.7+ leader uses information resources in an effort to form a department and/or organization with a corporate culture that focuses all employees on the organization's goals, values, and standards. He constantly emphasizes those common goals and values that unite the company, helping to overcome any conflicts and achieve the highest results. He is actively involved in the exchange of information with all employees, enabling them to stay abreast of all the organizational news. The 7.7+ style seeks to prevent an information deficit, which inevitably encourages rumours and gossip in the organization. He is convinced that access to all relevant information is an essential condition to achieve the best results.

Expert The 7.7+ style has very high professional competence in his field, as well as broad general knowledge. Therefore, colleagues and subordinates often turn to him for expert opinion or advice on the majority of institutional and professional issues. However, the 7.7+ style does not consider himself all-knowing, he appreciates the professionalism of each employee, and is ready to engage external experts in solving very complex problems. Realizing the limitations of any knowledge in the modern ever-changing world, the 7.7+ leader continuously strives to deepen his knowledge and to continuously improve his expertise.

Referent The 7.7+ leader usually has a considerable referent power and strong charisma. The 7.7+ style is confident, self-sufficient, persuasive, and consistent in his actions. He is unconstrained and purposeful, creating an atmosphere of optimism and positivity. He is genuinely committed to the organization, identifying himself with it, but at the same time he has his own standpoint and his own vision of work and life in general. All this involuntarily attracts others and encourages them to follow his ideas, values, and goals.

13.6   Cooperation Skills of the 7.7+ Style

Conflict Resolution

The 7.7+ style considers differences in opinions and conflicts as opportunities for improvement. The 7.7+ style expresses his disagreement openly to reveal the true obstacles in the way to efficiency. He carefully analyses the reasons for the differences and contradictions, trying to see a basis for cooperation beyond external differences. The honest, respectful, and confidential communication method allows the 7.7+ leader to be open and sincere, which helps overcome conflicts constructively, using power to improve the effectiveness and the spirit of cooperation.

The 7.7+ leader regards conflict as a vital component of progress, as a powerful source of energy and creative expressions. Most people do not like to participate in conflicts, but the 7.7+ style understands their importance for progress, so he tries to find the real causes of the conflict. He believes that the suppression of the conflict is much more harmful to the team and can cause an avalanche effect that will eventually lead to even more disastrous consequences. When people discuss and dispel their doubts, fears, and contradictions, they can overcome problems and move forward.

The atmosphere of sincerity, mutual trust, and respect that the 7.7+ leader tries to create helps to focus on the necessary resources and opinions of others. The principle of "What is right?" is critical to the optimal conflict resolution. People gain the courage to defend their ideas, take risks, and discuss emerging contradiction with each other if they are confident that all the ensuing consequences will be based on an evaluation of their correctness and optimality of the organization and the employees themselves. The 7.7+ style is convinced that an active and constructive way to resolve the conflict cannot be implemented in an atmosphere of avoidance, smoothing, searching for compromise, or forcing unilateral decisions. In such circumstances, people lose confidence that their views will be listened to and objectively and fairly assessed, and think to themselves: "why do I do anything? It can bring nothing but trouble." If the conflict is immediately articulated, the reasons are analysed in terms of objective and relevant facts, and then everyone can express his opinion.

The desire to avoid conflict is quite natural, since its emotional aspect brings discomfort. Usually the active defence of one's position is accompanied by anger, gestures, even shouting, and many actually prefer to smooth and extinguish the conflict in order not to mess with an angry employee. As is known, different people have different levels of resistance to alien manifestations of emotion. A kind of crying person often makes others uncomfortable and immediately causes a reaction of self-defence. However, avoiding emotions during the conflict can only worsen the situation. People should be able to speak out, and they want to be listened to, especially if they have concerns.

The 7.7+ leader's approach to the perception of emotional expressions of conflict implies an opportunity for everyone to speak, but attention should be focused on the facts and causes of the conflict. To ensure this, he can bring one or two colleagues to the discussion in the role of objective observers. An objective approach is particularly important if the people involved in the discussion have lost their ability to maintain impartiality. In such a situation it is useful to discuss the specific facts and logically sound arguments. As a consequence, the discussion will be focused precisely on the conflict resolution that will help prevent further confrontation.

If the principle of "What is right?" in resolving conflicts is shared by all team members, employees overcome contradictions by finding the facts, analysing the data, and identifying the causes. When a solution is found, it reflects the view that is somehow shared by all.

The 7.7+ leader's approach ensures the confrontation between ideas, not people. If all conflicting parties aim at identifying what is right, then the one whose idea is rejected will not feel offended. He will say to his opponents: "My idea was not entirely right. I hope that your idea will be more correct to solve our problem." This approach means no one will lose, as all participants will eventually benefit from a successful idea.

For the 7.7+ leader constructive conflict resolution is one of the possible ways to achieve synergy. By comparing and discussing different points of view, initially conflicting parties can find a solution that is better than their original ones. And although the new solution may present some elements of the original suggestions, it is a completely different solution, more profound, far from being a compromise. Synergy is the ultimate dream of any team. It is achieved only when the team is ready for conflict resolution, and does not try to gloss over conflicts or hide them. The 7.7+ leader always bears in mind that unresolved conflict robs collective energy, deprives the team from its commitment, necessary to achieve the best work results.

Communicative Competence

The 7.7+ style has a very high communicative competence. He tries to ensure that all staff is fully informed to make the right decisions. Employees are constantly aware of what is happening. Teamwork is always a result of the concerted and determined efforts of every team member. The 7.7+ leader attracts only those employees who really should be involved in solving the problems to discuss them. The 7.7+ style can hold meetings very rarely. In each case, the process involves only those employees who have the knowledge, skills, and experience necessary to achieve the results.

The 7.7+ leader seeks to organize an active exchange of ideas, to engage all available resources to achieve the best result. New ideas are welcomed, taken into account, and promoted. In order for the ideas and opinions of others to be compared and actively shared, methods of active listening are used. This ensures each team member's activity and a high degree of responsibility for the task. The 7.7+ leader is actively looking for accurate necessary information. He invites employees to dialogue and listens to their ideas and opinions carefully, even if they are very different from his own. He constantly checks the validity of his reasoning and decisions by comparing them to the approaches of others.

The 7.7+ style never tries to hide, downplay, or exaggerate on information. He is willing to share any information for objective analysis and unbiased review. This quality makes sincerity the main quality of the 7.7+ style as far as dealing with information is concerned. The 7.7+ leader tries to assess resources as appropriately as possible. But this is impossible if you do not have full and complete information. Since the 7.7+ leader seeks to achieve the best results, he is not afraid of going deeper and asking a lot of questions. If someone's professionalism is in doubt in any case, the 7.7+ immediately says: "I appreciate your initiative, but I'm not sure that you have sufficient knowledge and skills to do the job at a high level. Do you think maybe your enthusiasm and energy is expedient to strengthen the professionalism of our colleagues from the department of personnel, who are more experienced in this matter?"

If someone has problems on a project, the 7.7+ leader analyses them with the help of a method of direct information collection. He tries not to use closed questions, which imply brief yes/no answers. He makes extensive use of open-ended questions that invite to a discussion without imposing a point of view. This is especially important if the man asking question stands higher in organizational hierarchy than the one who answers. People have a habit of joining those who are more authoritative than they are, regardless of whether they agree with their views or not.

Active Positioning

The 7.7+ style always accompanies his views with weighty arguments. He defends his opinion with conviction and encourages others to do the same. However, even if the issue seems settled, he still asks others to express their opinions in order to achieve the best result. The 7.7+ leader is ready to give his opinion if the arguments of his opponents appear convincing. He is the initiator of such actions, which enhance the participation and commitment of other employees.

When defending his views, the 7.7+ leader clearly and confidently expresses his opinions. The high focus on the values of the organization together with a pronounced orientation towards people and results encourage the 7.7+ style not only to defend his standpoint in order to achieve the best results, but also to give him the opportunity to do so without attacking others. Powerful initiative does not mean that the 7.7+ leader breaks others in mid-sentence or stops all mouths. The 7.7+ leader is confident that there are no ideas that cannot be improved.

Arguments and defence often constitute a difficult dilemma: either victory or defeat. If the opinion is adopted by the team, this is victory, and if it is rejected, this is the defeat. The 7.7+ leader discards the win/lose model and invites everyone to move to a win/win model, that is, always look for "What is right?" instead of looking for the guilty ones. The 7.7+ style always strives to check whether his opinion is correct, discussing it with others. Such discussions enable a thorough analysis of the ideas from all perspectives. If the discussion shows that the 7.7+ leader was right, he can get down to work with even greater energy and with the team support. If there is a better idea, then the 7.7+ leader will not hesitate to change his opinion for a correct and optimal one. If colleagues do not agree with the 7.7+ leader, although he is correct, he will continue to work with the confidence that he has done everything possible and later again will try to convince others.

The 7.7+ leader actively takes the initiative, based on an objective assessment of the resources (R). He works showing respect and attention to other people. This approach helps other team members to assess the available resources and to plan their activities. The 7.7+ leader is well informed about the possibilities of his team and can assess the impact of specific actions for each individual. If the new initiative results in the need to work more for less money, the 7.7+ leader will recognize this contradiction and solve it. If the initiative stops production, the 7.7+ leader will consider the matter in advance.

The 7.7+ leader's faith in people's abilities encourages them to be more active, since the focus is on an objective assessment of the facts. The 7.7+ leader immediately finds the best course of action, and his enthusiasm is contagious. However, to show enthusiasm does not mean to act too quickly or ignore the circumstances and concerns. This means that you need to step back and assess the performance in terms of available resources, decision-making, and strategy. The active standpoint of the 7.7+ leader allows him to move forward, seek, find, and analyse information. The advantage of this approach is having a more optimal and realistic vision of the possibilities to defend one's standpoint, which is based on numerous facts, logic, and common sense.

The 7.7+ leader's standpoint is enhanced by the inherent sincerity. He is not afraid of analysing the facts. To complete the activities successfully it is necessary to consider all the circumstances and take appropriate measures in advance. The 7.7+ style shows his initiative in all stages of activity. He constantly evaluates the priority of a problem, analyses the possibility of implementing the plan and of its actual implementation, so that if necessary he can make the appropriate suggestions. While most members of the team prefer to go and start to do the work, the 7.7+ style establishes criteria and indicates the reference points on the way towards results. When the action is completed, the 7.7+ style initiates the evaluation of the work effectiveness to achieve the goals and makes the appropriate corrections necessary for the future work.

Decision-Making

The 7.7+ leader attaches great importance to making the right decisions that can help the organization to achieve common goals. He listens to other people's opinions on the subject and compares them to the established criteria; he is committed to understanding and agreement. The 7.7+ leader is not afraid of unpopular and/or tough decisions. Nevertheless, he always tries to solve problems on the basis of mutual understanding and high motivation.

The 7.7+ style's decisions are based on an open exchange of valuable ideas, opinions, and facts. As a result, decisions are made in an atmosphere of mutual understanding and agreement. Such an approach provides the best opportunity for success, as it allows identifying and resolving any latent and potential problems. The key to efficiency in the 7.7+ decision-making is a high level of involvement. The 7.7+ leader's notion of high quality involvement in the solution is that people are free to express their opinion, discuss alternative solutions, express interesting ideas, and discuss emerging misunderstandings and miscommunication. The quality of solutions is weighed and evaluated in accordance to their appropriateness and optimality. This approach leads to the final negotiated solution which appears as a natural result of a sincere debate. The high degree of involvement, characteristic of the style 7.7+, increases people's commitment to the decisions taken. People are willing to support those decisions, as they took part in their forging. Even if full agreement has not been reached, team members were informed of all the facts, opinions, and actions. They share a sense of commitment, since everyone had the opportunity to offer something different, his opinion, doubt, and concern. A commitment like this consolidates the team, because even if only one person has expressed an original idea, everyone else had the opportunity to support it and be responsible for the implementation of this idea.

According to the 7.7+ leader, the number of people involved in the decision-making process depends on the real necessity of this or that team member's participation. If an employee can contribute with his experience, skills, or responsibility, he must participate. Group decision-making may include both team members and third parties. In any case, the decision is easier to make, as the status and influence of each and every speaker matter less than the overall weight of his personal contribution to the process. If the most inexperienced member of the discussion brings the most valuable suggestion, it is accepted as the optimal solution. If the manager or the most experienced employee provides a poor solution to the problem, it is rejected as not optimal. This approach means that over time, all team members are somehow involved in the adoption of a number of decisions. However, some decisions may be made by one or two employees, who carry full responsibility for them.

Another advantage of the 7.7+ style decision-making is the simplicity of the process due to the high level of mutual trust and respect. Everyone knows that the decisions are made by the criteria of correctness and optimality, and a particular team member does not see the need to participate in the decision-making process, if he himself has nothing to offer. When fears, concerns, and barriers are eliminated, team members can make fair and quick decisions, no matter who is involved in the decision-making process.

Constructive Critique

The most important characteristic of the 7.7+ style is openness and honesty in relationships. This characteristic is particularly evident in the critical remarks and feedback. The 7.7+ style's critique involves constant study of the team effectiveness, and includes all types of critique: preliminary, regular, spontaneous, and subsequent. This sequence in the critical approach allows solving problems more quickly and efficiently just when they are detected; and if they still cannot be prevented, they are identified and resolved quickly, as soon as these problems emerge. This growing awareness within the team makes it possible to deal with the problem before it irreparably damages the organization.

With the help of critique that helps identifying all the problems and alternatives, the 7.7+ leader moves business forward. He always tries to use only objective critique, especially in difficult circumstances or when emotions emerge. The 7.7+ leader welcomes critique of him, as he seeks to identify all opinions and correct the mistakes to ensure continuous progress. People tend to consider critique as a final stage, which occurs only after the work is completed; often such critique is a celebration on the occasion of successful work completion. Most teams in general do not consider it necessary to trace the way to success. Instead, critique turns into a laudatory solemn event, aiming to maintain morale. This kind of celebration can lead to complacency, which is one of the most dangerous side effects of success. People start to believe in their success, considering themselves conquerors of the highest peaks. Over time this leads to a loss of quality standards and reduction of expectations. History is full of examples of companies that first experienced a period of extraordinary success, and then for a long time immersed in a prolonged period of recession and restructuring.

The 7.7+ leader's team also enjoys success and celebrates achievements, but at the same time, they analyse everything that happened in the context of initial expectations and the result which ideally could be obtained. And we should not be happy with increasing it by 20 %, since we could have increased it by 40 %. If the result is much higher than expected, most likely the targets were too low. Of course, success should bring joy, but the struggle to achieve higher work quality and greater commitment must never be forgotten.

Another common approach to critique is its use in searching for those to blame and punishing them. In this situation, the critical debate turns into a blame storming session. For those who lived through this kind of critique, the word becomes a stable backlash. In fact, it is not critique, but abuse used to find responsibility among the subordinates. The 7.7+ style critique is far from such improper and harmful practice. The purpose of critique is creativity, not punishment and humiliation. The 7.7+ style is equally willing to listen and to accept objective critique of him in the same way as he does in relation to other people.

The 7.7+ leader makes comments in an atmosphere of mutual trust and respect. This makes it easy to express negative comments, as well as to take them, as both parties realize the ultimate goal of critique, which is to find ways to improve performance. This approach supports the interlocutors and also helps to live through failure, as no member of the team feels lonely and abandoned. Despite the emerging contradictions and frictions, the 7.7+ leader always stresses common goals of employees: "We are a team!" But this does not mean that the 7.7+ leader cannot get mad or otherwise express his outrage. The difference is that even voicing negative comments, the 7.7+ leader does it in a constructive manner, with a focus on improving performance and development.

The 7.7+ leader tries to focus on specific examples of behaviour and the impact that this behaviour had on the team progress towards achieving the goal. He refuses to condemn critique and instead focuses on specific actions and their impact on the effectiveness of group activities. One of the major effects of the 7.7+ style critique is that it helps a person to become more efficient and to grow. This often leads to the fact that one's own person begins to ask other people to express constructive critique. If the critique helps the person to understand the interconnection between his actions and the results, he can understand how to change behaviour for the better, as he has a natural desire to get feedback again and again. As a result constructive critique becomes a natural, motivating, and necessary component of an effective joint venture.

13.7 Conclusions

The 7.7+ leader shares a concern for production and for people with a high focus on values. This style is characterized by high ethical self-exactingness and demonstrates a high degree of integration. This style is based on and implements such human values as justice, honesty, trust, and responsibility. These values are supported by every employee. The 7.7+ leader is objective and honest, he evaluates himself properly, he is modest and supportive, tries to think about the future, and acts with an eye towards it. He is solid and resolute in his actions. He does not try to initiate change for the sake of change, but treats it as a mandatory element of organizational development. The 7.7+ culture can be an effective management tool for the organization development and improvement.

The 7.7+ leader ensures a consistent achievement of the objectives and involvement of all the team's resources and energy. The 7.7+ leader embodies all the main principles of team effectiveness, as only this approach does not imply any dominance, opportunism, a rotten compromise, avoidance, instruction, and abuses. This attitude brings a fresh approach to the relationship, adds strength, and provides strong support to the achievement of results. The interaction organized by the 7.7+ leader allows not only to achieve the organizational goals, but also to form a sense of organizational commitment and individual self-fulfilment in employees.

The 7.7+ leader is well informed about everything in order to facilitate the efficient exchange of information. He gives another example of expressing his views openly and honestly on the basis of facts and identifying the reasons that make it easier to overcome any conflicts and contradictions. He is not afraid to admit his weaknesses or failures and welcomes others to express their best ideas. The atmosphere of openness contributes to the same behaviour in other team members who are willing to follow it.

The 7.7+ leader's actions are guided by the principle of "what is right?" and not "who is right?". This reduces the need for a fundamental attitude of political games, patronage, or control over the behaviour of people, as well as the fear of being involved in activities. This context inspires the team to work together and to achieve the best results, leaving no space to attempts to earn the recognition of the other. These individual achievements are estimated and recognized, but only in the context of collective achievements.

The 7.7+ leader gets involved in the work of everyone who is affected by the decision. This agreement, once installed, provides commitment which is necessary for the effective implementation of the plans. Results of collective interaction do not come by themselves, but require hard work. The 7.7+ style is not effective as long as team members do not form an atmosphere of mutual trust and respect; without trust, intensive exchange of information and really sincere relationships are impossible. No member of the team can expect that one day he will come to work and begin to demonstrate the 7.7+ style. The years of bad habits and bitter disappointments make this impossible, and the road to a better understanding of oneself is often thorny. Sincerity leads to critique, which may seem an insult. Attitudes, responsible for inefficient behaviour, are based on deeply rooted (and often hidden) values, which are very difficult to change.

Due to his increased freedom and responsibility, the 7.7+ leader, in fact, is considerably more demanding, but at the same time he carries a considerably greater satisfaction and compensation for anyone who is included in the job. The 7.7+ leader does not wait for being informed and spends a lot of effort trying to be completely in the know. It is very difficult to prove anything, explaining the reasons, seeking arguments, and evaluating opinions of other employees. Many managers are accustomed to authoritarian work methods, and so they do not like to explain and justify their actions.

The 7.7+ leader uses the existing conflicts as a source of energy for sustainable development and improvement of efficiency. Mostly this is possible due to the continuous strengthening of centripetal forces of cooperation. The purpose of the organization and individual goals come into harmonious interaction. Focus on achievements and focus on people become combined with each other, while the pursuit of profit becomes based on ethical norms, supported by the organization. The 7.7+ style convinces us that it is only through the involvement of all the existing resources that the maximum possible results may be obtained.

The 7.7+ leader usually attracts attention and is well respected in the organizational environment, as employees enjoy their open and confident leader. This does not mean that the 7.7+ style is infallible and never makes mistakes. He is also subjected to doubts and the impact of negative factors, but his constructive thinking and agility allow him to overcome those problems successfully.

Conclusion: From Optimal Leadership Towards Optimal Culture

The Synercube Theory together with the skills and knowledge that it is based on allows not only to optimally convert resources (R) into results (O) but also to determine the purpose of activities and the meaning of their objectives. The cultural value dimension gives the goals high social responsibility standards, fairness, and integrity that make them worthy in the highest sense of the word, since they have value and are useful for many people, uniting and motivating them. Can we call such purposes visionary? Yes, but only if visionary goal carries moral-value content. Even if visionary, the goal, first of all, is characterized by high predictability in achieving economic results. From this point of view, provoking the currency collapse, which can bring huge profits, can also be seen as the realization of visionary goals: the businessman was able to see and anticipate what the other did not anticipate. But is this a worthy goal? Therefore, we prefer to use the concept of decent visionary goal or just a worthy goal.

It does not matter who or what is at stake—an individual or a large corporation: success is not just the achievement of results on the basis of the available resources, but the achievement of good results with high social and personal meaning.

At the present time, when high human values are often devalued and even subjected to mockery, the notion of a worthy goal often seems something far too sublime. In fact, worthy goals, as well as decent human behaviour in general, can be understood more easily than we sometimes think. If a person is going to do something, first he has a clear idea of *what* he wants to do in his mind, but also the idea of *why* he wants to do this. The image of the future outcome becomes the driving force that motivates many people, only if this objective has some other meaning and is valuable to many people.

Thus, in the organization if work is to be done, everyone should understand what he is doing and clearly see the final result, its meaning, and value. And the more clear, understandable, and personal the importance of this goal is, the more committed each member of the team will be, and the greater the chance that people will be able to join together to achieve this goal and use all resources available to do it.

© Springer-Verlag Berlin Heidelberg 2016

A. Zankovsky, C. von der Heiden, *Leadership with Synercube*,

DOI 10.1007/978-3-662-49052-5_14

A worthy goal affects the motivation for yet another reason. If one has a clear idea of a worthy goal, how it can be achieved, even the idea that for some reason this worthy goal will not be fulfilled becomes unbearable. People are willing to overcome all obstacles and to fight in order to preserve and increase their dignity. When it comes to business, it is clear that if a company has a worthy goal it makes its competitors not only think about how to keep the pace, but also how to do it in a dignified manner.

Setting a worthy goal in itself may seem utopian, and its creator is usually afraid of possible troubles. Whoever sets a worthy goal may seem too bold, arrogant, or, conversely, overly idealistic and detached from reality. Because of these fears one starts to think about other factors that may prevent the achievement of this goal, to ponder all obstacles and fears: "What if this happens?" These fears often become a powerful barrier that blocks the activity. However, the more worthy the goal, the less reason for fears and doubts, and the greater the sense of employees' ownership and commitment to this goal. Team members support each other and express creative ideas which strengthen the confidence in the achievement of a worthy goal. There is also the possibility that a worthy goal and the efforts of the team on the path to achieve it will be able to involve those who make key decisions, and they will also support the goal. Each discussion on this subject reveals the potential for new actions, creative ideas, opportunities, and, ultimately, creates a synergy which would never have been achieved if the goal did not imply meaning and values that are shared by all.

A worthy goal has a values dimension. Today, this goal has become a key aspect for achieving long-term and steady success.

A decent strategy consists of three main parts. Firstly, the organization should be focused on forming a set of dominant values determining the overall ideology of the company. Such an ideology is a vital guiding force, which remains unchanged, even accompanied by other changes, including a change of management, range of products or services, the scope of activities, etc.

A fixed value basis allows formulating a wide range of purposes: from the simple and prosaic, designed to solve everyday human problems (e.g. to save people from snoring) to the most daring and ambitious aim, which currently can be seen as completely and totally cut off from life (e.g. to make everyone happy). The main thing is that the goal should really constitute a value to people, companies, society, and mankind. And the wider the range of people sharing this goal, the more motivating and personally meaningful it will be to the organization.

One of the most important components of a worthy strategy is a detailed and specific description of what is expected to be achieved within the framework of a worthy goal. The leader may possess unique knowledge and abilities, but even he cannot be as effective as a group of ten people committed to a worthy goal. Inspiring a worthy goal motivates all divisions and departments of the company to create their own worthy sub-goals and objectives, based on the common worthy goal. And it is not because senior management imposed it, but because everyone wants to find his rightful place among people, moving forward to new challenges.

Therefore, worthy companies realize goals that others regard as completely unrealistic.

A prerequisite to achieve a worthy goal at any level—be it individual, group, or corporate—is its constant actualization in the consciousness of team members. The task of the organization leader is not just to define this goal, but also to fix it on paper, to discuss ways to achieve it with employees, to show dignity in all actions, and ensure that all employees have adopted this goal and become its faithful followers.

It must be emphasized that a worthy goal is a motivating factor for people's development. And the more people are involved in the formulation of a worthy goal, the greater their commitment to achieving it, the more desire they have to see the results with their own eyes, and the less they are afraid to fail.

If we take particular people, leadership in the most concise definition implies creating and explaining a worthy purpose for the staff. Creating a foundation of values, people gain power to identify with and ultimately achieve their worthy goal. The company which does not have a clearly defined worthy goal and internal corporate values system will have problems with adopting Synercube values. These values and skills create the conditions for the team's desire to unite efforts for the achievements of a worthy goal, but only if this goal is supported by the worthy behaviour of a leader. Synercube values and skills reinforce the commitment of people to a worthy goal, "arming" them with such relationship skills that evoke the values of openness, sincerity and mutual trust, respect, and synergy. Synercube values create a solid foundation for confidence on the path to achieve a worthy goal.

The Darwinian model of natural selection, which has been influencing business development for many years, implied efforts to adapt to market changes and maximize profits. Today it is assuming a more and more civilized and socially oriented form: the one who will survive is the one who will manage to adapt to changing conditions, making it in a worthy way, achieving worthy goals.

The active standpoint of leadership based on shared values of employees can have a powerful influence on group norms and results. People tend to believe that their values and attitudes are purely personal, individual, and unique, but studies show that most individual principles arise from group norms. As a result, group settings determine the quality of individual labour efforts to a greater extent than many believe. Group norms are reflected in traditions, legends, habits, rituals, rules, regulations, policies, operating instructions, customs, taboos, and past experience.

These norms and standards are beginning to form in a process called convergence, when people working together eventually become more similar to each other, forming a specific language, jokes, habits, and attitudes. Convergence leads to the spontaneous emergence of rules by tuning individual behaviour in accordance with the common group template shared by every group member (Turner and Killian 1993).

Cohesion is one of the most significant phenomena of social organization. People tend to side with those who have similar experiences with them, as it allows them to better predict each other's behaviour, which is impossible with outsiders. They prefer to communicate with insiders. This convergence can be based on the same race, religion, common political views, socioeconomic status, education, etc. In organizational life other criteria are important, e.g. duration of employment, position, participation in trainings, and common experiences. If cohesion is high, people will treat each other with trust and show commitment to the group (Eisenberg 2007; Beal et al. 2003).

Conformity is a phenomenon that causes all team members to take the established group norms of behaviour. Conformity promotes the establishment of codes of conduct by creating a certain pressure, usually implicit, which makes a person not only follow the group norms, but also to promote its consolidation (Cialdini and Goldstein 2004; Bond and Smith 1996).

These norms cannot be overcome by a simple explanation, coercion, or authority. However, the understanding of the dynamics of group norms formation allows the head of the organization to ask a key question: "Do existing group norms and standards of behaviour help or hinder our work?" Conformity in itself is neither good nor bad; it is the usual dynamics of group behaviour.

Conformity can enhance effectiveness, but can also create barriers to increasing efficiency due to the fact that norms and standards can be inefficient, incorrect, or outdated.

The norms derived assume legitimacy only if they are based on values shared by group members. If the group norms are based on the wrong values or come into conflict with them, they can become a significant obstacle to organizational changes. This contradiction is typical of styles with a weak corporate culture.

Group leaders play a leading role in creating standards. By understanding the group dynamics and its principles, the leader can use these natural laws to support ongoing systematic changes. And in this moment the personal leadership style is of paramount importance. As soon as the organization attempts to change the existing situation, a large number of chaotic, contradictory, and confused responses immediately come. And this chaos gives the leader the opportunity to critique the situation and manage changes, as in this confusion lies priceless energy and emotional charge.

It is essential that leaders support the three types of energies mentioned above—convergence, cohesion, and conformity—throughout the process of organizational changes, using them productively.

Once the norm is formed, the group ensures its support, forcing team members to follow it. The 7.7+ leader is able to initiate changes and manage the transition from the rules that prevent development to progress.

Norms and standards can easily influence behaviour, but value-oriented leadership is able to start the process in the opposite direction, providing a powerful influence on the group rules and standards.

Achieving sustainable and effective changes requires a leader who can accomplish three major tasks:

1. To work out employees' fears of upcoming changes.
2. To create a basis for changes.
3. To set an example of effective and proper behaviour for himself.

Fears inevitably arise if the upcoming changes affect the personal sphere of habits, attitudes, and beliefs. Fear is further increased if the changes affect or call into question the people's self-esteem and personal values. In this situation, concern and fear are completely natural reactions. Changes are associated with loss of control over what's happening, and therefore are perceived as a threat to independence and everything that has been achieved. Another reason for the fear of change is the lack of awareness and lack of understanding of what is happening.

Individual fears and resistance to changes in an organization cause people to step back from the problem and pretend that they are not involved in decision-making, even if the decision depends on them. As a result, this leads to the well-known and ineffective group norms when members indifferently watch the development of a catastrophic situation and do nothing for its successful resolution.

People justify their inaction by fears of possible consequences, and also refer to factors such as the absence of clear regulations, insufficient effective procedures, defects in planning (when existing), habits, unwillingness to take action, the lack of support, and the lack of time. People tend to hide their fears from each other. They do not speak about their fears, as they fear to seem weak and immature. And the higher the status of the employee in the organization, the harder to confess his fears: doubts and fears are not worthy of a real expert.

However, everything can change dramatically if a person is able to affect change, if he fully understands the situation and has the necessary information. An understanding of the need and readiness for change is inadequate to implement these changes, as it is necessary to know how to do it.

The first task on the way of overcoming fears and internal resistance to change is the necessity to see your own fear, take it as something natural. This allows recognizing fears every time you try to change anything. Successful leaders capable of managing change must encourage sincere statements and be attentive to the concealed concerns of their employees, as well as work on their own fears. Despite the fact that the fear of change cannot be completely eliminated, you can control it if you create a framework that allows people to act in an objective, systematic, and coordinated manner. The Synercube Theory provides a framework for change, turning the fear of changes in a controlled process of development of skills, sincerity, and objectivity. This also contributes to the objective behavioural typology of leadership styles.

The styles and their description within the Synercube Theory allow people to use their own judgment to reach an agreement about what the correct behaviour is, and then to compare their behaviour with that model. This approach in itself is compelling because it allows people to assess the facts and reach their own conclusions about how to make decisions, resolve conflicts, or take initiative. Achieving real and lasting changes in the organization can be possible only when people see that their behaviour is wrong and want to change it for the better. If employees have discussed and formed a model of proper behaviour, change becomes quite realistic and feasible. Such models allow people to create their own relationship standards.

From the organizational perspective, the Synercube Theory is a kind of catalyst for commitment to the most profound changes. And as soon as people take on new values, individual changes take the form of group norms. And in the end, the changes will spread within entire organizational culture. If fears are discussed in advance and a model of effective leadership is accepted and shared by everyone, the team can totally focus on the conversion of resources R into the best output O. Shaping and implementing corporate values, attitudes, and taking into account the dynamics of group interaction, an organization can reach the level which is necessary to create a deep commitment to changes.

Important in order to gain the employees' commitment for future changes is the clear understanding that people only truly accept what they developed themselves or at least participated in developing. This means that it is imperative to engage those who will be involved in the implementation of changes in the discussion of upcoming changes.

The Synercube approach to changes includes several stages of organizational development, which allows building a relationship of mutual trust, respect, and sincerity. This process begins with individual changes, then affects the staff, then becomes the pattern for group relationships and finally rises to the organizational strategic level. Actions that are taken at the high-level of organizational hierarchy impact on all levels of the organization and all the relationships within it. Leaders influence changes with their own actions. It is very difficult to convince people of the success of any change if senior management itself does not accept and start it. It is human energy that triggers and promotes all corporate changes. Human energy is a powerful motivating and unifying force, if it permeates the entire organization from top to bottom.

Despite this obvious fact, many companies still look for obstacles to changes only at the lower levels of the organization. Strategic intentions, put on paper, are just a declaration of intent, which someone else is to implement. The striving of leaders for effective change forces them to push employees to behave correctly. But however good the management intentions might be, employees begin to resist changes and to feel fear and anxiety. People start to think that they are being used, exploited. Therefore, they will seek and find many ways to resist change.

In contrast to this method, change management based on the Synercube Theory of psychological and behavioural factors opens up real opportunities for continuous and effective organizational change.

References

Books

Eisenberg J (2007) Group cohesiveness. In: Baumeister R, Vohs K (eds) Encyclopaedia of social psychology. Sage, Thousand Oaks, CA, pp 386–388

Turner R, Killian L (1993) Collective behaviour, 4th edn. Prentice Hall, New York

Journals

Beal D, Cohen R, Burke M, McLendon C (2003) Cohesion and performance in groups: a meta-analytic clarification of construct relation. J Appl Psychol 88:989–1004

Bond R, Smith P (1996) Culture and conformity: a meta-analysis of studies using Asch's (1952b, 1956) Line Judgement task. Psychol Bull 119:111–137

Cialdini R, Goldstein N (2004) Social influence: compliance and conformity. Annu Rev Psychol 55:591–621

Printed in the United States
By Bookmasters